AS WE GO MARCHING

AS WE GO MARCHING

BY JOHN T. FLYNN

Preface by Ronald Radosh

41 UNION SQUARE WEST, NEW YORK, NEW YORK 10003

AS WE GO MARCHING

Copyright © 1944 by John T. Flynn. Published
   by arrangement with Doubleday and Company, Inc.

Introduction copyright © 1973 by Ronald Radosh.

This edition published 1973 by Free Life Editions, Inc.
   41 Union Square West, New York, N. Y. 10003

Library of Congress Catalog Card Number: 73-88237
ISBN: 0-914156-00-4

Manufactured in the United States of America
Faculty Press, Inc., Brooklyn, N. Y.

CONTENTS

Preface by Ronald Radosh   vii

PART ONE
THE SOIL OF FASCISM: ITALY

I	The Bad Word	1
II	The Democratic State	4
III	The Soil of Fascism	6
IV	Tax and Borrow and Spend	11
V	The New Industry	17
VI	The Magnificent Drug	20
VII	The Incredible Synthesis	27
VIII	Time for Greatness	33
IX	The Rise of Fascism	40
X	What is Fascism?	48

PART TWO
THE BAD FASCISM: GERMANY

I	The Impartial Microbe	74
II	Resetting the Scene	78
III	The Revolt of the Masses	81
IV	Old Devil Budget	87
V	The Supreme Project	98
VI	The Planned Society	100

VII	Machiavelli's Men	117
VIII	War	124
IX	Hitler	127
X	Good Fascists and Bad Fascists	160

PART THREE
THE GOOD FASCISM: AMERICA

	Permanent Crisis in America	166
I	The Good Deficits	172
II	The Righteous Autarchy	189
III	Democratic Militarism	203
IV	American Imperialism	212
V	The Last Mile	226
VI	The Final Note	251
VII	Bibliography	259
	Index	264

PREFACE

by Ronald Radosh

The former Presidential candidate for the American Independent Party remarked to *The New York Times* that he spent his nights reading John T. Flynn. The minority reactionary candidate in the 1972 election was undoubtedly referring to tracts made famous by Flynn in the early 1950's, from the million seller *The Road Ahead,* condensed by the *Reader's Digest,* to the McCarthyite diatribe, *The Lattimore Story.*

But to judge John T. Flynn by his last and most unrepresentative writings is akin to evaluating the work of Wilhelm Reich by concentrating only on his development of the mystical Orgone Energy theory advanced during his last and most bizzare years. In Flynn's case, it is a more serious distortion. To treat Flynn as a simple reactionary McCarthyite is to ignore the consistent anti-militarist and anti-imperialist strain always present in Flynn's writings. Most important, it allows readers to avoid confronting the theme advanced by Flynn in his most important, representative and analytical work, *As We Go Marching.*

The John T. Flynn one will find in the pages of that work is not the man read today by members of the new Right-wing. Flynn started his career as an economist, as an author of a score of successful books, and as financial columnist for the liberal *New Republic* since 1933. Writing for them during the days of the New Deal, Flynn's early admiration for Franklin Roosevelt turned to scorn, as he detected a drift towards corporatism at home and militarism and interventionism abroad.

In a short matter of time, Flynn became preoccupied with the growing drift of the Roosevelt administration towards an interventionist stance. As a result, Flynn became an active participant in the cause to keep the United

States out of war. He was to become leader of the militant New York branch of the America First Committee. This activity isolated Flynn from those he was once close to. At the time when interventionists were calling for defense of European democracy, Flynn was arguing that Germany and Italy threatened not England's "democracy, but her empire. What they covet is not her soil, but her colonies, not her liberty but her markets." It would be stupid, he asserted, "for Americans ... to permit themselves to be drawn into a war to save England's empire under the illusion that they are saving her democracy."

During the last half of 1940, when liberal opinion began to shift towards intervention, *New Republic* editor Bruce Bliven dismissed Flynn as a columnist for his journal. As of November 1940, Flynn's caustic anti-war comments had become too controversial to be admitted into the dialogue about America's future. As Bliven and others supported entrance in a new war, Flynn continued to argue that the world war was one "between empires and about imperialism;" simply another "chapter in the long, age-old struggle of European empires about dividing up the world." Flynn then made known his opposition to any and all Empires, including "American Empires." Predicting new deals by the imperialist powers at the war's end, Flynn stated back in January 1941 that "it is out of this abominable world of imperialism, the scramble for dominion, the fight for trade backed by armies and guns, that I want to keep this great peaceful democratic world of ours."

Flynn was not to be successful in his effort to avoid intervention in a new imperial conflict. His effort to oppose intervention led instead to lonely political isolation from former associates. Writers like liberal Max Lerner went so far as to note that he had more sympathy with Henry Luce and his concept of an American Century than with anti-war liberals. "I prefer him infinitely," wrote Lerner, "though our purposes are as far removed as the four corners of the winds, to men like ... John Flynn." Others began to condemn Flynn as pro-Fascist and an appeaser of Nazism. These calumnies only led Flynn to redouble his work to preserve an America that would remain non-imperial and that could maintain a prosperous economy without recourse to war.

It was the wartime experience, and the growth of decision-making in foreign policy by a small elite, that led Flynn to show concern about the erosion of the basis of popular government. A long opponent of fascism, Flynn first developed his line of argument about domestic fascist tendencies in 1943. The United States, he argued in a speech presented that year, was "little by little adopting first one and then another policy that is beginning to make us look more like a National Socialist government than a democracy." Blaming fascism in Germany on the "old social democratic and republican governments that preceded" Hitler, Flynn argued that these regimes had "developed and cultivated all of the essential elements of Fascism." These included corporatism; "The organization of the economic society as a planned economy under the supervision of the State"; a "Planned Consumption Economy"; "Militarism as an economic Weapon"; "Imperialism," and finally "Dictatorship."

All these characteristics, he claimed, had been developed in Italy and Germany by civilian leaders. The old German Weimar Republic had engaged in planned consumption, and had plunged Germany into debts on top of debts which caused ruinous inflation. They also developed cartelization of industry and government partnership in industry. Under Article 31 of their Constitution, the government had the power to initiate rule by emergency decree. When Hitler took "power all he had to do was to add ... the old militarism and imperialism of the Empire" and to consolidate a new strong dictatorship. Flynn's analysis bore striking resemblance to the explanations put forward by contemporary Marxists like R. Palme Dutt, author of *Fascism and Social Revolution.*

The essence of Fascism, Flynn argued, was not to be found in the ugly and obvious episodes of storm troopers and book burnings. It was in the commonplace elements which existed as well in the United States. In particular, Flynn saw the threat of strong central government and "a plan for blank-check" rule in the efforts of the National Resources Planning Board under Alvin Hansen, which sought to initiate national planning. With F.D.R.'s third term, Flynn warned, the New Deal was "forging the last link in the chain of American national socialism."

At a time when American soldiers were fighting Hitler's armies in Europe, an attack on President Roosevelt for harboring Fascist tendencies was not warmly received in the United States. Yet Flynn's analysis was given some positive attention by individuals who were not part of the Right-wing. Socialist Party chieftain Norman Thomas, for one, was highly impressed. "In the most effective possible fashion," he wrote Flynn on August 31, 1943, "you have made a very strong case." Thomas thought that Flynn had "dismissed some of the side-show features of fascism a little more summarily than I would." He also disagreed with Flynn's "negative" view that "the world drifts to fascism anyhow through processes which private capitalism has accepted to its own hurt." Thomas, of course, saw "an alternative to fascism" but believed it could not "be a return to private capitalism that has steadily evolved toward the present situation." Yet the Socialist leader informed Flynn that he had "quoted your definition of fascism in a footnote in my own book."

Flynn was trying to warn Americans of a basic point that the seeds of fascism lay within the United States; and they could not be eradicated merely by winning the fight against Nazi armies abroad. Sensing the need to elaborate upon this theme, Flynn wrote what was to be his most important book. Until publication of this paperback volume, *As We Go Marching* has remained neglected and relatively unknown. Yet it was Flynn's most informed and perceptive contribution to discussion about the nature of American society. Its purpose, he explained, was to define the meaning of fascism and "then to search for its elements in America."

Flynn would find that few would understand his intention in writing it. Because he had opposed U.S. entrance into World War II, he was forever tainted with the label of "appeasement." When he appeared to speak at the University of Illinois in Urbana in May 1944, thirty members of the faculty and student body protested against his appearance, "on the ground that he was anti-semitic, that he had trafficked with seditionists, was pro-fascist and that it was not good for the war effort to have him there."

Despite the opposition Flynn faced from those apparently on the political Left, his arguments bore close resemblance to Marxist arguments about the nature of fascism. The contents of his book would give scant comfort to those on the Right—who themselves were so blinded by anti-Communism that they often acquiesced in fascist efforts of repression. Flynn, after all, was attempting to battle against the domestic seeds of fascism, which he feared were rapidly developing within his own native land.

It was Statist institutions solidified by the New Deal, he argued, that produced an American version of fascism—a "good" fascism rather than the "bad" kind all Americans detested in Nazi Germany. The elements of fascism had been planted in corporatist institutions such as the N.R.A. People liked the term "planning," but New Deal planners thought "of a change in our form of society in which the government would insert itself into the structure of business, not merely as a policeman, but as partner, collaborator and banker." The economy would be planned and coerced rather than free, "in which business would be brought together into great guilds or an immense corporative structure, combining the elements of self-rule and government supervision with a national economic policing system to enforce these decrees."

These corporatist tendencies reached fruition with the New Deal. World War II further consolidated the new business collectivism, which was based upon "an economy supported by great streams of debt and an economy under complete control, with nearly all the planning agencies functioning with almost totalitarian power under a vast bureaucracy." The New Deal also tried to extend this system into the realm of foreign affairs. Government spending was most prolific for military systems. Neither Congress, business or labor found fault with spending for national defense. "Thus militarism," Flynn wrote, "is the one great glamour public-works project upon which a variety of elements in the community can be brought into agreement."

Militarism and war, however, were components of both fascism and imperialism. And both were clearly present within the United States. Flynn, unlike many pro-war liberals, held few illusions about the supposedly unique characteristics of American democracy. He was especially concerned about administration efforts to impose conscription under the guise of "civilian training." There were arguments on behalf of a big army, he wrote Senator Arthur Vandenberg on October 30, 1945, but nations always tried militarism, "supposing it would advance some special objective not necessarily connected with war, only to find that militarism in the end rides the countries. It sets in motion forces and pressures too powerful to be controlled."

Flynn presented Vandenberg with a copy of *As We Go Marching,* informing him that he "tried to depict the current of pressures and forces that slowly drew Italy and Germany along the road to Fascism." Flynn always felt, he explained, that America "occupied a unique position in the world." It was not only the one remaining non-imperialist nation, but it was "the only great power which did not use its strength for aggression." But now Flynn was growing "even more apprehensive that we may be lured along the road to imperialism—under the pious pretensions and false declarations as to our purposes." Flynn hoped that his letter would "lure" Vandenberg to read his "chapter on American Imperialism." Vandenberg, who was soon to become an arch interventionist and Republican architect of Cold War concensus, obviously learned little from Flynn's chapter—if he ever read it.

For those who did take the time, they found a scathing critique of American foreign policy. America, Flynn maintained, had become an Empire. Like any other Empire, it would not be exempt from the rules of imperial decline. Having gained its wartime goals, the large nations sought only preservation of the *status quo.* They appealed for support to well-meaning idealists who hoped to create a peaceful world. But their own goal was to build an order "in which they, all leagued together, will preserve a world which they have divided among themselves and in which the combined forces and might of the allied aggressors will hold for each what they have." Imperialism would be disguised under "phrases of benevolence and as a dream of world peace."

Thus, Flynn predicted, Americans "will do what other countries have done. We will keep alive the fears of our people of the aggressive ambitions of other countries and we will ourselves embark upon imperialistic enterprises of our own." There was no doubt that the germs of a vigorous imperialism are here among us ... the moral germs. And if the economic problems of the nation should seem ... to lead us off into some imperialist adventures, the moral support of such ventures will not be lacking."

America, he noted, had "managed to acquire bases all over the world." There was "no part of the world where trouble can break out where we do not have bases of some sort in which ... we cannot claim our interests are menaced. Thus menaced there must remain when the war is over a continuing argument in the hands of the imperialists for a vast naval establishment and a huge army to attack anywhere or to resist an attack from all the enemies we shall be obliged to have.... We must have enemies," Flynn added sarcastically, "they will become an economic necessity for us."

Hence the ingredients for fascism were present at home. Public debt-supported autarchy had to be operated by a totalitarian government. America was moving in that direction. Centralized power was growing stronger as more of it became concentrated in the Executive branch of Government. "Despite many differences in the character, customs, laws, traditions, resources of the people of Italy, Germany and America," Flynn wrote, "we have been drifting along identical courses and under the influence of the same essential forces." Free enterprise and constitutional government had been eroded, and a new Statist capitalism had replaced it. Flynn warned that "the test of fascism is not one's rage against the Italian and German war lords."

> The test is—how many of the essential principles of fascism do you accept and to what extent are you prepared to apply those fascist ideas to American social and economic life? When you can put your finger on the men or groups that urge for America the debt-supported state, the autarchical corporative state, the state bent on the socialization of investment and the bureaucratic government of industry and society, the establishment of the institution of militarism ... and the institution of imperialism under which it proposes to regulate and rule the world ... and proposes to alter the forms of our government to approach ... absolute government—then you will know you have located the authentic fascist.

The American fascist was an individual who believed in "marshalling great armies and navies at crushing costs to support the industry of war and preparation for war which will become our greatest industry," all conducted under "a powerfully centralized government in which the executive will hold in effect all the powers with Congress reduced to the role of a debating society."

Flynn's prototype American fascist was not a thug in brownshirt or SS uniform; it was the American statesman who sought to erode the people's power in Congress and to concentrate undue authority in the hands of the President. Flynn warned against militarism and imperialism; yet his cry for constitutional government was to become purely a rallying cry for the Right-wing in American life. Liberals then defended the tradition of Presidential power, which was conceived as the repository of all virtue in political life.

As Flynn surveyed the emerging post-war world, he concluded that his worst fears had come to pass. His concern about autocratic Presidential power being exercised against Congress, and his fear that imperial germs would develop to escape domestic economic problems, colored his response to Harry S. Truman's Korean intervention. While liberals were beating the interventionist drums, and arguing that a strong stand "would defeat communism in Asia and advance democracy at the same time, Flynn was pointing out that war production was producing what the President "calls great prosperity." It was not, Flynn argued on June 18, 1950, a "natural prosperity." Given a choice between risking war or facing "the danger of a frightful economic collapse in this country," Flynn assumed that American political leaders would choose war, which was "politically safe." Economic collapse would ruin those responsible; while war would cause the populace to "rally around" those who caused it.

As to Truman's assertion that the Korean War was a "police action," Flynn asserted boldly that "the first casualty of war is Truth," and that a myth had been perpetrated to gain a legal excuse to justify Truman's refusal to go before Congress and ask for a declaration of war. He had no right to send in American troops, Flynn argued on July 16, because "in the Korean case, we were not attacked."

Viewing the conflict as a "civil war," Flynn warned Americans against being influenced by "warriors infatuated with war." He asked, at a time when all most Americans heard was propaganda advocating defeat of Communist aggression via military victory, "what can possibly be gained from victory?" And he urged that Americans find a way to "disentangle ourselves from these grim and tragic necessities." Unlike the liberals who supported the Truman intervention, Flynn called the depiction of the war as a United Nations action nothing but a "pathetic comic opera." Trying to give an American war a UN cover was a "supine sham." And Flynn worried that "hotheads" would try to use Korea "as a jumping off place into a wider and longer struggle somewhere else."

That place turned out to be Indo-china. And it was in early 1951 that

Flynn first warned that "ahead of us lie more Koreas. We could be at war in Indo-China," he stressed. If the U.S. won *or* lost, "the price would be appalling." In the context of increasing United States imperial penetration of Asia, John T. Flynn cogently and calmly applied the logic of *As We Go Marching* to post-war developments.

American leaders, he stated on September 15, 1953, were "borrowing from Fascism." That doctrine's popularity among liberal intellectuals was not unique. Flynn listed the many notables who once had been admirers of Benito Mussolini. He included in his list former Columbia University President Nicholas Murray Butler, Congressman Sol Bloom, diplomat Richard Washburn Child and financier Thomas W. Lamont. Fascism was popular because it promised jobs and security through the technique of spending large amounts of money, to be raised by taxes and government borrowing. The money was then to be spent on arms production.

Mussolini, Flynn continued, had initiated "a kind of statism in which the government should be responsible for the material welfare of the people." Flynn would have called it socialism, but he noted that Mussolini called it fascism because that "didn't have a bad name." Yet the only new industry that kept Italy prosperous was "militarism and war." By 1937 Mussolini was spending 37 billion lire on the armed forces. Now Americans, Flynn noted, were emulating Mussolini. Since 1939 America had been floating on government military spending. The lesson to be learned was that in Italy such a path led only to war.

In June of 1954, Flynn accused the Eisenhower administration of "seriously thinking of leading the United States into another war with Asia." Eisenhower was contemplating such a course, Flynn thought, because he faced "the same trap that President Roosevelt" faced in 1939. In times of economic depresssion, only war saved the nation from unemployment. Since 1941, Flynn sadly reported, America had "been living on the big business of war."

Without a new war to maintain prosperity, the 1950's business boom would collapse. Eisenhower had been unable to find any substitute "for war to keep fifteen or sixteen millions employed." The national debt was up to 274 billion dollars, and the government was spending two billion per month on munitions production. Without a new war, that business would drop. War spending could not be stepped up "if you don't have a war." It was a fact, Flynn insisted, that "war has become the basis of the prosperity of the United States." The domestic cost was the "slavery of militarism for millions of young men," increased debts piled upon debts, high wages and prices, and continuing spiraling inflation.

It was the expression of such views that soon showed Flynn that he was not to be a welcome member in the ranks of the new Right-wing. On October 22, 1956, William F. Buckley Jr. rejected an undated article submitted to *The National Review* by Flynn. In the piece, Flynn had repeated his fondest arguments. Militarism, he wrote, was a "job-making boondoggle." Its purpose was not to defend, but was to bolster "the economic system with jobs for soldiers and jobs and profits in the munitions plants." Presenting figures for military spending between 1939 and 1954, Flynn argued that there was no "authentic 'center' with a socialist sector and a capitalist sector on either side" of the economy. There existed only the "racket" of military spending "with the soldier-politician in the middle—unaware of the hell-broth of war, taxes and debt." Flynn protested that the administration was spending $66 billion per year, most going for defense and only a "small fraction" spent on "the legitimate functions of government. The biggest item is on so-called 'national security.' "

Flynn's piece was rejected by Buckley on the grounds that its author did not understand the nature of the Soviet military threat—just as Bliven and the 1930 liberals had rejected his arguments because he did not perceive the supposed nature of the Nazi military threat to America's security. In both cases, Flynn remained true to the analysis put forth most clearly in *As We Go Marching*. The threat was not abroad; it was internal. It was not Soviet Communism that menaced America—it was the Statism at home and the growth of domestic fascist trends, all based upon dependency on war production for attainment of domestic prosperity.

Hence John T. Flynn ended his public career isolated from both the New Right and the Old Left. Liberals and the Left, he thought, had long ago deserted anti-imperialism on behalf of an effort to build a liberal American Empire. Now, in the name of conservatism, a new American Right was propagating globalism and perpetual intervention abroad. Removed from all sides of the Cold War consensus, John T. Flynn continued to point out—to the few who would listen—that the real threat was the militarism and fascism within ourselves. Those who now read *As We Go Marching* will have the opportunity to confront for themselves his most forceful exposition of this theme.

August, 1973

Author's Note

THIS BOOK is divided into three parts. One is about Italy, another about Germany, a third about the United States. But actually the book from beginning to end is about the United States. It has to do with the direction in which America has been drifting and in which she now moves with accelerated pace under the drive of war. When the war ends, in what direction will she go? Toward socialism or fascism? Or into some heroic struggle to reinstate the capitalist society? What socialism is, is fairly well understood. But this is not true of fascism. And we cannot have an intelligent answer to this question unless we know precisely what fascism is.

This book is about fascism in America. The fascism of Italy and Germany is examined because that is the only way in which we can decide what fascism is. Having examined it in Italy and Germany, not to tell again the ofttold story of Hitler and Mussolini but to isolate the essential ingredients of fascism, we will be in a position to put our own society under the glass to determine whether any or all of those essential ingredients are here.

Books about Mussolini and Hitler are countless. Mostly they deal with the foreign aggressions of these men and the brutalities with which they maintain their regimes at home. Those offering a sober analysis of the whole structure of the societies they have built are not nearly so numerous. I have, I believe, examined patiently all or nearly all of these volumes. I have treated them as the testimony of witnesses and I have sought to study, to sift, and to arrange these testimonies in order to make the picture as clear as possible, so that the reader may himself apply the tests to his own or any other country to identify there the fascist state or partisan.

The European war may end quickly. But we must not make the mistake of supposing that because Mussolini has been unhorsed or that when Hitler is finally destroyed this will mark the end of fascism or national socialism in Italy or Germany. Fascism, as we shall see, is nothing else than an expansion of forces and techniques in government which have been developing in Europe for decades. It is something we shall have to fight for many years to come—long after the war is over—here as everywhere. We are not fighting fascism when we fight anti-Semitism. They are quite different evils though they may be found together. We probably shall see men set about the impossible task of purging fascism of its ugly features, cleaning it up, offering us a polite, religious, democratic fascism. It is a hopeless task. But we cannot have intelligent opinions about the problem today or in the future unless we know first what fascism is. The first objective of this book, therefore, is to define it and then to search for its elements in America.

JOHN T. FLYNN

Bayside, L. I.
October 19, 1943

AS WE GO MARCHING

PART ONE

THE SOIL OF FASCISM: ITALY

I · The Bad Word

FASCISM HAS ATTAINED to the dignity of a cuss word in America. When we disagree with a man's social or political arguments, if we cannot reasonably call him a communist, we call him a fascist. The word itself has little more relation to its original and precise object than a certain well-beloved American expletive has to the harmless domestic animal it actually describes. But fascism is something more than a bad name. If we are to have an eye cocked for fascism and fascists in this country we had better be sure we know a fascist when we see one. Of course we will recognize him in an instant if he will go about in a Bundist uniform or storm trooper's black shirt. But what if he wears no such uniform, has never learned to goose step, speaks with no German gutturals or Italian gestures but in excellent seaboard English and is, in fact, a member of a patriotic American society or labor union and actually hates Hitler and Mussolini and wants them trapped, tried, and strung up—how then will we detect him?

There is a difference between a fifth columnist working in America for Hitler, Mussolini, or Stalin, and an American who would give his life for his country but would also like to see its social and economic life changed in the direction of the fascist pattern. You will get no such American to admit that what he believes in is fascism. He has other and more agreeable names for it. He would be provoked to knock you down if you called *him* a fascist. That is because he does not know what fascism is and makes the mistake of supposing that a fascist is one who is on the side of the Führer or the Duce. Dollfuss was a fascist and so was Schuschnigg, but neither of them was noticeably on the side of Hitler and one was assassinated and the other seized and imprisoned by Hitler. Metaxas in Greece was a fascist, but he was far from being a champion of his warlike neighbor who finally drove him from his fascist dictatorship and his country.

There are far too many misconceptions of the meaning of this explosive word. Many suppose that fascism is just a trade name for the modern, streamlined dictatorship. Hence they see little difference between the fascist Hitler and the communist Stalin. Both are dictators. They preside, however, over very different systems of society. They are despots ruling over totalitarian states, but the social structure of Russia is no more like the social structure of Germany and Italy than the State of Stalin resembles the State of Nicholas II.

Because our attention is fixed upon the element of dictatorship—which is just one ingredient of that order—we dismiss the whole thing as merely a form of gangsterism. Hence we hear such loose and superheated definitions as this: that it is a "revolt against Western culture" or "an attack upon our civilization." It is, alas, not a revolt against Western culture but a fruit—bitter and poisonous—of that culture.

We get far too much of our information about fascism from the daily reports of its dramatics—its marching black or brown shirts, its saluting legions, its posturing leaders, its violent techniques for obtaining power, its persecution of Jews, its suppression of free speech, and, finally, its inevitable adventures in the dark field of imperialism. These are the products of regimes that are built on violence; and violence is the essential weapon of every kind of dictatorship whether it be the dictatorship of the royal Louis XIV or the proletarian Joseph Stalin. It is violence and force that create the incidents and episodes that make the material of news. There are other weapons and instruments of policy in the arsenal of the fascist besides the castor-oil bottle, the torch, and the sword. What we must seek are those other instruments which distinguish the fascist dictatorship from all other dictatorships. What we must understand is that these fascist dictators are popular dictators, by which I mean dictators who, though by no means loved by the people, nevertheless hold their power through them. They are demagogic dictators as distinguished from purely military dictators. The regime includes a group of social and economic ingredients without which the dictatorships could never have been established and without which they could not have lasted so long.

There is a whole library of pamphlets, books, and orations produced to prove that fascism was caused by the Treaty of Versailles or by the greed or stupidity of Britain and France, or by the ingrown wickedness of the German or the supine flabbiness of the Italian, by anti-Semitism or munitions profiteers, by the conspiracies of business magnates or the rising hatred of the free world of the scholar. Yet fascism grew up in Italy without any push from anti-Semitism and it flourished there before it did in Germany, which is supposed to be the peculiar victim of Versailles. It has made its appearance in Greece and the Slavic Balkans as well as in "Nordic" Germany and Latin Italy and in Portugal where there were no munitions magnates to stir the broth.

You may hear any day angry discussions of the course of events in Washington. You will hear ardent New Dealers assert that the government is building a great buttress around the crumbling walls of democracy. Others tell you, with equal assurance, that the order being fashioned there is obviously National Socialism, while still others are quite as sure that it is communistic. Certainly it cannot be all these things. It is, I fear, reasonably certain that most of those who damn the present Washington regime look upon it as Red—and take Mr. Dies's revelations of the number of Communist party members and fellow travelers who have penetrated the bureaus as evidence that we are on our way to bolshevism. The fears of these critics are very much alive, and they grow in virulence. Yet we cannot afford to be in doubt about the real meaning and direction of our policies.

If we have any doubt, therefore, about what fascism is we would do well to resolve them. And the best way to do that is to examine it in the land where it began. If we will look at it in Italy, how it rose, what produced it, and what it in turn created as a system of national life, we cannot possibly be in doubt about what it is. It was in Italy where it was first established, where it reached its full flower and had its longest experience. If we will look at it there we can isolate its essential elements. And when we do this we will perceive that its roots run deep and long through the very structure of that society; that they are roots not indigenous to Italy but are to be found in all Western societies.

What follows, therefore, is not a history of fascism or the story of Mussolini's rise to power, but rather a search for the elements of this outrageous growth in order to make a list of those elements that must be united to produce it in America.

II · The Democratic State

SOMETHING over eighty years ago eight diminutive states were huddled together in that bootlike peninsula which is thrust into the Mediterranean from the Alps to the African sea. Generally it was referred to as Italy. But actually there was no such nation. Then in 1859, as the culmination of a great patriotic movement, inspired by Mazzini, directed by Cavour, and precipitated by Garibaldi, they were united in a single state called Italy. Half a dozen years later this movement was completed when Venetia joined and Rome was subdued. Thus Italy as a state had an existence from its union to the march on Rome of only sixty-two years. But in those sixty-two years and in the twenty which followed under Mussolini, it became the laboratory of the most dangerous and explosive collection of principles in modern history.

Out of this Italian laboratory came the thing we know as fascism. Its influence has spread throughout the continent of Europe and into parts of this hemisphere. And the world today struggles in a vast crisis which, in one sense at least, is the culmination of this fatal experiment.

The society which the apostles of the *Risorgimento* fashioned took the form that is now called a democracy. The history of Italy during the next sixty-two years became part of that adventure in representative government that characterized the continental scene after 1848. Italy became a constitutional monarchy. It included a king, a constitution, a chamber of deputies, with a premier responsible to the King but dependent on the deputies for funds, an aristocratic senate appointed for life, along with grants of freedom of discussion and the press which, despite certain legal modifications, were exercised extensively. It was, in the true sense, not a democracy any more than any European state was a democracy. The people did not exercise direct authority and there were extensive limitations on the right of suffrage. There was a property and literacy test which, in a country where everyone was poor and two thirds were illiterate, resulted in a voting registration of only 2 per cent of the population. This was liberalized in 1882, which brought a registration of 7 per cent. Universal male suffrage did not come until 1913.

Moreover, Italy, like every European state save Switzerland and France, recognized the principle of the elite through an aristocratic senate, which was, however, not so essentially aristocratic as the British House of Lords, since appointment was for life only.

The term "democratic" has been used rather loosely of late. But generally it may be said that in these new European states the power of the people was recognized in fact as the ultimate authority. Their control over the purse gave them an immense authority and there was a more or less continuous extension of this power through the growing place of the parliament in the structure of the state. In Italy the habits and practices of parliamentary popular government began slowly to affect the life and thinking of the people. The press could be limited under special conditions until 1896 when this power was repealed. However, save on one or two occasions, the power was used sparingly though it did indeed exist as a background for restraint. Nevertheless, there was a kind of traditional tolerance for free speaking which is not easy to define. Mr. G. A. Borgese describes it best as follows:

> There had always been a considerable breath of tolerance in modern Italy, at least in the large cities and in the conflicts among leaders. The hereditary dogmatism of the Italian intelligence had found a countercheck in the equally hereditary and almost instinctive trait of the old nation, which had

learned in hundreds of years the best lessons of history, namely that intellectual passions vanish, while benevolence lasts, and that the suggestions of the heart are safer than the pretensions of the mind. This sweetness of Italian life, in spite of poverty and strife, of ecclesiastical and social tyranny, had ever been inspiring to foreigners visiting the country and it was this rather than imitation of English parliamentary institutions that made up the peculiar kind of Italian liberalism which was more psychological than theoretical and political.[1]

I quote this because it helps to balance the significance of the repression that lay hidden in the statute. Italy began to discuss her problems with growing freedom and even fierceness. The Premier, though named by the King, had to gather behind him a majority in parliament to govern which included the power of the purse. The liberal parties grew continuously in numbers and power. And generally Italy must be accepted as an authentic section of the whole experiment in representative government that now faces the bar of the world to give an account of its stewardship.

It is not possible to review the history of this experiment in government and the people it covered without concluding that Italy was in no sense a field especially fertile for the cultivation of the totalitarian idea. The Italian states were among the last in Europe to form themselves into a unitary nation. And long after they did that the people remained far more citizens of their several small provinces than of the central state. They looked always with a mixture of indifference and suspicion on Rome. They resented regulations emanating from the center. The slow development of a stronger central government had to make its way in Italy against the normal and habitual attitudes of the people.

III · The Soil of Fascism

THUS we behold the body into which the fatal germ of fascism will insert itself—a parliamentary, constitutional monarchy con-

[1] From *Goliath: The March of Fascism*. Copyright, 1937, by G. A. Borgese. By permission of the Viking Press, Inc., New York.

forming to the general pattern of Western civilization. In one other respect it followed that pattern. It was what is commonly called a capitalist society—a society in which the instruments of production and distribution were owned and operated by private persons or groups for profit and within the framework of the money economy. That is, it was like the other countries of western Europe.

Of course the Italy of the *Risorgimento* was a more simple form of society than that of the fascist squadrons. But so also was the America of the Civil War compared with the more complicated system of Mr. Coolidge's New Era or Mr. Roosevelt's New Deal. As Italy grew and the machine invaded the world, and the techniques of corporation organization and modern finance were perfected, Italy adopted them, though less extensively than Germany or Britain since she remained largely an agricultural country. Italy, however, developed and exhibited very quickly the characteristic defects of her economic system. These were persisting poverty, inadequate income, interrupted employment, crises.

The men who united Italy into a nation were preoccupied not with her economic problems, but with the dream of liberation and unity. There was a deeply rooted popular notion that Austria was at the bottom of all Italy's troubles, including her poverty. The country was supposed to be divinely favored by Providence with abundance which only the suppressive hand of Austria held away from the people. "Where is there another country in the world," said Cesare Correnti, "endowed with such smiling, well-navigated coastlands, with so many ports, a land so rich in every blessing of nature, so fertile, so healthy, suitable for every form of agriculture, bearing oaks and northern trees as well as Syrian palms and other tropical plants, enlivened by a bracing, invigorating climate, by life-giving streams, by shores rich in fish, by pastoral and wooded mountains, by lovely prospects of land, water, and sky?"[1]

The leaders of the *Risorgimento*, knowing little of economics, believed that if a united Italy could be liberated from the Austrian yoke, she would be free to put her resources to work for a better life. But when the Austrian had gone and the honest Piedmontese

---

[1] Quoted in *Development of Political Ideas in Italy in the 19th Century*, by Luigi Villari. Proceedings of the British Academy, February 17, 1926, Vol. XII.

monarch, Victor Emmanuel II, ruled over a free and united Italy, the government soon revealed that it had little notion what to do about the persisting poverty and recurring crises. They were not unique in Italy. But poverty was a graver problem there than in other western nations. "The Italians," said Ferrero, "have been used for two centuries to live upon half a loaf." The living conditions of Italian peasants during the first years of the new nation were held to be at as low a point as at any time in the previous 2,000 years.[2] They were poor not merely compared with American standards but with those of the European nations around them. As late as 1891, measured so much per head, the Englishman got $150 a year, the Frenchman $130, the Prussian $85, and the Italian only $35. He subsisted on only half as much wheat flour as a Briton or even a Spaniard.[3] This was the condition which confronted the victorious leaders of the *Risorgimento* and their successors.

Of course Italy in the fifty years up to 1914 shared in the development of the great age of machinery. Industrial workers increased from 188,000 to 2,330,000. The great silk industry rose from nothing. Foreign commerce trebled. Railways were built. The nation's savings rose from 980,000,000 lire to 5,822,000,000 lire.[4] These statistics do not accurately measure the economic well-being of the country. They do, however, indicate material progress. But that progress was not sufficient to end the dark poverty that flourished in the midst of her progress. A larger number of persons enjoyed a higher standard of living. But also the number of peasants and poor workers who failed to share in this increase remained fatally large.

The causes of this poverty were not essentially different from the causes in other similar societies. They had two sources: one, the defects of the economic system. The other lay in Italy's natural conditions. The system of production and distribution by private owners using money as a means of distribution develops certain difficulties in operation. There has been a good deal of popular discussion of these defects in recent years. They arise out of the opera-

[2]*The Corporate State in Action*, by Carl T. Schmidt, Oxford University Press, 1939.
[3]*Italy Today*, by King and Okey, Nisbet & Co., London, 1909.
[4]*Mussolini's Italy*, by Herman Finer, London, 1935.

tion of economic laws and out of certain human characteristics—savings, debt, the idiosyncrasies of money, the habits of income on one hand and the presence of so many hostile interests among human groups on the other. This is no place to examine these laws. We must be content with the fact that they exist. And the operation of these laws was producing in Italy much the same effects they were producing everywhere else. In Italy, however, the impact of these laws was greater because Italy herself was a poorer country. She was behindhand in the development of a modern industrial society. Her agricultural system was antiquated. The peasant proprietors' holdings were too small. The share croppers were shamelessly exploited. The illiterate peasant farm worker was cheated, starved, and underpaid.

In other words, the rulers of the new nation, from first to last, faced the problem of the modern capitalist state, growing ever sharper and more critical, of utilizing its powers to ensure its people a decent share of the necessities of life. It faced also the problem of protecting its more fortunate citizens from the adversities of recurring depressions. The problem was no different from that of other countries. It was merely more pressing because Italy was poorer and the diseases of the system had eaten more deeply into her vitals.

The condition of Italy was, in a sense, no worse as the century ended than it was before Italian unity was established. Indeed in many respects it was better. What had changed was the people. Now they expected their government to do something about it. The people, whatever the degree of social sluggishness in the south, were becoming more literate. The old population, which, as Mr. Borgese observes, had lived through twenty centuries of servitude and misery, restrained by their civil servants and soothed by their religious teachers, had been willing to surrender to the hard fate of inescapable poverty because it was accepted as their lot in the natural and supernatural order of things. But this was no longer true. Two thirds of the people were illiterate in 1871. Less than half were illiterate in 1900. And this number rapidly declined in the succeeding years. The schoolhouse was doing its work, as it was everywhere in the world. And so was the newspaper. The Italians were discussing their problems. As election after election was debated and ideas flowed in upon the people—and from other parts of the world stories of the better life in other lands were retold—a wholly new temper displayed itself.

The rise of the socialist movement played a powerful role in all this. Socialism arrived late in Italy—around 1890. At first it was a revolutionary party, but by the beginning of the century it became a reformist party collaborating with the liberals for reforms not essentially socialist—universal suffrage, pay for deputies, full liberty of the press and of religion, government neutrality in labor disputes. The alliance with the liberals lasted until two years before the Great War. Together these groups submitted the capitalist economic philosophy to merciless analysis. Socialism grew, but the effects of socialist preaching grew far more than the party. Labor organized. Unions, dominated by the socialists, became numerous and powerful politically. Employers organized in trade associations with their budget of claims upon the government. Even the Catholics abandoned indifference to the political scene and were summoned to action by the famous encyclical *Rerum novarum* of Leo XIII, which contained some sentences that read like excerpts from socialist literature.

Everywhere there was the ferment of ideas that characterized the late nineteenth century. Anarchism and syndicalism, along with co-operative movements, focused attention upon the growing problem of poverty and crisis. The poor said: "We were better off when we were worse off." The middle classes, better off, became acutely aware of their own problems, namely the retention of what they had against the onslaughts of depressions and the programs of the reformers. Labor, businessmen, farmers, all sorts of minorities organized and produced those indefatigable pressure groups that rob modern governments of their rest. Thus the government was under ceaseless demand for further solutions.

A serious phenomenon appeared that one day was to devour much of the effective strength of the parliament. The new Germany was a federal state. The individual states that formed the empire held fast to the power to legislate upon and administer their local affairs. The task of government was split into many fractions, each reasonably within the mental grasp of human beings. In Italy, though, there was only a single parliament. It worked well enough while the population was small and life simple. But as Italy grew and the social structure became more complex, every province and commune pressed its problems upon the parliament. In time it attempted to legislate upon an array of subjects utterly beyond its capacity. Thus the parliament was forced to abdicate many of its powers in favor of commissioners, bureaus, and bureaucrats who assumed the role of legislators and executives. The bureaucratic state began to proliferate. And as power grows by what it feeds on, the central government reached out for ever more power. Dr. Salvemini says one of the worst stains of the old pre-fascist government was the Home Office control over local affairs. Mayors were elected. But the Home Secretary put a "prefect" into each province who could dismiss mayors and disband town councils. "Thus the prefect was in a position to put pressure to bear upon the mayor and town councilors, especially in the backward sections of the country," says Dr. Salvemini. "The mayors and town councilors who used their influence in favor of the government's candidates during election programs remained in office, even if they were the worst rascals. Those who supported the opposition . . . were replaced by 'commissioners.' Thus slowly power was drawn toward the center—power which exceeded the ability and grasp of the central government to administer intelligently."[5]

IV · Tax and Borrow and Spend

WE ARE NOW ABLE to see that this Italian society had set in motion certain streams of thought. We will see still others come into being. First we see the conviction of the people that there were economic and social problems affecting them that ought to be solved, that foremost among these problems were those of poverty

[5] *What to Do with Italy*, by Gaetano Salvemini and George La Piana, Duell, Sloan & Pearce, New York, 1943.

and of crises and that they were determined that the government do something about these problems. So deeply rooted were these convictions that no man could arrive in power who did not adopt them as part of his polity.

This situation became itself the parent of another settled conviction that began as a little trickle and finally cut its way deep into the terrain of Italian public thought. It began to flow as a full current in the regime of Agostino Depretis, who rose to power as Premier in 1876.

From the beginning of united Italy the country had been ruled by the Right, some of them able statesmen and patriots inspired by the principles of liberation and unity. They were under the dominion of political rather than economic ideas. Meantime taxes rose, centralization became a specter to the liberals, the demand for private security through social-welfare measures and public security through preparedness was ignored. The nation's prestige abroad was said to be deteriorating. The end of this was a political uprising against the cautious regime. And on the crest of this uprising Depretis rode into power. He was a journalist-politician who had allied himself in parliament with the Left. When he came into power it was as the leader of the Left, and as such he ruled as Prime Minister, save for a brief interlude, for most of the eleven years from 1876 to 1887.

He promised every sort of reform without regard to the contradictions among his promises. He promised to reduce taxation and increase public works. He promised greater social security and greater prosperity. When he came to power, he had no program and no settled notion of how he would redeem these pledges. His party was joined by recruits from every school of political thought. He found at his side the representatives of every kind of discontent and every organ of national salvation. The oppressed tenants along with the overworked and underpaid craftsmen of the towns crowded around him, beside the most reactionary landowners and employers, to demand, as one commentator said, the honoring of the many contradictory promissory notes he had issued on his way to office.

He was supposed to be a man of personal integrity so far as

money was concerned. But he proved to be a leader of obvious intellectual dishonesty. He was shallow measured as a statesman, with only the most rudimentary knowledge of the grave problems of economics and social reform. But as a politician he was a craftsman of the first order. He had a cunning knowledge of men. If he understood only superficially the weaknesses and evils of the social system, he knew instinctively the frailties and vices of political leaders. He practiced a policy of pleasing everyone. He entered office with no settled plan of government, depending on day-to-day improvisation to meet the multiplying difficulties.[1]

A depressing fate has seemed to dog the footsteps of so-called leftist ministries of Italy. Depretis, with fellow liberals in key positions of his cabinet, adopted, when he came to power, the policies of his conservative predecessors and called them his own. He increased indirect taxation, dodged the solution of the problems he had promised to attack by naming commissions. When he entered office the budget was balanced. It remained so until 1884. However, the inevitable depression arrived and Depretis, the promiser of the better life, not knowing what else to do about it, turned to the oldest and most reactionary device—public works financed by government borrowing. He adopted the policy which in our own time has been called "tax and tax, borrow and borrow, spend and spend." The budget was thrown out of balance in 1884 and remained so for thirteen years.

The budget had been unbalanced from 1859 to 1876, but Depretis' predecessors had ended that condition. Depretis unbalanced the budget in 1885-86 and now adopted this as a deliberate national policy. Living from hand to mouth to keep himself in power, seeking to placate groups of every sort, Depretis used the public funds freely. Roads, new schools, canals, post offices, public works of every sort were built with public funds obtained by borrowing.

Depretis now discovered he had got hold of a powerful political

---

[1] Bolton King and Thomas Okey, in their excellent account of the Italy of these years, say of Depretis' government that "nominally it was more liberal than the Right, but it had inherent weaknesses which robbed its liberalism of reality . . . It drew its strength from the south and the south was the home of all that was unhealthy in political life. Most of its leaders, though patriots in a way, had small scruples as to methods." *Italy Today*, by King and Okey, Nisbet & Co., London, 1909.

13

weapon. Political life in Italy was notably corrupt. Deputies could be bought. But Depretis found that instead of buying the *deputies* he could buy their *constituents*. Every district wanted some kind of money grants for schools, post offices, roads, farm aid. The Premier found that he could buy the favor of the constituency by spending public money in the district. The deputy had to prove to his people that he was sufficiently in the favor of the Premier to bring such grants to them. The philanthropic state was now erected in Italy and it was never to be dismantled.

Miss Margot Hentze describes the system thus:

> Pressure was brought to bear through the organs of local administration, who were given to understand that "favorable" districts might expect new schools, public works, roads, canals, post and telegraph offices, etc.; while the "unfavorable" might find even their existing institutions suppressed. And the effect of these tactics was great. Many of the most eminent men on the Right lost their seats.[2]

The Encyclopaedia Britannica, 14th Edition, 1929, title "Italy," thus alludes to this episode:

> In their anxiety to remain in office Depretis and the finance minister, Magliani, never hesitated to mortgage the financial future of their country. No concession could be denied to deputies, or groups of deputies, whose support was indispensable to the life of the cabinet, nor, under such conditions, was it possible to place any effective check upon administrative abuses in which politicians or their electors were interested.

The press was subsidized secretly. Journalists were flattered and some of them paid while others obtained handsome berths for their relatives. Indeed it was over a scandal connected with the press that Depretis was forced on one occasion to resign. His supporters were fond of speaking of him as "the incorruptible." He was styled by some of his enemies the "incorruptible corrupter of all." Thus the first liberal government in Italy made to its public life the dubious contribution of control with public funds and the policy of borrowing and spending.

Those who imagine that the device of spending deficit money is

[2] *Pre-Fascist Italy*, by Margot Hentze, G. Allen, London, 1939.

an invention of present-day reformers may be interested in the record of Italian deficits:

	Deficits	Balanced Budgets
From 1859 to 1876	17 years	
" 1876 to 1884		8 years
" 1884 to 1898	14 "	
" 1898 to 1910		12 "
" 1910 to 1925	15 "	
	46 years	20 years

Thus in sixty-six years of national life up to 1925 the budget of Italy was unbalanced for forty-six years. The first seventeen years of this record arose out of the assumption of the debts of the several constituent states and the great burdens attending organization of the new nation. But after Depretis the deficits were the product of a definite policy of spending borrowed money on public works to avert economic disaster and enable ministries to remain in power.[3]

The result of these spendings and borrowings, of course, was to create a great and ever-growing debt. By June 30, 1914, Italy's national debt was 15,766,000,000 lire—a huge sum in the purchasing power of that day for a country of Italy's size and poverty. The consequence of this was that Italy found herself, as she entered the war, under the necessity of immense war expenditures financed by huge borrowings on top of the already staggering public debt. The effect of this debt, even before the war, was to impose an exhausting burden of taxation on a people too poor to live in decency. By 1913 the interest on the debt alone made up a fourth of all the public revenues. And by 1914, when people were grumbling about the oppressive cost of the army and the navy, the interest on the debt amounted to almost as much as both these sums.[4]

[3] The figures used here are based on the following:

Pamphlet issued by Provveditorato Generale Della Stato, Rome, 1925. *Italian Government Finances*, by H. C. McLean, for 1923 and 1925. Trade Information Bulletins Nos. 116 and 130, Commerce Reports, U.S. Dept. of Commerce. *Italy's International Financial Position*, by Constantine McGuire, Macmillan, New York, 1926, p. 63, *et seq. Cambridge Modern History*, Vol. XII, pp. 232, 233. *Fascist Italy*, by William Ebenstein, American Book Company, New York, 1939. *The Fascist Experiment*, by Luigi Villari, London, 1926. Encyclopaedia Britannica, title "Italy," 14th Edition, Vol. 12.

[4] *Italy's International Financial Position*, by Constantine McGuire, Macmillan, New York, 1926.

The debt and the servicing of it became the most harrying problem of the government. King and Okey said in 1909 that "the country is weighed down by taxation because the state has undertaken burdens beyond its strength," and added that "the financial question is at the bottom of half the difficulty in Italy."[5] Certainly it intruded itself upon the discussions of every other question. Once having committed themselves to keeping things afloat by government spending there was no escape from it. The device having been discovered as a means to power there were always leaders who were willing to use it. Against them the more prudent and honest statesmen who counseled a sane financial policy were powerless. Good advice was unavailing against grants of money. Italy could never repay the debt. She could never hope to make a substantial reduction of it. And as the deficits mounted prudent men could see no end ahead save disaster. The interest charge became so intolerable that when Giolitti was able to refund the debt at a lower rate of interest the achievement was hailed as Italy's "financial *Risorgimento.*"

It is interesting to find the late Guglielmo Ferrero sounding a warning against Italy's borrowing-spending policy as far back as 1899. In a little-known volume called *Militarism* he told how the government had opened new roads, built public works on an elaborate scale, set up banks, organized great public services, spending on all this "fabulous sums" and "contracting heavy debts." These novelties, observed Ferrero, were copied from the French parliament and as a result the Italian parliament "finally grew to resemble the French parliament and became an instrument in the hands of an oligarchy." Then he called attention to the approaching denouement:

When the fountains of government abundance began to dry up, when through lack of funds and the impossibility of negotiating fresh loans the state was forced to check the extension of bureaucracy and to put a stop to public works, then and then only did the Italians realize what it meant to have allowed themselves to be made one of the most heavily taxed nations in the world.

Italy enjoyed a respite for twelve years from deficits after 1898 up to 1910. During that period she had a windfall in the shape of

[5]*Italy Today*, by King and Okey, Nisbet & Co., London, 1909.

great remittances of cash from her emigrant citizens who had settled in America and who kept a continuous flow of funds back to the old folks at home. That played a very great part in balancing her budget, for there was a steady stream of emigrants leaving Italy—very poor people who contributed very little to the purchasing power of her population and whose departure removed a considerable army annually from among those who stood in need of government assistance, draining away large numbers of the unemployable population. Those who left became, by Italy's standards, heavy earners in the New World and were transformed into contributors to her national income rather than unproductive beneficiaries of it. The balanced budget despite this passed away definitely in 1911 not to return again until a great war and a subsequent revolution had swept from the people of Italy their freedom.[6]

V · The New Industry

WE HAVE NOW SEEN that out of the chronic economic difficulties of Italy the politicians had recourse to the practice of state spending of borrowed money. This practice could not have continued for so long a period as to be practically habitual without the approval of the people. It imposed burdens because the debt service charges added to the tax rate of an overtaxed people. Men of all sorts grumbled at it. Politicians of all sorts disapproved it. But most of them resorted to it as an inescapable evil. Italians were like the economy-minded husband who demands that his wife spend less money on the household but without curtailing any of his comforts.

[6]Dr. Gaetano Salvemini, whose contributions to the examination of the whole fascist experiment in Italy have been so great, makes one statement about the debt which does not correspond with the above account at one point. In a debate with Dr. Roselli, a fascist apologist, before the Foreign Policy Association, he said: "We were able during the fifteen years before the war to balance the budget always with a surplus." Mr. Constantine McGuire gives the following figure as the over-all deficit for the years 1898 to 1914: Revenues, 31,991,000,000 lire; expenditures, 36,804,000,000, a deficit for the sixteen years of 4,813,000,000 lire. The budget was balanced from 1898 to 1910. But this record ended in 1911 and was not resumed for another fifteen years. In the fifteen years before Italy entered the war the budget was balanced ten times and unbalanced five times.

The policy developed for itself a peculiar support among people who opposed it in principle in much the same way as our tariff. Congress has always been full of statesmen who make speeches against the tariff but work incessantly for higher duties for the products of their own states. Thus in Italy, while individuals murmured against the growing debt, they continued as members of cities or villages or farming districts to fight valiantly for their share of the spendings. The people as beneficiaries were always more powerful than the same people as citizens. However, the whole history of the policy had the effect of setting up a stream of opinion and desire respecting government spending. It was not something new that ran across settled beliefs. It became a habit and, in moments of public economic difficulty, was the first thing great masses thought of and clamored for. No man in Italy would find himself on unfavorable ground as a rule by promising bigger budgets at the cost of bigger public debts. As a rule the statesman riding that vessel would find himself sailing with and not against the stream of public opinion and tolerance. The presence, therefore, of this stream in the consciousness of the people of Italy is one of the most important to be noticed and kept in mind as we search for the roots of fascism in Italy or any other country.

But this policy does run into resistance—and resistance in very influential quarters. The large taxpayer is against it. He acquiesces reluctantly. And as the debt grows and he looks with growing fear on its future proportions he begins to exert his full influence against it. In different countries the basis of resistance takes different forms, but it comes chiefly from the conservative groups. Hence it becomes increasingly difficult to go on spending in the presence of persisting deficits and rising debt. Some form of spending must be found that will command the support of the conservative groups. Political leaders, embarrassed by their subsidies to the poor, soon learned that one of the easiest ways to spend money is on military establishments and armaments, because it commands the support of the groups most opposed to spending.

There is no other policy of European governments about which there is so much innocent misunderstanding in America as the institution of militarism. The American criticism of this evil has been directed almost wholly at the ambitious chieftains, the warlike statesmen, and the thrifty munitions barons who are supposed to be behind it. They are, of course, behind it. But they would not get very far were it not for the fact that a large military establishment draws countless thousands annually out of the overstocked labor market while it enables the government to set up and support a large industry which employs even more men than are in the army. Among all the means for producing government-created income none is so successful as militarism.

In 1895 Italy was spending five times as much on the army and navy as on public works. To ask an Italian statesman to agree to disarmament before the Great War would have been to ask him to liquidate the largest industry in Italy. Nothing could have been more futile than to offer such a proposal to an Italian government always on the edge of the precipice of economic disaster. And while there was always a certain amount of agitation against militarism and conscription in Italy, the system in fact always had the approval of the liberal and labor leaders. The aggressive supporters of large military expenditures, however, were the conservatives, also the most aggressive enemies of the policy of spending. Thus it was because the government could get public agreement for loans for this purpose and because such loans were essential to the policy of spending which kept the floundering economic system going that the militaristic policy remained so vital and vigorous an institution in Italy—and in every other continental country. It is estimated that the costs of the army and navy plus the indirect costs arising out of debt charges incurred for this purpose accounted for 63 per cent of all the costs of government.

I must not leave this whole subject of spending and the means employed to spend, including militarism, without observing that there is nothing new in it. It is as old as civilized government. And, what is more, the protagonists of it have understood precisely what they are doing.[1]

[1] The following excerpts from Plutarch's *Pericles* in the *Lives* make very clear how well these two instruments of state policy were understood by that early republican statesman. "Pericles, finding himself come short of his competitors in wealth and money, by which advantages the other was enabled to take care of the poor, inviting every day some one or other of the citizens that was in want to supper and bestowing clothes on the ancient

VI · The Magnificent Drug

AFTER Agostino Depretis came Francesco Crispi. Thus, oddly enough, after the liberal statesman who introduced the policy of spending, perfected the techniques of corruption, and committed the nation to the institution of militarism, came the liberal statesman who infected Italy with the virus of imperialism. For imperialism flows as logically from militarism as militarism from spending. Practical Italian politicians perceived that they could not induce their tax-burdened people to support large armies and navies—whatever the real purpose—without persuading them that they stood in need of these costly weapons. They could not do this without providing the people with an adequate arsenal of fears. If the country had no natural enemy to be cultivated, then an enemy had to be invented. There is no answer to the proposition that a nation must be strong enough to repel the ambitions of powerful and greedy neighbors. Hence the powerful and greedy neighbors become

people, and breaking down the hedges and enclosures of his grounds, that all that would might gather what fruit they pleased, Pericles, thus outdone in popular arts, by the device of one Damonides of Oea, as Aristotle states, *turned to the distribution of the public moneys.*"

How he used these "moneys" is revealed in the following paragraphs of the Roman biographer: "Pericles, at that time more than any other, let loose the reins to the people, and made his policy subservient to their pleasure, contriving continually to have some great public show or solemnity, some banquet, or some procession or other in the town to please them, coaxing his countrymen like children, and with such delights and pleasures as were not, however, unedifying. Besides that every year he sent three score galleys, on board of which there went numbers of citizens, who were in pay eight months, learning at the same time and practicing the art of seamanship.

"He sent, moreover, a thousand of them into the Chersonese as planters, to share the land among them by lot. . . . And this he did to ease and discharge the city of an idle, and by reason of their idleness, a busy, meddling crowd of people. . . .

"That which gave most pleasure and ornament to the City of Athens and the greatest admiration and even astonishment to all strangers . . . was his construction of the public and sacred buildings.

"It was good reason, that now the city was sufficiently provided with all things necessary for war, they should convert the overplus of wealth to such undertakings as would hereafter, when completed, give them eternal honor, and, for the present, while in process, *freely supply all the inhabitants with plenty.* With their variety of workmanship and of occasions for service, which summon all arts and trades and require all hands to be employed about them, *they do actually put the whole city, in a manner, into state-pay;* while at the same time she is both beautified and maintained by herself. For as those who are of age and strength for war are provided for and maintained in the armaments abroad by their pay out of the public stock, so, it being his desire and design, that the undisciplined a national economic necessity. Then in good time defense calls for the seizure of some neighbor's territory or of some remote strategic island or the rectification of frontiers for military purposes. The raw materials of war must be accumulated and these perhaps are found in the hands of weaker small peoples with whom quarrels are quickly brewed. National pride, the dignity of the race, patriotism —all these well-known and well-exploited emotions are played on. And of course, as the apprehensions of the people grow, the army grows with them, and so, too, the unbalanced budget—acclaimed by the most energetic conservative enemies of big budgets.

These policies, of course, could not be developed in Italy without the aid of the purple people, the inflammable spirits who love adventure and the dangerous life, who swell to ecstasy when the war drums roll but whose zeal for high emprise would be unavailing if harder and more cynical motives did not inspire the realists in power.

Many explanations of this phenomenon have been offered. In Ger-

mechanic multitude that stayed at home should not go without their share of the public salaries, and yet should not have them given them for sitting still and doing nothing, to that end, he thought fit to bring in among them, with the approbation of the people, *these vast projects of public buildings and designs of works*, that would be of some continuance before they were finished, and would give employment to numerous arts, so that the part of the people that stayed at home might, no less than those that were at sea or in garrisons or on expeditions, have a fair and just occasion of receiving the benefit and having their share of the public moneys."

Plutarch then enumerates the trades that were aided by this: "The materials were stone, brass, ivory, gold, ebony, cypress-wood; and the arts of trades that wrought and fashioned them were smiths and carpenters, moulders, founders and braziers, stone-cutters, dyers, goldsmiths, ivory-workers, painters, embroiderers, turners; those again that conveyed them to the town for use, merchants and mariners and ship-masters by sea and by land, cart-wrights, cattle-breeders, wagoners, rope-makers, flax-workers, shoemakers and leather dressers, road makers, miners. . . . Thus to say all in a word, the occasions and services of these public works distributed plenty through every age and condition."

Here was an authentic PWA four hundred years before Christ. But this would not be complete if we did not name the source whence these moneys came. The Delian League, composed of the Greek cities opposed to Sparta, had created a fund to be preserved for use in the event of the inevitable war against Sparta and Corinth. This fund consisted of yearly contributions of coin by all these cities. Athens was entrusted, as leader of the League, with the custody of this great and ever-growing treasure which was kept on the Isle of Delos. It was this fund, and not taxation, to which Pericles turned to finance his public works and other government spending activities. And so we understand when Plutarch says: "This [the public works program] was of all his actions in the government which his enemies most looked askance on and cavilled at in the popular assemblies, crying out how that the Commonwealth of Athens had lost its reputation and was ill-spoken of abroad for removing the common treasure of the Greeks from the Isle of Delos into their own custody."

many it is ascribed to the "German disease." Mr. Herbert Agar, one of our own purple philosophers, who sees ahead America's "Time for Greatness," explains the evil of aggression among the Germans as due to the historic fact that Germany grew up "outside the stream of Latin culture." This handy diagnosis, of course, cannot be applied to Italy, which has wallowed in the stream of Latin culture. So in Italy it is ascribed to some peculiar weakness in the Latin soul, the love of glory, the nostalgic yearning for the ancient renown of the Romans, their addiction to dramatics. Others see in it the dark fruit of the arms industry or of dynastic ambitions or old racial feuds. Mr. G. A. Borgese, an eminent Italian scholar and a bitter critic of fascism, which he justly calls the Black Age, sees the sense of inferiority of his countrymen at the bottom of their sins—imperialism as well as fascism. In a brilliantly written volume in which he has communicated to his recently acquired English something of the florid energy of his native tongue, he traces the long genesis of Italy's spiritual degeneracy to those poets and scholars from Dante to d'Annunzio who have unwittingly fed her sense of frustration. She had lived through the centuries under the shadow of the long-extinguished glories of the past so that even in her moments of resurgence she could lift her sights no higher than "Renaissance" or "*Risorgimento*"—the resurrection of some former eminence. The long subjection to Austria had been a "delirium of inferiority" and had finally become "an inferiority—an actual one."[1]

But we need not look for special explanations of Italy's hesitant steps in imperialism. In the eighties there was no people in Europe less concerned about international adventure than the Italians. They had achieved their independence about a score of years before. Most of the men in public life were the old veterans of *Risorgimento*, including Depretis and Crispi. The Italian mind was still under the dominion of those passionate appeals for natural rights on which the followers of Mazzini and Garibaldi had been nourished. Italy, which had seen most of her people under the heel of the worst of the continental aggressors—Austria—had fed her spirit too long on the arguments against despotism not to have still a deeply rooted hatred

---

[1] From *Goliath: The March of Fascism*. Copyright, 1937, by G. A. Borgese. By permission of the Viking Press, Inc., New York.

for imperialism. For eighteen years, while the chief European powers and some of the smaller ones—Teuton, Saxon, Latin, and Slav—had struggled over territories in Africa and Asia, Italian statesmen still talked eloquently of the rights of man and of small peoples. They were preoccupied with their internal difficulties—the battle against poverty, crisis, and debt. These were Italy's real enemies, not the Lion of Judah in Abyssinia. What, then, could be more insupportable than to ascribe the rise of imperialist ambitions in Italy to peculiar characteristics of the Italian character when there was nothing either peculiar or unique about them save their sluggishness? Every country in Europe had been practicing the dark art for many years. Italy was the last to feel the contagion.

A more rational explanation is to be found in the fact that imperialism became a realizable policy against the background of economic distress, the spending of money, the resistance of the people to spending and debt. When the economy-minded conservatives began to object to "wasting the public money on schools and roads and subsidies to farmers," the practical politician who did not dare make an end of spending and borrowing found militarism and its inevitable companion suitable and feasible forms of activity to be substituted for a peacetime works-project administration. The easy opportunity for this policy in all European countries arrived when Africa was opened by explorers and Asia by traders and naval officers—two vast continents, one filled with treasure and the other with customers.

England, France, Germany, the Dutch, and little Belgium, and even feeble Spain sent their ambassadors of good will on warships and opened the era of new imperialism. The behavior of these countries calls for no unique diagnosis. When Italy belatedly took her place at the counter we need not explain her behavior by motives more fantastic than those which moved her fellow marauders. The example of her neighbors furnished her statesmen, struggling with insoluble budget and labor and social problems, turning more and more to militarism as a form of spending, with a happy suggestion for escape. They mixed and offered to their perplexed and impatient people this glamorous opiate—this magnificent drug. They are not written down as wicked men for this in other countries and need not be in Italy. Indeed the architects of imperialism in Britain and France are immortalized in marble and bronze. The effect of the policy, however, upon their countries and upon the whole world has been as evil as any misfortune that has come upon men.

It is interesting to find two recent arrivals from Italy confirming this view. Eleanor and Reynolds Packard, United Press correspondents in Rome until the war, in their memoir *Balcony Empire,* make the following comment on the present-day Italian:

> With all these years of training, both physical and mental, that the average Italian had forced on him, it seemed strange that every Italian youth did not develop into an ardent fascist. But the fact is that the so-called fascist ideals ran counter to the Italian character. Fundamentally the Italian is non-militaristic by nature and he loathes all forms of regimentation. All the uniforms and fascist regalia with which Mussolini bedecked Italian boys could never change this; so that as soon as fascist precepts were hard to follow—that is when they involved hardships and sacrifices as in wartime— the average Italian instinctively turned against them.[2]

Mr. Herbert Matthews, of the New York *Times,* in a very recent book affirms that years later, even after Italy's rigorous tutelage in militarism under Mussolini, she did not want the war and listened with pathetic credulity to the Duce's lying protestations of peace; that, indeed, in spite of the bloodthirsty tone of the press, the people loathed the war.[3]

It is, in fact, not in the alleged affinity of the Italian soul for the devil that one sees with apprehension the true menace of the fascist disease. It is indeed in the very opposite of that fact that we discern its danger. It is in the fact that the devil could seduce a people so little addicted to the drug he offered that we must derive our greatest concern. If this were something to which the Italian was peculiarly susceptible and against which our robust American nature offered a stout resistance, then we would have no need to trouble our heads about it. But as we observe the onset of the fascist illness in Italy—and elsewhere—we will be more and

[2] *Balcony Empire,* by Eleanor and Reynolds Packard, Oxford University Press, 1942.
[3] *The Fruits of Fascism,* by Herbert L. Matthews, Harcourt, Brace & Co., New York, 1943.

more impressed by the disturbing fact that no nation or race exhibits any immunity to it.

The man who was to turn Italy's eyes in this direction was one of those who had been most ardent in the championship of the old Mazzinian ideals of national freedom. There is perhaps nothing a free people has to fear more than the labels public men pin on themselves and with which they wriggle into power. Beneath the skin of many a well-advertised liberal lurk the blue corpuscles of a hardened tory. The tragic evil of these misbranded liberals is that they are able to put into effect reactionary measures that conservatives longed for but dared not attempt. When the conservative statesman seeks to adopt some atavistic policy, liberal groups can be counted on to resist the attempt. But when a liberal premier, marching under the banner of liberalism, attempts this there is no opposition or only a feeble one. He paralyzes the natural resistance to such measures by putting a liberal label on them and by silencing or dividing his followers who constitute the natural opposition to his misbranded product. No end of print has been devoted to the story of how the reactionaries imposed fascism on the Italian people. The march of fascism would not have been possible had it not been for the leadership it got from men who were known as liberals or radicals. Fascism was a leftist job.

Francesco Crispi, the father of Italian imperialism, was not only a devoted follower of Mazzini, the republican patriot; he was one of Mazzini's favorite lieutenants. He wanted to see the new Italy a republic. He began life as a conspirator in Sicily, as an admirer of the old Jacobins who had cut off the head of Louis XVI. He was not only a republican but a pacifist who called war the greatest of crimes. It must not be assumed, however, that Crispi was a fraud. He was a man of dignity and ability and of strong character. But he was not a true liberal. This is one of the baffling paradoxes of political leadership—this foggy perception even of honest and intelligent men of their own fundamental philosophies. Like many of the stanchest defenders of the *status quo* in America who began life in the socialist societies of their colleges only to graduate as the apologists of the most deeply rooted evils of reaction, Francesco Crispi was, at bottom, always a conservative. Young minds are frequently fascinated by the intellectual adventure of radicalism, a phase of thought from which they recover when they face the realities of coming to terms with the world. Beginning as an intellectual liberal but emotionally a conservative, as time went on the intellectual convictions were subdued by the more deeply rooted emotional bias. This is a common plight with many thoughtful men in whose minds there is waged an incessant struggle between their intellectual processes and their spiritual bias, who arrive at liberalism by logic, yet never quite break away from the conservatism of their inner souls and who in the end surrender to the solidly rooted prejudices of the spirit.

Many of these so-called liberals are crusaders rather than liberals, and the crusader is not always a liberal. A man may crusade for the most reactionary objectives. But as he is usually expending his energies against superior force he cultivates the impression that he is a liberal because he fights for the right against established evil.

Crispi came into power at a moment of profound economic distress. Italy was again in economic trouble and once again launched on a long flight of unbalanced budgets. Against these new difficulties he struggled in vain. He had denounced unbalanced budgets, but floated now on the uncertain bosom of continued deficits. Then, as disorders and clamors for relief filled the air, the statesman who had been a republican revolutionary turned to suppression and the old Mazzinian pacifist turned to imperialism.

While he was Foreign Minister in the cabinet of Depretis, Crispi began to hatch some small schemes of colonial adventure. He began to stir up suspicions of his neighbors. He was always detecting signs of danger in France and Germany. He told the Italians that colonies "were a necessity of modern life. We cannot remain inert and do nothing so that the Powers occupy by themselves all the best parts of the earth." He sowed seeds of future irritation by aiding small settlements of Italians in Egypt, Tunis, Constantinople, and Salonica, "to revolatilize their culture." He organized a colony on the Red Sea, calling it Eritrea. He founded Somaliland. He ended by launching an attack upon Menelek, the Lion of Judah in Abyssinia. He succeeded in exciting some of the people for a brief period into an imperialist fever, drawing their minds away from their crushing internal troubles. He provided a pretext for enlarging the army and borrowing more money. Then came the disastrous climax of war upon Menelek at Adowa, where 4,600 officers and men were wiped out. The tragic collapse of this tawdry spectacle in imperialism brought the Italians, who did not really like it from the start, to their senses. People poured into the streets crying, "Down with Crispi!" "Away with Africa!" Parliament repudiated him. He died at the age of eighty still hated and ostracized by his people. Crispi had gotten the Italians whipped and himself cast out, and for the moment they turned away from the colonial dream. But he had planted in the minds and hearts of the Italians the first seeds of colonialism, buried for the moment under what Borgese called "a deep furrow of frustration." For fifteen years their minds remained poisoned by the humiliation at Adowa, and the Italian imperialist had now in his possession that potent emotion called *revanche*. Adowa became a symbol of Italy's lost honor.

VII · The Incredible Synthesis

WE COME NOW to a fact of central importance. What I have been trying to say thus far is that out of the condition of Italian society sprang certain streams of opinion and of desire that governments acted on and that people accepted or at least surrendered to with little resistance, even though they may not have approved or even understood them. Bewildered statesmen turned to government debt as a device for creating purchasing power. No one approved it in principle. But there was no effective resistance because people demanded the fruits it brought. Another was the ever-growing reliance on social-welfare measures to mitigate the privations of the indigent, the unemployed, the sick, the aged. The instruments of debt and spending became standard equipment of politicians. And this need for spending opened the door to an easy surrender to the elements most interested in militarism and its handmaiden, imperialism.

These drifts or currents of opinion seem obvious enough. But they must not be dismissed because they are obvious. Much of our confusion in the understanding of national problems begins with our superior refusal to notice the obvious factors that lie at their roots. It would not be true to say the people as a whole wanted these things. Indeed it is entirely possible that as a whole they did not want them. But powerful minorities wanted them, and the people accepted them because they were in the dark as to a better course.

Little by little another stream of thought began to insert itself into the general mind. This was a growing suspicion that there was something fundamentally wrong with the system of capitalism itself. Hitherto no one questioned its eternal continuance. Welfare measures, lower taxes, better land laws, wiser finance, more honest officials—these would one day make it work better. As for poverty, that within reason was part of the order of nature. But gradually the notion got about that the trouble lay nearer the roots of the economic system. Presently the idea began to take hold that this challenge must be met with some kind of over-all regulation.

One of the most baffling phenomena of fascism is the almost incredible collaboration between men of the extreme Right and the extreme Left in its creation. The explanation lies at this point. Both Right and Left joined in this urge for regulation. The motives, the arguments, and the forms of expression were different but all drove in the same direction. And this was that the *economic system must be controlled in its essential functions and this control must be exercised by the producing groups.*

The first steps in this direction were, of course, the trade-unions and the trade associations. Manufacturers and merchants came to the conclusion that their troubles grew out of overproduction and excessive competition. They turned to various devices to control prices, limit production, mitigate competition. The cartel came into use. The cartel is an agreement among producers to set up central control of some factor in their common business—exchange or prices or output or territory or accounting practices or raw-material purchases. At bottom each cartel is an attempt by businessmen to subject a sector of the economic system to government by themselves. The movement marked a turning point in the history of the capitalist society. It is an attempt to get rid of the risks inherent in business by planning and direction. Karl Pribram, in his study of collective monopolies in Europe for the Brookings Institution, points out that unlimited free competition was never accepted in Italy as the basis of the economic order as it was in America. Monopolies created by agreement were enforceable in the courts.[1] And he agrees with another authority that the cartel was a revolution against risk, the central driving force in the capitalist system.

Nothing seems to be more deeply ingrained in the human mind than the old guild idea that those who produce should be permitted to set up the laws under which production is carried on. However bitterly competitors may battle each other for business there is a common ground upon which they can and will always unite against the consumer and the rest of society. For years the liberal has fought the cartel movement—and the American equivalent, trade combinations—as the sinister fruit of sheer greed. But that attack has made little headway. The most serious aspect of this movement has nothing to do with morals. It comes down to a question whether the functions of distribution and production ought to be planned and directed and by whom. Singularly a powerful group of so-called liberals in this country, long the inveterate foes of this idea, has now become its most vehement advocates. Italian businessmen took the view that production and distribution ought to be planned and that they should perform that function. That idea spread among capitalists and, though freedom of trade along with the Rights of Man were guaranteed by the old constitution, as Dr. Pribram points out, this did not prevent eighty-four cartels from operating to limit freedom of enterprise.

On the side of labor a similar drift was in the making. The General Confederation of Labor was in fact under the domination of the Socialist party. Thus the leaders of the labor movement in Italy adopted the socialist diagnosis of the capitalist system; namely, that it suffered from a group of basic flaws that made its indefinite

[1] *Cartel Problems, an Analysis of Collective Monopolies in Europe*, by Karl Pribram, Brookings Institution, Washington, D.C.

continuance impossible and that it was moving toward ultimate disintegration.

While believing this, the socialist movement contented itself largely with reformist activity in favor of a group of reforms upon which it was able to unite with the non-socialist liberal elements. This fraternization led to a good deal of tolerance for the socialist diagnosis among liberals. And thus, while liberals were not willing to adopt the socialist cure—the overthrow of the system—they did tinker extensively with the idea of planning and control. By degrees the conviction that the economic system was fundamentally defective and needed remolding or repair with a greater degree of conscious control was almost universally adopted among the laboring groups, the liberal elements allied with them, and the conservative capitalist groups. Out of Italy had gone definitely any important party committed to the theory that the economic system should be free.

Into this state of affairs drifted a new group with a new theory—the syndicalists. And this is perhaps the most important single development in the long march of society toward the fascist state. We need not concern ourselves with the ultimate springs of syndicalism. Its origins are endlessly debated. But certainly it was Georges Sorel, a French engineer turned economic reformer, who brought this latest *ism* on a vital scale into European affairs and who supplied it with a logic and a dialectic. Sorel, famous as the author of *Reflections on Violence* and *The Decomposition of Marxism*, nevertheless accepted the central doctrine of Marx, that the tools of production belonged to the workers, the inevitability of class war and the expropriation of the capitalists. To this extent syndicalism sprang out of socialism. But there the agreement ended.

The old socialists had argued for the taking over of the instruments of production by the state which would manage them for the benefit of the people. Sorel saw in this an evil worse than capitalism. It was, in fact, state capitalism or statism. The tools of industry should be owned, not by the state, but by the workers. Society, now organized in geographical groups, should reorganize in economic groups. Thus, for instance, the steel industry would be organized as a great economic province. It would be under the dominion of the workers and all would be workers. The citizens of that province would be its workers. Every industry and economic group would be organized on the same model. The political state would disappear. Order would be obtained by a central council composed of the representatives of all these economic provinces. This central "council would estimate capacities and necessities of the region, co-ordinate production, arrange for the necessary commodities and products inward and outward. A species of economic federation would thus replace the capitalist system."

Sorel's syndicalism therefore involved the extermination of the capitalist state which he and his followers denounced as an instrument of oppression that would become an even more formidable engine of oppression if its powers were enhanced by possession of all the industries of the nation.

The syndicalists added to this theory of society another that had to do wholly with the technique of revolution. They rejected political action. They urged direct action—violence, including sabotage and actual revolt when the time was ripe. The syndicalists formed a separate organization but as an organized movement made little progress. Its teachings, however, exercised a powerful influence on the old socialist movement. The Socialist party of France became almost wholly syndicalist. In Italy the party developed a syndicalist wing that was only a small minority. But the syndicalist idea penetrated and permeated socialist thinking until it dominated the socialist mind though not the official organs.

Everywhere socialists were talking like syndicalists. Emile Vandervelde, socialist leader of Belgium, pointed out that the political state will retain only the most rudimentary powers while the economic life of the nation will be taken over by the people organized in a structure completely separated from the political state. What syndicalists did was to focus the attention of socialists upon the fact that with the coming of their order a new kind of state would be needed. "It is not true," said Vandervelde, "that the socialists wish to entrust the operation of the principal industries to the government of the state," despite the fact that the communist manifesto had said that "the proletariat will use its political supremacy to wrest by degrees all capital from the bourgeoisie, to centralize all instruments of production in the hands of the state; that is the proletariat organized as the ruling class." Vandervelde said "the function of the government is to govern, not to manage industrial enterprises. . . . We shall come to a social system in which the functions of the state, organ of authority, are reduced to a minimum, *while the functions of the state, organ of management, are carried to a maximum.*"[2]

This development was inevitable. The great terror of the world had been the tyrannous state. The old Italian republicans had sought to build a friendly state whose powers were so limited by constitutional restrictions and the counterbalancing of functions among king, commons, and senate that it could not be used as an instrument of oppression. The socialist proposals to arm the state with all the instruments of production led logically to a plan to escape the inevitable consequences of that program.

Here in syndicalist-socialism was the catalytic agent that was bringing together a number of hostile elements in society and gradually uniting them, however little they perceived it, in agreement upon the following set of principles:

1. The renunciation of the old principle of liberalism in fact, though of course the language of liberalism continued to be used. The unions were as far from liberalism as the nationalists.
2. The economic system must be subjected to planning.
3. This planning must be done outside the political state.
4. It must be committed to the hands of the producing groups.

All—employers through their trade associations and cartels, workers through their unions, socialists through their gradual indoctrination with syndicalism—were approaching a common ground by different routes while all the time it seemed to observers that they were moving farther apart. They were growing more violent about the points on which they disagreed while all the time that very violence was drawing them together on the central idea of syndicalism. Syndicalism, in the end, was the agent which, modified to suit the necessities and the coming crisis and the interests of various groups, would produce that incredible synthesis—the ultimate getting together of radicals and reactionaries, the revolutionary leaders

[2]*Socialism Versus the State*, by Émile Vandervelde, Chas. Kerr & Co., Chicago, 1919.

of Milanese syndicalism and the rich magnates of the north, the little middle-class shopkeepers of the towns, and the great numbers of trade-unionists and farmers, to produce the final result in Italy that has brought so much misery to the world.

VIII · Time for Greatness

ITALY, moving along the current of ideas described here, floated into the first decade of the century with all the elements of disaster in her body. An economic prophet might have predicted doom for Italy in a few years. Yet that doom did not come for twenty years, and then only after an interlude of seeming prosperity and the impact of a great war. But that war, which postponed the catastrophe, rendered it more inevitable and darker in the end.

The man who was to preside over the most critical of these years was Giovanni Giolitti, described by Benedetto Croce as the greatest Italian of his era. Yet history must record that he was in no sense a great statesman. He was a master politician. He little understood the dark forces that were undermining his world. He was one of those ministers whose first aim is to remain in power. His business was not to solve problems but to settle disputes and to win the votes of deputies. This he did by avoiding fixed principles and relying on an ever-shifting opportunism. He spent and borrowed freely and without scruples. He promised with liberality. He was all things to all men, took no firm stand against any school, compromised, soothed, wheedled. If he failed to solve any of the problems of Italy he at least won in four elections, in 1902, 1904, 1909, and 1913. The secret of his tenure of power was that he listened attentively to the tremors of the soil, located every stream of thought and ran with those streams, cajoling all the powerful minorities of labor, capital, and farmers, talking with firmness but taking no firm position on any subject save as votes demanded it. He was a leader of the Left. He made an alliance with the socialists, and, by virtue of that alliance, his spending, and his wars, remained in power through the greater period immediately preceding the Great War.

Mr. Borgese observes, and perhaps justly, that this period was the happiest in the limited years of Italy's existence as a nation. A steady stream of emigrants poured out of Italy to America and other lands, relieving the pressure on her glutted labor markets. The millions who left sent back a steady stream of remittances to alleviate the poverty of those who remained. The army and the war industries absorbed a large number of men who otherwise would have sought jobs.

But under the surface all the old evils were growing in malignance. The national debt was rising ominously. The army, navy, and social services were absorbing half the revenues of the nation. Italy was the most heavily taxed nation in proportion to her wealth in Europe.

In these years a new, malevolent force intruded itself into the life of Italy. It was at this point, not after the war, that what Mr. Borgese calls the Black Age began. People can grow weary of poverty. This is particularly true of young people who have been taught to read, to listen, and to think. The time when men accepted want as the continuing condition of their class under an ordinance of God was past. Many devout peasants still did. But everywhere among the working classes this day was over. The experience of hundreds of thousands who had gone to America and who sent home their riches and the story of the realization of abundance confirmed the growing belief at home that something could be done about their hard lot, if only the right men were in power. That lot had been a hard one for centuries.

The socialist and the syndicalist had penetrated the minds of the workers. If he did not convert them all to his philosophy he at least shook their confidence in the existing order of things. The intellectual groups—journalists, teachers, many professional men of all kinds—became profoundly distrustful of the economic system. What was quite as serious was that great numbers began to harbor the impression that the men who led Italy did not know what they were doing.

There was a weariness of politicians and of public corruption. There was a deep resentment of the soiled pool of justice in courts that knew no justice save for the wealthy and in the big cities, for the corrupt politicians who ruled them. It is a fair statement that in Italy, where parliamentary government had come late, there was an early disillusionment about that republican government of which so much had been said. Great numbers lost faith in it. It is not possible to overestimate the gravity of this phenomenon—where among the ablest and most fortunate so many had been shaken in their belief in the absolute soundness of the economic order under which they had flourished.

Such a society, marked by a sense of frustration, loss of faith in existing institutions and existing leaders, is of course a fertile soil for the cultivation of another phenomenon, full of menace, which now appeared in Italy—the cult of the crusader and the adventurer. Benedetto Croce, Italy's foremost contemporary philosopher, hailed it but with misgivings. He called it a reaction against positivism. New voices cried out with disgust against all the grubbers in the sciences, in technology, in finance and economics built on the humdrum life of facts and figures, wages, profits, interest, taxes, security, and work. All this was sordid. Men were made for better things—what the better things were remained obscure. Croce noted all this as "a reawakening of national trends of thought." And this he defined as "a widely diffused spirit, half romantic, half mystical, to which the crude simplifications of positivism were intolerable."

There was a greater interest in great ideas. It was a time for greatness. But he had to concede that the mind thus turned loose, thus emancipated from facts, took unexpected directions. "In the luxuriant revival of speculative enthusiasm," he said half apologetically, "there crept a dangerous and morbid element."[1] Croce, the one-time socialist, had forsaken that path for the heady heights of romantic philosophy. He had rejected humanitarianism and pacifism and had approved Georges Sorel, at least for his opposition to these ideals. He could imagine a philosophical use for violence and thought perhaps the Inquisition was such an instance. Giovanni Gentile, another liberal philosopher, second in fame only to Croce, was also fascinated by this neo-idealism. He called it "faith in the necessity of the advent of an ideal reality, *a concept of life which*

---

[1] *History of Italy*, by Benedetto Croce, translated by Cecilia M. Ady, Clarendon Press, 1929.

must not enclose itself within the limits of fact, but progress and incessantly transform itself and make itself adequate to a superior law which acts upon the spirit with the force of its own intrinsic worth."

The Italian professors, like their English contemporaries, produced no end of what we would now call glamor phrases to express in verbose obscurity this release of the spirit from the constricting prison of fact and law. Out of the mouths of men like Croce and Gentile and a lesser throng of writers and poets and teachers, many of whom had once been liberals, were pouring strange ideas such as Americans were more familiar with in the writings of Nietzsche, Barrès, Maurras, Houston Stewart Chamberlain, and Kipling, the trumpeters of the neo-imperialism of the nineties. The heroic ethics of the romantic age, they moaned, had vanished. The merchant and the money-maker, they whimpered, had taken over the soul of the Italian. They proclaimed that life was without meaning unless it was dedicated to some high, mystical experience, such as trouncing some of their weaker neighbors.

Giovanni Papini, once an ardent socialist, but known now to Americans as the author of a *Life of Christ,* turned to the cult of the dangerous life. The romanticists were right in their indictment of "the dying materialism" in one particular which did not interest them. The materialistic philosophy of the latter nineteenth century had extinguished in a large section of the Italian soul and dimmed in others the flame of religion without supplying it with any alternative ethical mooring. Brought now to his knees by the relentless force of economic law, summoned by the torches of the crusaders to the higher morality and bereft of his moorings and his moral standards, he was ripe on the bough for some lawless aggression in the name of action. Of course it all pointed to war. Papini glorified war as "the great anvil of fire and blood on which strong peoples are hammered." He proclaimed that, "as the small democrats cry out against war as a barbarous return to extinct cruelty, we conceive of it as the great reawakening of the enfeebled—as a rapid and heroic means to power and wealth."[2] Behold the final phrase—the short cut "to power and wealth." Here is the new idealism that

---
[2] *Il sindicalismo di Enrico Corradini,* by Vincenzo Amoruso, Palermo, 1929.

must not enclose itself within the limits of fact and which must also not enclose itself within the sordid limits of the bourgeois laws against assault, larceny, and murder.[3]

The great cult soon found in Italy the voice it needed in Gabriele d'Annunzio—evangelist of Life with a capital L, the "great round life"—life of the coursing blood, the unbridled will, heroic enterprise for the sake of heroics. He was a man without morals, without principles, and with no notion of what was Italy's real disease. He got himself elected to the Chamber on the Right. But one day, as Borgese describes, inflamed by the shouts and roars of the socialists, he marched over to that side, saying, "I go toward life." He it was who, more than any other single individual, touched the Italian imagination with this new spirit and held up the torch of war and imperialism and the reckless life.

Through these years the divisions between labor and capital were becoming deeper. Giolitti was kept in power by a socialist-liberal coalition. This quickened the alarm of the conservatives. Strikes grew from 1902 to 1912. They penetrated the farm districts. In 1904 the Labor Exchanges proclaimed a general strike as protest against the government's resolve to maintain order. There were riots in Milan, Genoa, Venice, Naples, Florence, Rome. Conservatives charged they were part of a revolutionary movement. The conservatives in 1910 formed the Nationalist Association. It proclaimed a group of principles. But actually its chief objective was to fight "the exploitation of labor by the socialists." The rich upper middle classes, businessmen of Milan and Turin and financiers of Rome, army officers and nobles, flocked to its banner. Labor by this time, through a series of amalgamations, had formed the General Confederation of Labor. The battle lines were formed in Italy. She was confronted with the baffling problem of two powerful social armies—labor and capital—organized for economic warfare, each

---

[3]These fevered phrases were not peculiar to Italy. In England, Dr. J. A. Cramb, one of her foremost philosophers of the new spirit, had spoken earlier with the same gaudy fustian. To Englishmen at Queens College he said: "If ever there came to any city or nation, clear through the twilight spaces across the abysses where the stars wander, the call of Fate, it is now." The call, of course, was to go forth and grab in Asia and Africa. "Imperialism," he said, "is patriotism transfigured by a light from the aspirations of universal humanity . . . a phase of the life effort of the state toward complete self-realization; a phase of the eternal nisus, the perpetual omnipresent strife of all beings toward fulfillment."

almost as powerful as the state. Italy had the problem of every modern state—how to function as a state with these two giant hostile forces struggling for mastery within its body.

The end of all this was inevitable. Giolitti had exhausted the possibilities of spending and debt, social welfare, and of political maneuvering. Across the Mediterranean was Tripoli. And to Tripoli the bewildered Premier who did not want war led his people to war as the refuge of a nation which, unable to solve its problems, fled from them.

Nationalism was in the air. Britain, France, Spain had been busy gathering the remnants of Africa. Italy had been encouraging Italian settlements in Tripoli for some years. The nationalists and the romanticists raised the cry for the occupation of Tripoli. Certain socialists and liberals—from the side ordinarily opposed to war—were for it. Labrioli, socialist leader, had clamored for it for years. Signora Sarfatti, Mussolini's authorized biographer, tells how Turati and Treves, also socialist leaders, were disposed to go along with Giolitti on the theory that by playing his imperialist game they would cash in on their domestic policies, but that Anna Kuliscioff shamed them out of their weakness.[4] The pacifists Moneta and Voce, opposed to colonial expansion, saw good in it and Colaganni called it a baptism of Italian unity. In the state of mind of Italy, with the uneasy spirit infecting all classes, it was an easy matter for the war-minded imperialists to create the necessary support for the Tripolitan adventure. And so Giolitti, who looked for every stream of opinion and moved with that stream, took Italy to war with Turkey for Libya.

Croce says Italy went to war because the Italians wanted to go to war, could not sit idle while other powers took the whole African coast, and because Italy could not endure the odium of the Ethiopian disaster. "Giolitti," he added with a soft, sentimental touch, "who understood what Italy wanted, like a father who sees that his daughter is in love, and thereupon, after due inquiry and precaution, takes steps to secure for her the husband of her choice, took her to war."

That war was undisguised aggression, which is bearing its poison-

[4] *Life of Benito Mussolini*, by Margherita G. Sarfatti, Frederick Stokes, New York, 1925.

ous fruits for Italy now. Yet the elite, the youth and "loudest of all," as Borgese scornfully observes, "a few writers who in the intoxication of politics tried to find forgetfulness of their mediocrity, and some groups of apostates from revolutionary socialism," went gaily to the great nationalist festival of war. "Aggression and slaughter" were praised as beautiful in themselves; war was supreme, the most delightful form of life. The war began in September 1911. It was over by October 1912. Turkey was ingloriously defeated. Tripolitania and Cyrenaica, along with the Dodecanese and Rhodes, were conquered. The vengeance of the Italian spirit upon Fate was not appeased. Instead the appetite for glory was whetted. And once more glory did its work upon the budget. But once more peace—dreadful and realistic peace—peace the bill collector, heavy with all her old problems—was back in Rome. The deficits were larger. The debt was greater. The hostile camps of labor and capital glowered at each other across a still-wider gap. Militarism and imperialism were in full flower. The various economic planners were more relentless than ever in their determination to subject the capitalist system to control.

Italy thus floundered into the year 1914. Then in June a conscript soldier fired at a colonel and was arrested. All the liberal and radical elements rose in support of the conscript. At this point a well-known socialist editor of the *Avanti*, named Benito Mussolini, demanded the freedom of the soldier. He talked of revolution. What followed, so far as it was organized, was the work of Mussolini and his close associate, the anarchist Malatesta. Borgese says they planned to seize the Rome–Milan railroad, disunite northern and southern Italy, and control the state. Disorders broke out in many places. In Milan, Turin, Bologna, other large cities, general strikes were called. In other places—Ancona, Rimini, Ravenna—improvised committees of action seized the towns, sacked dairy farms. Republics were proclaimed in some small towns, called chicken republics, because chickens were sold for a lira. Mussolini summoned his followers in Milan to meet at the Piazza del Duomo to begin the insurrection. The meeting was broken up by the police. With that the Red Week ended. The reformist wing of the socialists called a truce. This was on June 10, 1914. At that moment a Serbian patriot was priming his revolver, and a little more than two weeks later he shot the Austrian Archduke in Sarajevo. In a month World War I had begun.

It was not a peaceful and prosperous Italy upon which the Great War descended. It was an Italy with all the ingredients of fascism in her system. It now becomes necessary for us, out of what we have seen, to isolate these essential elements of fascism. The word itself with its future evangelist, Mussolini, appeared at this time. Italy did not enter the war for eleven months. Meantime a battle was waged among the friends of the Allies and the Central Powers and the neutralists for possession of Italian policy. Mussolini, editor of the socialist *Avanti*, quit that post and established his own journal, *Popolo d'Italia*. He became the most vocal and violent advocate of intervention on the Allied side. Mussolini was in fact a syndicalist, and, like many syndicalists, saw in the war an opportunity for revolution. He organized in January 1915 what he called the *Fasci di azione Revolutionaria*. It was made up, in his own words, of "men of heresy, ready for anything from the trenches to the barricades." In all of them he said "there is the hate of the *status quo,* the scorn of the Philistines, the love of adventure, and the zest for peril. Today it is war. It will be revolution tomorrow."

IX · The Rise of Fascism

HOW Italy wriggled herself into World War I and what happened on her battlefields is not germane to this discussion. It is merely necessary to chronicle that she did go in and emerged victorious.

But, the war over, she soon found herself infinitely worse off than before she entered it. She had lost 600,000 dead, a million wounded. For this she expected much and got little or nothing. Slowly her people awoke to the sobering realization that all the old problems that vexed the nation before the war were still there, only many times multiplied in extent and intensity—poverty, unemployment, debt, the bitter clash of the economic armies, the frustration and helplessness of her leaders.

The soldiers streamed back to the cities to find factories discharging, not hiring, men. Unemployment rose to unprecedented levels. The economic war was resumed. But now the conservatives found their old power gone. Organized labor doubled its membership. The General Confederation of Labor, which had 1,159,000 members before the war, now had 2,200,000. The Italian Confederation of Workers rose from 200,000 to 1,250,000. The Left wing parties were more powerful. The Socialist party, which got 1,849,000 votes in 1919, got 3,500,000 in 1920 and won 156 seats. The Popolari—Christian liberal groups—now deeply infected with radical notions, got 101 seats.

Italy's Old Man of the Sea—the debt—was now a monster. The prewar debt which had frightened the conservatives and menaced the state with bankruptcy looked trivial in the presence of the mountainous load after the war. The prewar debt was 15,766,000,000 lire. When the war ended, the debt was 60,213,000,000 lire. Italy was back in the old holes save that they were deeper and darker than before.

The Socialists and the Popolari combined forces and returned the aging Giolitti to power. He had a four-point program. To state it is to reveal the futility of the old prewar leaders as they returned to the graver problems after the war. He was for (1) confiscation of war profits, (2) investigation of war expenditures, (3) parliamentary control over declarations of war and the making of treaties, (4) increased taxation of the rich. Save the proposal to tax the rich all this had nothing to do with the economic problem, which was to find the secret of making the economic system work, the creation of enough income to enable the people to produce and buy what they produced. As usual, however, the pressure of events and not the deliberate planning of statesmen shaped their programs. Under that pressure Giolitti turned again to the old reliable welfare devices. One law after another was passed, celebrated always with brave words. Italy had an old-age pension law. To this was added unemployment insurance and insurance for the aged and disabled. A system of health insurance was being worked out—Italy's "Beveridge Plan," twenty-two years ago. Public funds were provided to aid workers' co-operatives. The government began to concert measures to divide the great landed estates among the peasants. Laws were passed recognizing the principle of collective bargaining and of collective contracts between employers and workers. The liberals shook hands with themselves at the appearance of a new deal in Italy.

Of course all this brought a resumption of the spending and borrowing policies. The following is a table of the postwar yearly deficits:

                1919–20........11,494,000,000 Lire
                1920–21........20,955,000,000 "
                1921–22........17,169,000,000 "

Thus in the single year of 1921–22 the deficit was five billion greater than the accumulated deficits of the old prewar spenders over a period of fifty years. By 1922 the national debt had risen to 92,643,000,000 lire—six times the whole prewar debt and 50 per cent greater than the debt as the war ended.

It should be said, of course, that all these huge sums were not spent on ordinary welfare projects and that a great part of them represented outlays arising out of the war directly and still another part rising indirectly from the war. Thus the government had to rebuild the devastated areas of northern Italy. It restored 163,000 dwellings, 346 town halls, 255 hospitals, 1,156 schools, 1,000 churches, and an immense amount of roads, railways, drainage and irrigation works, etc., including the restoration to farmers of 450,000 head of cattle. These alone cost eight billion lire. However, the effect upon the government and the society was the same, no matter what causes lay behind the expenditures. Whether useful or not, these vast borrowings enabled the government to spend fabulous sums to provide work and increase income.[1]

[1] *Under the Axe of Fascism*, by Dr. Gaetano Salvemini, Viking Press, New York, 1936. Dr. Salvemini is supported in his contention that the war caused most of these expenditures by Mr. Constantine McGuire in his *Italy's International Financial Position*, as well as by Signor di Stefani, Mussolini's Finance Minister, who said that "the budgets of the last few years do not result solely from the discrepancy between current revenue and current expenditures, but from the fact that the deficits are swelled by many exceptional items dependent on the war. These, instead of being acknowledged in budgets of their own years, weighed down the balance sheets of succeeding years." That is to say, many of the items of expenditure did not represent expenditure at all in those years but in preceding years. We shall have to conclude, therefore, that these budgetary figures give a somewhat exag-

Over all this the great Russian bolshevist revolution had thrust its ominous shadow. Partly out of the dislocations and price chaos of the war and partly promoted by revolutionary spirit, a wave of strikes swept over the country. In the four years preceding the war, strikes had caused the loss of 4,000,000 man-hours. In 1919 they caused the loss of 22,000,000. In 1920 it was 30,000,000. They involved over a million workers in industry and as many in agriculture. The climax came in September 1920. A dispute over wages in the machinery industry of the north brought the threat of a lockout by the employers. The union officials ordered the workers to remain in the factories. Half a million men in 600 plants held possession of their shops. They seized the plants, hoisted the Red flag, and proceeded to operate the plants. Everywhere this was looked upon as the long-awaited revolution in Italy.

The enraged industrialists urged Giolitti to use the army. But he merely waited. Wiser than they, he knew that these suddenly socialized factories, without credit, cash, materials, power, or sales force, could not operate in an environment that was wholly capitalist. The economic system simply closed in around them, isolated them utterly. In a few days their ill-advised experiment collapsed. And with it the Red terror in Italy collapsed.

The enemies of communism made a powerful use of the whole Red episode and particularly this event. Liberal chroniclers of the period brand the anti-Red agitation of the conservatives as fraudulent. But it would not be true to say that the fear of bolshevism had departed. What had happened once might happen again. The socialists were still in power. We have but to observe the situation in America. With not a single avowed communist in Congress, with no communists in our state legislatures, with the party itself a diminutive fraction of the electorate, we manage to keep alive a pretty active anti-communist terror. At the very moment when Italy was passing through these disorders, the presence of three moderate socialists in our New York legislature produced an unseemly furor and the ejection of the socialists even against the protests of Al Smith. What

gerated picture of the extent of the deficits. What the real deficits were we have no way of knowing, save that even after these corrections they were enormous and resulted from expenditures which, however necessary, performed the service of swelling national income and mitigating the difficulties of the Giolitti regime.

would we have done if we had had 156 socialist congressmen, if they, teamed with some liberal Democrats, had gotten possession of the machinery of Congress, if the Red flag flew over the steel and heavy-goods mills of Pennsylvania and Illinois?

In the midst of all these events Benito Mussolini, whose small *Fasci di azione Revolutionaria* had vanished with the war, now called another meeting. Somewhere between 45 and 145 men attended in a room in the Piazza San Sepolcro. They were mostly persons of complete inconsequence. Mussolini himself was then the editor of a small newspaper—*Popolo d'Italia*—since his expulsion from the Socialist party. Here again he organized a fascist fraternity which he called the *Fasci di Combattimento*. Why he did this, how he did it, and what relation it had to the dark events that were to follow we shall now see. And as we see this audacious man put together his fascist order in the light of the events and circumstances that have been described here, we will see with clarity precisely what that fascist order is made of.

Mussolini was admirably formed to do the job. He was a complete opportunist. On one occasion, after he had established the fascist order, he said: "Fascism has no armory of theoretical doctrines. Every system is a mistake and every theory a prison." Signora Sarfatti, his adoring collaborator and biographer, relates how one day she found herself surprised at some statement of Mussolini and said: "But yesterday you said——" Mussolini interrupted: "Signora, yesterday was yesterday. Very well. But today is today." It is a fair statement to say that when Mussolini organized his little fascist band in the Piazza San Sepolcro he had in his mind no picture of the kind of society he would finally organize.

The second important point in his character was that his chief aim was power. In pursuit of that object he was completely unmoral. As he was imprisoned by no theories of government, neither was he constricted by any principles of public morals. He went the whole way with Machiavelli. In an essay which he later printed he wrote:

> I affirm that the doctrine of Machiavelli is more living today than it was four centuries ago. If the external aspects of life are greatly changed no profound modifications are perceptible in the merits of individuals or races.

He made it plain that he had no reservations in his acceptance of the philosophy of his hero. He adopted Machiavelli's doctrine that morals have no application whatever to the ruler. And he quoted with approval Machiavelli's advice that the ruler "must suppose all men bad and exploit the evil qualities in their nature whenever suitable occasion offers."

This does not mean that Mussolini did not have opinions about social and economic subjects. Quite the contrary. He was ready to expound his doctrine on any subject from religion and literature to the social sciences. But these opinions were not chains around his wrists. Starting as a dogmatic socialist, he had drifted far from their central doctrine. In so far as he had any convictions on economic society he was a syndicalist. Signora Sarfatti says he was influenced most by the syndicalist Georges Sorel. He had been deeply impressed by Pareto, whose lectures he had attended while working at Lausanne. He got his idea of the elite—the free circulating elite—from Pareto. He began to talk early in 1919 about a new aristocracy, an aristocracy created by the war, one of fighters, of "men of the trenches." He accepted with passionate approval the doctrines of Nietzsche whose works—at least *Zarathustra*—he had devoured. Also he had drunk at the spring of Gustave Le Bon, whose *The Crowd: a Study of the Popular Mind* is the only book he mentions in his autobiography. Thus equipped, Mussolini launched his movement.

Here is the eleven-point program which the *Fasci di Combattimento*, under Mussolini's leadership, adopted at its first meeting:

1. Universal suffrage.
2. Election of national assembly that would prepare a new constitution.
3. Abolition of the senate.
4. Nationalization of arms and munitions factories.
5. Establishment of national militia.
6. Control of the factories, railroads, and public services by workers' councils.
7. Minimum wages and eight-hour day.
8. Extension of social insurance.
9. Confiscation of war profits.
10. Confiscation of certain church property.
11. Heavy inheritance and income taxes.

Various declarations were made in connection with this. One was:

We have so little concern for the bourgeoisie that we have put at the head of our program a demand for the (1) confiscation of fortunes, (2) confiscation of war profits, (3) heavy taxation of capital.
We will accept no form of dictatorship.

Another announced that "the budget must be balanced by means of rigid economies and the suppression of all useless expenditure." Put differently, the new fascist reformers said "demagogic finance must be eliminated, savings encouraged, subsidies to parasitic organizations withdrawn."[2]

In this platform of principles there is no sign of what shape fascism would actually take. What we are now concerned with is what fascism actually turned out to be. For this fact—that the announced program of its founders and the system of society which they put into effect were oceans apart—is one of the profoundest significance for us.

As we survey the final result, we cannot escape asking ourselves why Mussolini announced one program and put into effect a wholly different one. Can it be that, instead of Mussolini molding the minds and the plans that were stewing in the fevered minds of the people of Italy, it was the people of Italy who molded Mussolini's plans? Here we are confronted with a demonstration of the fact that what was done in Italy was not wholly the work of Mussolini. We cannot conclude that had there been no Mussolini there would have been no fascism in Italy. The materials of fascism were there, as we shall presently see. Of course it is an obvious fact of history that it was Mussolini who organized fascism in his country. It is probably certain that had there been no Mussolini all that followed would have been quite different. He invented its nomenclature, its jargon; he composed its incidental music and arranged the scenes. Had there been no Mussolini fascism in Italy might well have been as different as two performances of Shakespeare's *Hamlet* directed by two different stage managers and with different stars.

We cannot escape the conviction that fascism came to Italy because the most powerful forces there were driving in that direction.

[2]*The Fascist Experiment*, by Luigi Villari, London, 1926.

Mussolini, whose chief aim was power, began his movement with one set of objectives and ended with a wholly different one. Events, conditions, the demands of powerful groups, the streams of thought and desire running deep and strong among the masses forced him to follow their course or be washed under. Had Mussolini not modified his program he would have been discarded. But the thing we know as fascism might well have come, sooner or later. A different leader would have given it a different color, different tempo, different rhetoric, and perhaps many different incidental characteristics. But he would have given fascism or *he* would have been discarded, because at that moment events and circumstances had become more powerful than parties or leaders, the decision over events had passed out of the hands of the people; the rushing currents were carrying Italy along. Only he who moved with them could lead.

I must be careful not to infer that Mussolini did what a majority of the Italian people wanted. He had made one important discovery —a principle that most successful politicians in a parliamentary state understand and that is perceived by few of their intellectual critics. It is that parliamentary societies are not governed by majorities but by combinations of minorities. "Majorities are inert," Mussolini said to his faithful Boswella, Signora Sarfatti, "but minorities are dynamic." He had perceived that society is composed of groups profoundly concerned about their several group interests. They are all minorities. Each minority is far more interested in its special minority objective than in those vague, general subjects that concern the state as a whole. It comes about, therefore, that two seemingly hostile minorities can be induced to unite upon a third proposal of a general nature provided they are each rewarded with a promise of fulfillment of their own special desires. Mussolini climbed into power, as all such men climb into power, not by having a hard and fast program, not by becoming "prisoners of theories," but by locating the streams of intention and thought and desire running strong among the masses and moving with each of these streams.

I have failed signally in what I set out to do if I have not made clear that for many years certain deeply fissured streams of thought and desire and demand were running among the people; that these streams of thoughts represented the efforts of powerful minorities to serve some important end of their several class purposes and interests; that Minister after Minister had perceived these currents and had run with them, that Italy had descended with a kind of doom-like inevitability into social and economic bankruptcy and that Mussolini, filled with a passion for power, coming on the scene in a moment of despair and chaos, perceiving obscurely the intentions and desires of the people, quickly enough located them, rose to power, and then proceeded to put into effect a program not conforming to his own opinions, as he set out to do, but conforming to the opinions of these controlling groups among the Italian people. There remains now merely to show clearly what, out of the conditions we have been describing, he finally adopted and put together to make up that special form of society we call fascism.

X · What Is Fascism?

MUSSOLINI became Premier in October 1922. With the innumerable arguments about the march on Rome or with the story of the violent, lawless, and outrageous tactics he used to come to power we are not concerned here. That history has been told many times. Our business is to see the use he made of his power to fashion a new form of society.

He did not have a majority in parliament. He had to form a coalition cabinet which included a moderate socialist and a member of the Popolari. Some liberal politicians saw the hope of a stable government and the General Confederation of Labor (socialist) agreed to collaborate. Mussolini, of course, began to move toward dictatorship. But the full dictatorship did not come until 1925, after the assassination of Matteoti.

We will now see the elements of the fascist society emerge—point by point. First we must note one important difference between communism and fascism which becomes clear here. Socialism has a definite philosophy, based upon clearly enunciated principles which had long been debated and were widely understood. Socialists disagreed among themselves on certain points and upon programs of action. But socialism as a system of social structure with an organized body of doctrine was well understood. This was not true of fascism. Whether it was capitalist or anti-capitalist, labor or anti-labor, no one could say until the leaders themselves decided upon a course of action. It was improvised as the movement went along. Therefore we cannot define fascism as a movement committed to the collection of principles enunciated in its formal proclamation of principles and objectives—the Eleven Points of San Sepolcro. Mussolini, being in pursuit of power, made that objective the mold by which his policies were formed. Behold now the erection of the great fascist edifice.

1. He had been a syndicalist and hence anti-capitalist. The original program included a demand for confiscation of war profits, confiscation of certain church property, heavy inheritance and income taxes, nationalization of arms and munitions plants, and control of factories, railroads, and public services by workers' councils. These, Mussolini said, "we have put at the head of our program." But in power he did none of these things. Signora Sarfatti quotes him as saying:

> I do not intend to defend capitalism or capitalists. They, like everything human, have their defects. I only say their possibilities of usefulness are not ended. Capitalism has borne the monstrous burden of the war and today still has the strength to shoulder the burdens of peace.... It is not simply and solely an accumulation of wealth, it is an elaboration, a selection, a co-ordination of values which is the work of centuries.... Many think, and I myself am one of them, that capitalism is scarcely at the beginning of its story.[1]

On another occasion he said: "State ownership! It leads only to absurd and monstrous conclusions; state ownership means state monopoly, concentrated in the hands of one party and its adherents, and that state brings only ruin and bankruptcy to all." This was indeed more in conformity with his syndicalist faith, but it completely negatived the original fascist platform. The first point we shall have to settle, therefore, is that fascism is a defense of capitalist society, an attempt to make it function. This view, which Mussolini did not entertain when he began, he came around to as he saw that

[1] *Life of Benito Mussolini,* by Margherita G. Sarfatti, Stokes, New York, 1925.

Italy, in spite of all the disorder, had no mind to establish a socialist state. Moreover, he attached to himself the powerful industrialists and financiers of Milan and Rome along with many of the nobles, two of those powerful minorities essential to his general aims. Thus he molded fascism into a powerful weapon to beat down the Red menace. But it was Italy which molded him to this philosophy, new for him, the man who, when the factories were occupied, had applauded the act of the workers.

2. Next Mussolini had denounced "demagogic finance" and promised to balance the budget. However, he lost little time in turning to the time-worn favorite of Ministers—the unbalanced budget. As late as 1926 he wrote in his autobiography: "The budget of the nation [as he came to power] had a deficit of six and a half billions. It was a terrific figure, impossible for an economic structure to bear. . . . Today we have a balanced budget." The surface facts supported that statement. His first budget showed a deficit of 4,914,000,000 lire; his second a deficit of only 623,000,000; and his third (1924-25) a surplus of 417,000,000 lire. It is entirely probable that Mussolini believed a balanced budget a good thing and consistent with his other promises. But Mussolini's policies were made for him by the necessities of power, not by the laws of economics. At the very moment he was boasting of a balanced budget he was on the eve of a huge deficit of nine billion, in 1926-27. The year after that he balanced the budget once more so far as his books showed, and this was his last. From then on Italy was to float upon a sea of deficits, of spending and ever-rising national debt.

But as a matter of fact Mussolini never balanced a budget. Immediately on taking office he proceeded to spend more on public works than his predecessors. Dr. Villari, fascist apologist, says that between 1922 and 1925, despite drastic economies, Mussolini spent 3,500,000,000 lire on public works compared with only 2,288,000,000 lire in the previous three years. He also spent more on the army and navy and continued to increase those expenditures. How Mussolini could spend more than his predecessors on arms and on public works and yet balance the budget excited the curiosity of Dr. Gaetano Salvemini, who investigated the subject with surprising results.

Dr. Salvemini discovered that Mussolini resorted to a subterfuge to pay contractors without increasing his budget. He would make a contract with a private firm to build certain roads or buildings. He would pay no money but sign an agreement to pay for the work on a yearly installment plan. No money was paid out by the government. And hence nothing showed up in the budget. Actually the government had contracted a debt just as much as if it had issued a bond. But because no money passed, the whole transaction was omitted from the Treasury's books. However, after making such a contract, each year the government had to find the money to pay the yearly installments which ran from ten to fifty years. In time, as the number of such contracts increased, the number and amount of the yearly payments grew. By 1932 he had obligated the state for 75 billion lire of such contracts. The yearly payments ran to billions. What he did by this means was to conceal from the people the fact that he was plunging the nation ever deeper into debt. If these sums were added to the national debt as revealed in the Treasury admissions, the actual debt was staggering ten years after Mussolini's ascent to power on a promise to balance the budget. According to Dr. Salvemini's calculations, the debt of 93 billion lire, when Mussolini took office, had grown to 148,646,000,000 lire in 1934. To what breath-taking sum it has now risen no one knows.[2] But an Associated Press dispatch to the New York *Times* (August 8, 1943) announced that the Italian debt was then 405,823,000,000 lire, and the deficit for the year was 86,314,000,000 lire.

Mussolini made no secret of the fact that he was spending. What he concealed was that he was loading the state with debt. The essence of all this is that the fascist architect discovered that, with all his promises, he had no formula for creating employment and good times save by spending public funds and getting those funds by borrowing in one form or another—doing, in short, precisely what Depretis and Crispi and Giolitti had been doing, following the long-settled practice of Italian governments. Thus spending became a settled part of the policy of fascism to create national income, except that the fascist state spent upon a scale unimaginable to the old

[2] For a full and interesting discussion of this weird chapter in fiscal policy see "Twelve Years of Fascist Finance," by Dr. Gaetano Salvemini, *Foreign Affairs*, April 1935, Vol. 13, No. 3, p. 463.

premiers save in war. But in time the fascist began to invent a philosophical defense of his policy. What the old prewar ministries had done apologetically the fascists now did with a pretension of sound economic support. "We were able to give a new turn to financial policy," says an Italian pamphlet, "which aimed at improving the public services and at the same time securing a more effective action on the part of the state in promoting and facilitating national progress."[3] It was the same old device plus a blast of pretentious economic drivel to improve its odor. Thus we may now say that fascism is a system of social organization which recognizes and proposes to protect the capitalist system and uses the device of public spending and debt as a means of creating national income to increase employment.

3. The third point to be noticed has to do with industry. For decades, as we have pointed out, men of all sorts believed that the economic system ought to be controlled. Mussolini accepted completely the principle that the capitalist economic system ought to be managed—planned and directed—under the supervision of the state. By this he did not mean that kind of state interference we employed in America before 1933—that is, regulatory commissions to prevent business from doing certain unlawful things such as combining to restrain trade. What he had in mind was what so many in Italy had in mind, that some force should be brought into being to direct and manage the movement and operation of economic law—controlling such great glandular energies as production, distribution, labor, credit, etc.

In doing this Mussolini was again complying with a general though vague desire of the people. And in doing it he had in mind two generally favored objectives. First, there was a growing weariness of the eternal struggle between employers and employees. Second, people wanted in some general way the functions of production and distribution managed in the interest of better times.

Nothing that Mussolini did fell in with his own ideas more than this. He was a syndicalist. And, as we have pointed out, it was the central principles of syndicalism that were making their way un-

[3]*The Italian Budget before and after the War*—pamphlet issued by Provveditorato Generale Della Stato, Rome, 1925.

noticed into the thinking of all sorts of people. The syndicalist believed that industry should be controlled. So did Mussolini and so did most other people. The syndicalist believed that this control should take place outside the state. So did Mussolini and so did almost all others. The syndicalist believed that society should be organized for this control in craft groups. So did labor, industrialists, the people. And so did Mussolini. The syndicalist believed that industry should be dominated not by consumers or citizens as such but by producers. So did most others including the Duce. There was only one point on which they differed. That was the meaning of the word "producers." The employers considered themselves the producers. The syndicalists believed the workers were the producers. One way to resolve that question was to call them all producers. After all, outside of the doctrinaires of various groups, the masses among them had in mind very practical ends. The bosses wanted to curb competition, protect themselves from what they called "overproduction," and from what they also called the unreasonable aggressions of labor. The leaders and doctrinaires among the laboring groups had theories about workers' councils, etc. But what the membership wanted was higher wages, better working hours, job security, etc. The seemingly wide gap between the employers' and the workers' definition of the word "producers" was not so great. An organization that would form all the producers—the employers and employees—into trade groups under state authority in separate groups but brought together in some sort of central liaison agency or commission, in which the rights of workers to bargain with their employers would be preserved, while the employers would have the opportunity to make, with the backing of the law and upon a comprehensive scale, regulations for the planning and control of production and distribution, came close to satisfying the desires of many men in all parties.

All this did not correspond completely to the Sorel syndicalist's blueprint for society, but it drew most of its inspiration from that idea. So much is this true that the system has come to be frankly called Italian syndicalism, and fascist historians and apologists like Villari now refer to Italy freely as the syndicalist state.

It would not be true to say that this is precisely what employers and labor leaders and their union members wanted. The point I make is that at the bottom of it was the central idea that these groups held in one degree or another, and that while it certainly excited the opposition of many, it corresponded sufficiently with a general drift of opinion to paralyze any effective opposition to it. It was moving in the direction of a current of opinion—of several, in fact —and not wholly against such a current.

Out of all this came the Fascist Corporative System and then the Corporative State. Briefly, it is built on the old syndicalist principle that there is a difference between the political and the economic state. The political state is organized by geographic divisions and has as its function the maintenance of order and the direction of the defense and progress of the nation. The economic state is organized in economic divisions, that is according to craft or industrial groups, and has as its function the planning and direction of the economic society.

Employers are organized into local trade associations called syndicates. The local syndicates are formed into regional federations, and all these regional federations into a National Confederation. The same holds true of the workers. In each locality the local labor syndicate or union and the local employers' syndicate or trade association are brought together in a corporative. The regional federations are brought together in a regional corporative. And the National Confederations of Employers and of Workers are united in a great National Corporative. I refrain from going into any details about the functions and techniques of these bodies. It is conceivable that in different countries they might differ widely—as indeed they have. But the central principle will be the same—that through these federations and corporatives employers and workers will plan and control the economic system under the supervision of the state. Mussolini himself called this "self-regulation of production under the aegis of the producers."

In time Mussolini went further and made this the basis of reorganizing the state. Instead of abolishing the Senate as he had promised in his original platform, he abolished the Chamber of Deputies and substituted for it the Chamber of Fasces and Corporations, the members of which are supposed to represent the great trade and professional estates along with the representatives of the fascist state. This Mussolini has called the Corporative State. He looks upon it as his greatest contribution to the science of government.

At this point we can say that fascism is (1) a capitalist type of economic organization, (2) in which the government accepts responsibility to make the economic system work at full energy, (3) using the device of state-created purchasing power effected by means of government borrowing and spending, and (4) which organizes the economic life of the people into industrial and professional groups to subject the system to control under the supervision of the state.

4. Mussolini, having incorporated the principle of state-created purchasing power into his system, turned naturally to the old reliable project of militarism as the easiest means of spending money. It is scarcely necessary to dwell on this since our newspaper files are well supplied with statements of returning American travelers since 1935 telling, some with an accent of approval, how Mussolini has solved the problem of unemployment in Italy by means of expenditures on national defense. Some of our own high officials have found occasion to comment on this fact, contrasting his accomplishment with our own failure to put our people to work.

Money was spent on highways, schools, public projects of various kinds, and on the draining of the Pontine Marshes, which became in Italy the great exhibition project not unlike our TVA in America. But this was not enough, and so he turned more and more to military expenditures. It must also be said that this fell in with his own tastes and temperament and with certain other objectives he had in mind, such as the elevation of the Italian spirit by this display of warlike power.

William Ebenstein gives the following figures for fascist outlays on the army and navy:[4]

1924–25	3,240,000,000	Lire
1934–35	4,330,000,000	"
1935–36	10,304,000,000	"
1936–37	12,865,000,000	"

[4] *Fascist Italy*, by William Ebenstein, American Book Company, New York, 1939.

Compared with Great Britain, which spent 20 per cent of her budget on defense in 1936, and France, which spent 27.2 per cent, Italy spent 31 per cent. In 1939 she spent 52 per cent.

The militarization of Italy became an outstanding feature of the new regime. And the economic value of this institution in relieving unemployment while inducing the population to submit compliantly to the enormous cost became a boast of fascist commentators.

5. It is not necessary to comment on the fascist brand of imperialism. What we have already observed on that head—the intimate connection of militarism and imperialism—applies with full force here. It is unthinkable that Mussolini could induce the people of Italy to bear with patience the load of deficits and debt and taxes which this policy forced without supplying them with an adequate reason. Of course the reasons were the same old ones—the necessity of defense against enemies and external dangers daily magnified by propaganda, the economic necessity of colonies, and the appeal to the purple spirits in the population, the lovers of action and danger and glory. The extent to which Mussolini worked all these instruments is too well known and too recent to call for any further comment. The very nature of his regime called for action, ceaseless action, like a man on a bicycle who, if he stops, will fall. Imperialist ambitions, the re-creation of a new Roman Empire became an essential part of the whole scheme of things, intimately bound up with the policy of spending and with the propaganda of egoism and glory directed against the imagination of the people.

In 1929 the depression which struck every capitalist nation hit fascist Italy. Foreign and domestic trade was cut in half. Factories cut their output in half. Unemployment rose 250 per cent. The problem of the fascist magician was to reverse all this. Mussolini blamed it not on the defects in fascist doctrine, but on the "bourgeois spirit with its love of ease and a career" which still lurked in Italy. What was the remedy? "The principle of permanent revolution," he cried in a speech March 19, 1934. He repudiated the doctrine of peace. "War alone brings up to the highest point the tension of all human energy and puts the stamp of nobility upon the peoples who have the courage to meet it." This he called "dynamism." What he meant was that he had no weapon against the inevitable economic crisis save that ancient one—more and more military expenditures paid for with borrowed funds and supported by the evangel of heroism and high adventure ending in war.

To sum up we may say, then, that fascism in Italy was and is a form of organized society (1) capitalist in character, (2) designed to make the capitalist system function at top capacity, (3) using the device of state-created purchasing power through government debt, (4) and the direct planning and control of the economic society through corporativism, (5) with militarism and (6) imperialism imbedded in the system as an inextricable device for employing a great mass of the employables.

There is one more ingredient. But before we look at it let me point out that none of these activities or policies already described involves moral turpitude according to the codes of the great nations of the West. It is entirely possible for an ordinarily decent person to approve and defend both public debt and spending, the corporative or guild system along with militarism and imperialism. In my view both militarism and imperialism are evil things, but not in the view of Western culture. There is no revolt against Western culture in any of these things, for all of them have been present in it for centuries, and the West is well peopled with the bronze and marble statues of heroes who have been associated with their advance.[5] It is for this reason that it is an easy matter for ordinarily good citizens to look with indifference or tolerance or even approval upon the juncture of these several forces in our midst. My own opinion, however, is that no state can undertake to operate these separate devices all together to save the capitalist system without sooner or later finding itself confronted with the necessity of employing force and suppression within its own borders and upon its own people. It is a fact, as we have seen, that Minister after Minister over many years used the policies—spending and borrowing, militarism and imperialism, and that business control was attempted by private business organizations—but the use of these devices never succeeded,

---

[5]"The transformations undergone by business organizations in those countries which have revamped their national systems along totalitarian lines are fully consonant with and may be considered the logical outgrowth of previous trends in structure, policies, and control within the business world itself." *Business as a System of Power*, by Robert A. Brady, Columbia University Press, 1943.

first because they were never tried on a sufficiently large and persistent scale and second because within the framework of the constitutional representative system it was not possible to carry them to their full and logical lengths. The difference between Mussolini and his old parliamentary predecessors and precursors is that he used their devices upon the grand scale and organized the internal force that was necessary to give them an ample test. And he was enabled to do this because of the extensive and demoralizing collapse of the whole system which had been slowly degenerating for several decades and whose degeneration had been completed by World War I. We can now examine this sixth and final ingredient.

In all that we have seen thus far there is the familiar pattern of the man devoted to power and in possession of that power fumbling about for the means of meeting the problems of the society that pressed on him from every side. There is complete evidence that Mussolini when he began his march to power had no program. Both Professors Volpe and Villari, fascist apologists, admit that the original program was "confused, half demagogic, half nationalist, with a republican trend." He dropped one after another of his original principles as he found it expedient to make his policies conform to the great streams of public opinion and demand as soon as he recognized them. When he took power his program had changed to the point where he was committed to an attempt to make the capitalist system work. The anti-monarchist became the pillar of the Crown. The syndicalist revolutionist became the savior of capitalism. The anti-clerical became the ally of the Church. But how he would make this capitalist system function was a point on which he was far from clear. His position was wholly different from that of Lenin and Stalin, who overthrew an existing economic and political order and faced the task of establishing a new one whose fundamental principles and objectives and techniques were all supposedly well understood. Mussolini was committed to making the existing economic system work at the end of several decades during which it was crumbling to ruin.

Mussolini was certainly no absolute dictator when he took office as Premier in 1922. He was summoned to office in a constitutional manner, though he had created the condition which ended in that summons by violent measures which could not be called civilized. He did not have a majority in the Chamber. He had to function with a coalition cabinet containing a socialist and a member of the Popolari. It was in every sense a parliamentary government that he headed. Few looked for the absolute dictatorship which ultimately developed. As usual men were deceived by their own inveterate optimism and the words of politicians. One of the most exasperating features of political movements in the last twenty years has been the habitual use of meaningless words by the Machiavellian leaders.

There has always been a tendency among politicians to juggle with words. But in the last dozen years, when the art of propaganda has been developed to a high degree and all sense of moral value has evaporated from public pronouncements and documents, leaders of democratic countries make statements so shockingly at variance with their convictions and intentions that the casual listener is almost wholly defenseless against them. It is difficult to believe now that Mussolini ever prattled about democracy. Yet he did. Only two years before he took power he boasted that the Great War was a victory for democracy. Of fascism he said, when he took office, "that a period was begun of mass politics and *unqualified democracy.*" Mussolini had been an anti-monarchist. When first named to the legislature he, with some of his colleagues, remained away from the Chamber on the occasion of the King's speech as a gesture of disdain of the monarchy. The year before he assumed power he declared fascism was ready to co-operate with the liberal and socialist groups. He urged freedom of speech for the socialists who, he declared, were no longer dangerous to the state and should be permitted to carry on their propaganda. Ivanoe Bonomi, who preceded him as Premier, says that he tried to recall his party to its original republicanism and that he insisted the use of force must be abandoned against the organization of the proletariat. Mussolini's party showed its distaste for these attitudes at the party congress in November 1921. But these were taken as an indication of Mussolini's own position.

It is also possible that Mussolini himself, though he was hungry for more power, did not believe he could attain to absolute power. It seems probable that he underestimated the feebleness of the political system he attacked. And the moderate gestures toward democracy which he made for public consumption were beyond doubt lip service to a force he believed to be stronger than it was. But corruption and traffic with evil polity had weakened the structure of the old republican spirit. In the past it had been possible for Ministers to attain a degree of power which could be more or less loosely called dictatorship. We know that within the framework of democratic controls an enormous amassing of power can be created. Americans who have seen men like Croker, Murphy, Quay, and Penrose, and, at a later period, Huey Long and a number of other autocrats at work know how it is possible through the manipulation of patronage, appropriations, the courts, the police, and the election machinery for one man to gather into his hands powers only inferior in degree to those of a dictator. This had happened in Italy. Thus we find the Italian publicist Romondo, before the Great War, referring to Giolitti's regime, writing:

> Under the shadow of a democratic flag we have insensibly arrived at a dictatorial regime. . . . Giolitti has nominated nearly all senators, nearly all the councilors of state, all the prefects, and all the other high officials which exist in the administrative, judicial, and military hierarchy of the country. . . . With this formidable power he has carried out a grouping together of parties by means of reforms and a working agreement of individuals by means of personal attentions. . . . Now when the parties forget their programs . . . when arriving at the threshold of the Camera they leave at the door the rags of their political convictions . . . it is necessary for the majority to support itself by other means . . . as all personal powers support themselves, with tricks and corruption. . . . Thus in practice one arrives at the annulment of parliamentary institutions and the annihilation of political parties.

I quote Romondo's lament because it was uttered by one who perceived these phenomena at the time. We have in these pages already seen how power had been leaking out of every community and out of parliament into the hands of the Premier. Prefects had been planted in the provinces who had reduced the mayors and local officers to subjection. Decisions on local matters were thus transferred to Rome. Business, labor, farmers, communes—every class and every section—rushed with their difficulties to Rome, which encouraged the illusion that it could handle them. Parliament, overwhelmed by these multitudinous issues, sought escape by creating commissions to make rules and to manage them. Thus Rome got into its hands jurisdiction over every part of the political and economic system and undertook to manage that through a bureaucratic state dominated by a Premier who held his power through the incomparable power of a philanthropic treasury which kept public funds flowing everywhere. Italy became a highly centralized philanthropic bureaucratic state in which parliament became an instrument in the hands of the Premier.

Italy had become accustomed to this sort of thing—a Minister who could gather into his hands all the strings of power. It was of course by no means an authentic dictatorship. The right of opposition remained. The right of criticism continued. The Premier had to gather the support of many minority parties in the Chamber, and his insecure dictatorship lived from hand to mouth at the mercy of unstable and contentious and bargaining parliamentary groups. Yet Giolitti could get a vote of confidence of 362 to 90. It could be called a dictatorship only by analogy. But it represented a loss of power by the republican organs of state, and these losses constituted a serious erosion of the republican foundations. And this erosion was the prologue to the swelling theme of Mussolini's imperial act. Italy under Mussolini did not have to leap at one wide stride from pure representative government to dictatorship. The legislature and the people had been partly conditioned to the so-called dictatorship principle.

Mussolini had to have more power and he set out to get it. Few sensible men defended the condition that had grown out of numerous parties so that seldom did one party win a clear majority in the Chamber. The Premier had to govern with the support of a collection of hostile elements drawn together behind him by coalitions of several minority parties. When proportional representation for parliament was introduced, the situation became worse. Parliament became a hopeless, brawling society with the power of clear decision almost destroyed. The public was exasperated with parliament. Even the parliamentary system was discredited and blamed for everything.

There was an incessant demand for parliamentary reform. That reform took the course of less power for the Chamber, more for the executive. It was not called "streamlining the government" because that word was not yet invented. Mussolini had to rule with a Chamber split many ways and with his enemies in the majority. He determined to correct that condition at once. He did not cease in the process until he had made himself an unrestrained tyrant. Here is what he did.

He used three devices: (1) the electoral law of 1923, (2) the use of the military party, (3) the capture of all agencies of modern propaganda.

The electoral law was called a reform. Members of the Chamber were elected by proportional representation under a reform forced through by Premier Nitti. Socialists had rejoiced in this reform because it enabled them to get so large a vote in the Chamber. But this became the basis of Mussolini's electoral law and his electoral system. He adopted the proportional representation system with the provision that would enable a party receiving a fourth of the votes to have two thirds of the seats in the Chamber. How did he succeed in doing this? It was passed by the same Chamber that had been elected under the sponsorship of Giolitti in 1919. Villari says it passed both houses by substantial majorities. On this he bases his claim that no objection can be made to its constitutionality. Having done this, Mussolini now held two thirds of the votes in the Chamber.

Many, however, defended this law. The Italian Chamber was split into numerous parties—fractional parties. A stable government was next to impossible in this situation, and many felt that some change should be made by which the party with the most votes, even though it had a minority, should be able to carry on the government. Thus Mussolini got plenty of highly respectable help along the first steps to absolute rule. The balance of the support was obtained by intimidation.

The other weapon of dictatorship was the party. The characteristics of this party were that it was (a) limited in numbers and (b) subject to quasi-military discipline. There is nothing unique about this. In this respect it followed the socialist model, which is in all countries a party calling for a rigidly disciplined membership limited necessarily by the very nature of the discipline it enforces. The military character of the party had no precedent in the socialist political forms. The military character, however, has been found in other countries and takes its form from the intention of the organizers to employ force as an instrument of attaining power. In this respect it followed the syndicalist theory of violence. Thus the form of political organization, like so much of the economic doctrine, was borrowed from the strategy of the Left. The quasi-military character of the party, with its black-shirt uniforms, was merely one form of using violence—an instrument of coercion and intimidation and confusion which is not unknown in the history of political parties.

Few Americans are familiar with a department of human art in which European radicals have specialized for many years—the art of revolution. Revolution through the barricades or by mass proletarian attack upon a regime is no longer thought to be a practical art. Revolution by procedures within the framework of the existing constitutional system has been for many years the accepted technique. There is a considerable literature on this subject which Americans, little concerned with revolution, have ignored. But we know that Mussolini's reading had been largely devoted to this very literature. The central objective of this type of revolution is to produce confusion. Groups of all sorts unfriendly to the regime must be encouraged and activated whether they are in agreement with the revolutionists or not. They add to the divisions and the sense of hopelessness. Violence is a second arm of action. It intimidates the weak and creates disorder that harries the indifferent citizens. Within this atmosphere of division, intimidation, and disorder it is possible for an audacious and assertive and cocksure minority to force itself into power by quasi-constitutional means after which it can use the parliamentary and constitutional instruments it then controls to work its will upon the whole fabric of the society. The Fascist party performed this function.

When Mussolini became Premier and obtained a majority by means of the electoral law, he was still hesitant in his assumption of absolute power. There remained in the Chamber a large number of critics —vocal opposition. Most aggressive of these was Matteoti, socialist leader. The constant attacks within the Chamber upon Mussolini drove fascist black shirts to further outrages against the enemies of fascism, and as the culmination of a series of criminal assaults Matteoti was assassinated by men holding high place in the Fascist party and the charge was made that Mussolini had ordered the crime.[6] The incident presented Mussolini with a real crisis. He met it with an extraordinary exhibition of assurance and audacity, assumed full responsibility for the state of the country, while denying complicity in the murder, and defied his enemies. He then unloosed upon all opposition the same relentless persecution and suppression he had meted out to the socialists. The more intrepid critics who refused to comply with the new order were assaulted, jailed, or exiled. Mussolini assumed the role of despot. To complete this, the Grand Council of the Fascist party was made "the supreme organ of coordinating all activities of the regime." All its members were appointed by Mussolini and he alone could summon them to meet. Later the Chamber decreed its own dissolution and a new Chamber, in accordance with the principle of corporativism, was established. Its members were chosen as follows: The fascist syndical organizations chose 800 candidates and other fascist groups chose 200. From these 1,000 the Fascist Grand Council named 400 to be the party candidates for the Chamber. Their names were submitted to the electorate, which voted "yes" or "no." Thus all opposition was completely extinguished. But the regime began with a compliance with parliamentary forms and used that form to destroy the constitution.

There is a third weapon the dictatorship uses with deadly effect. This is the weapon of modern propaganda, which is quite different from that mild and old-fashioned thing which in America was once known as "publicity." Complete control of the press is of course a vital element of this along with suppression of all critical elements. But this modern propaganda is something more than the negative force inherent in suppression. It is a positive assault upon the mind of the people. I have said that these modern dictatorships are popular or demagogic. I do not mean that they are popular in the sense of

---

[6]The evidence against Mussolini on this point has been collected and presented in great detail in Mr. George Seldes' *Sawdust Caesar*, Harper & Bros., New York, 1935. A very full and reliable record of the depredations of the fascist gangsters is made in Dr. Gaetano Salvemini's *Under the Axe of Fascism*, Viking Press, New York, 1936.

commanding the love of the people. But for reasons associated with the structure of modern societies these dictatorships must have their roots running deep into the populations as the final source of power. They rise to power by running with all the streams of thought in the population. They are committed more or less to do those things which the powerful minorities among the people wish. But when they face the necessity of doing these things, immediately powerful countercurrents press against them. Thus spending involves taxes and borrowing which in turn involves more taxes which sets up powerful resistance from all quarters.

Corporative control means regimentation of business which, when attempted, involves stern compliance measures which also provoke another powerful group of irritations and enmities. In the end the dictator must do things which the population does not like. Hence he must have power—power to subdue criticism and resistance. And this necessity for power grows by what it feeds on until nothing less than absolutism will do. And so the popular mind must be subjected to intense conditioning, and this calls for the positive and aggressive forms of propaganda with which we are becoming familiar in this country. The chief instruments of this are the radio and the movies. In the hands of a dictator or a dictatorial government or a government bent on power the results that can be achieved are terrifying. Along with this, of course, goes the attack upon the mind of youth. The mind is taken young and molded in the desired forms. It is at this point the dictatorships develop their attitude toward religious organizations, which cannot be permitted to continue their influence over young minds.

The dictatorship element of the fascist state has accounted for two sets of facts: (a) a collection of theories upon which the totalitarian organism is founded, and (b) a collection of episodes that have grown out of it.

The fascist organizers have felt the need to fabricate a philosophical basis for their system, which is a recognition of the popular stake in the experiment. They have, therefore, invoked the principle of the elite. This is not new in Europe. Almost every existing government at the time recognized the principle of monarchy and the principle of aristocracy, including the government of England, which to this day dedicates its upper chamber to the aristocracy or the elite. Long before the last war the principle of the elite was extensively discussed. Pareto was one of those who had subjected this institution to minute analysis. He criticized the static or hereditary elite that existed in most countries. In Britain and Germany there was an effort to mitigate this by providing for fresh infusions of new members into the elite by conferring of nobility upon candidates for the distinction from time to time. But the old hereditary elite remained and continued to dominate its class. Pareto played with the idea of a fluid or a circulating elite, as he called it. And Mussolini, who had listened to Pareto at Lausanne, had heard him with approval. It would be a simple matter to get an endorsement of this idea from large numbers of thoughtful people in every European country. It was this principle Mussolini adopted—the Fascist party being the instrument for the creation of this new elite. Hitler adopted the same idea in Germany. At the bottom, the idea is defended upon the theory that men are not equal in their intellectual and ethical endowments and that society should seek to isolate those who represent the highest development of the race and give them special functions in the exercise of social power.

Out of this, therefore, might be said to grow the idea for the exclusive party, limited in membership and exercising a determining influence on the social structure and the government, while according the masses a share in the power through the elected Chamber. In fact, however, the Fascist party did not grow out of any such theory. The theory instead is a rationalization to provide the Fascist party with an ethical basis. The party is a pure instrument of absolute power. But the idea invoked to defend it is not without its appeal to great numbers of people.

The other principles of fascist policy are the totalitarian government and the principle of leadership. They are not the same. Our own government is almost unique in its proclamation of the idea that the government shall not possess complete power over all human conduct and organization. The only powers possessed by our government are those granted by the Constitution. And that Constitution grants it very limited powers. The powers not granted to the central government are reserved to the states or to the people. Totalitarian government is the opposite of this. It defines a state whose powers are unlimited.

However, a state with unlimited powers need not necessarily be a dictatorship. While equipping the state with unlimited powers those powers may be diffused through several organs of government such as the legislature, the monarch, the courts, and the states. In Italy the leadership principle is invoked to concentrate all the powers of the state in a single head. The principle of hierarchy may define it also—a structure in which at each level of authority the powers, such as they are, are lodged in a single person—a leader—who in turn is responsible to another leader above him who possesses all the power deposited at that level, such leader being finally accountable to the supreme leader—the dictator.

As we survey the whole scene in Italy, therefore, we may now name all the essential ingredients of fascism. It is a form of social organization

1. In which the government acknowledges no restraint upon its powers—totalitarianism.

2. In which this unrestrained government is managed by a dictator —the leadership principle.

3. In which the government is organized to operate the capitalist system and enable it to function under an immense bureaucracy.

4. In which the economic society is organized on the syndicalist model, that is by producing groups formed into craft and professional categories under supervision of the state.

5. In which the government and the syndicalist organizations operate the capitalist society on the planned, autarchial principle.

6. In which the government holds itself responsible to provide the nation with adequate purchasing power by public spending and borrowing.

7. In which militarism is used as a conscious mechanism of government spending, and

8. In which imperialism is included as a policy inevitably flowing from militarism as well as other elements of fascism.

Wherever you find a nation using all of these devices you will know that this is a fascist nation. In proportion as any nation uses most of them you may assume it is tending in the direction of fascism. Because the brutalities committed by the fascist gangs, the suppressions of writers and statesmen, the aggressions of the fascist governments against neighbors make up the raw materials of news, the public is familiar chiefly with the dictator element in fascism and is only very dimly aware of its other factors. Dictatorship alone does not make a fascist state. The dictatorship of Russia, while following the usual shocking techniques of tyranny—the concentration camp and the firing squad—is very far from being a fascist dictatorship. In any dictatorship the dictator attacks such internal enemies and coddles such internal allies as suit his purposes, and so his suppressions and propaganda will be directed at different groups in different countries. Hence while Hitler denounces and persecutes the Jews, it was two Jews—Theodore Wolff and Emil Ludwig—who acclaimed Mussolini, because the latter did not find it profitable to attack them. The central point of all this is that dictatorship is an essential instrument of fascism but that the other elements outlined here are equally essential to it as an institution. In different countries it may alter its attitudes on religion or literature or races or women or forms of education, but always it will be militaristic and imperialist dictatorship employing government debt and autarchy in its social structure.

The commonly accepted theory that fascism originated in the conspiracy of the great industrialists to capture the state will not hold. It originated on the Left. Primarily it gets its first impulses in the decadent or corrupt forms of socialism—from among those erstwhile socialists who, wearying of that struggle, have turned first to syndicalism and then to becoming saviors of capitalism, by adapting the devices of socialism and syndicalism to the capitalist state. The industrialists and nationalists joined up only when the fascist squadrons had produced that disorder and confusion in which they found themselves lost. Then they supposed they perceived dimly at first and then more clearly, in the preachments of the fascists, the germs of an economic corporativism that they could control, or they saw in the fascist squadrons the only effective enemy for the time being against communism. Fascism is a leftist product—a corrupt and diseased offshoot of leftist agitation.

It is equally superficial to assume that this job was the work of the practical men and that the world of scholarship remained aloof, ignoring the dark currents that were rushing beside it eating away its foundations, as one fatuous American writer has asked us to believe. Far from being the work of the practical men, it was much more the achievement of a certain crackpot fringe—the practical men coming in only when the work of confusion was well under way. They came in on the tide of confusion. As for the scholars and poets—remote from the evil smell of politics and economics—Italy's foremost philosopher and historian, Benedetto Croce, had long before created a tolerance for the syndicalist ethic in Italy. He wrote approvingly of Sorel. He went so far as to say that the Inquisition may well have been justified. Certainly Mussolini and Gentile believed up to 1925 that he supported fascism. Later he was to have his house burned over his head when the practical politicians took the scholar at his word.

If there was a second to Croce among the scholars it was Giovanni Gentile, who became Mussolini's Minister of Education. It was Gentile who brewed most of the nasty draughts which were offered to the lips of the scholars—such as first taking the fascist oath and later joining the Fascist party under compulsion. Mussolini himself, says Borgese, stood reluctant before these proposals for two years because of his awe of the mysterious world of the mind and the academy, since he yearned to be thought of himself as an intellectual. But Gentile finally persuaded him. And when the professors were presented with the demand to take the oath and join up, of all the thinkers and teachers in Italy, only thirteen refused. After that, having taken the first step, caught in the spiritual necessity of defending themselves in the forum of their own consciences, they proceeded to out-fascist the fascists in their fabrication of ethical and philosophical supports for the new order.

No one will wish to mitigate the dark colors of this evil episode in the history of our civilization. But it will not do to say it is just the work of bad men. Too many men who lay claim to being called good citizens have proclaimed their approval or at least a warm tolerance for the performances of Mussolini. Mussolini's black shirts had clubbed socialists into flight and the timid into submission. One might suppose that the use of the cudgel would have called at least for an apology from some of those men like Gentile who entered the fascist movement at the head of a group of liberal academicians and writers. Mussolini had boasted that his fascist revolution was made with cudgels. And the philosopher Gentile was so far from being horrified at this that he actually said that in the days before the march on Rome "the cudgels of the *squadristi* seemed like the grace of God. The cudgel in its material brutality became the symbol of the fascist, extra-legal soul. . . . That is holy violence." Here is the dread cult of violence which becomes holy the moment it appears in support of one's own special cult. Let no man suppose that it is only in Italy that a liberal philosopher can hold a brief for "holy violence."

It was after the vulgar brutalities of the march to power, after newspapers had been burned and editors beaten, political clubrooms sacked, after the sacred cudgel by God's grace had done its holy violence on its enemies and others had been gorged with castor oil, after thousands had been thrown into concentration camps and countless other brave men had been driven from their country, after Matteoti had been assassinated and Mussolini had proclaimed that democracy was "a dirty rag to be crushed under foot," that Winston Churchill, in January 1927, wrote to him, saying: "If I had been an Italian I am sure I would have been entirely with you from the beginning to the end of your victorious struggle against the bestial appetites and passions of Leninism." He assured the Duce that were he an Italian he would "don the Fascist black shirt." And a year later, in *Collier's Magazine,* he wrote extolling Mussolini above Washington and Cromwell.

Does this mean that Churchill approves of beating and suppressions? Hardly. Its significance lies in the revelation of the extent to which evil deeds will be excused or tolerated or even defended when some cherished public or religious or social crusade is the excuse. Man's capacity for cruelty—even the good man's capacity for cruelty—in the prosecution of a spiritual crusade is a phenomenon to affright the soul.

Mussolini—the same Mussolini whose career of violence and aggression and tyranny had been widely advertised—has testimonials from many Americans. Mr. Myron C. Taylor, until recently envoy to the

Vatican, said in 1936 that all the world has been forced to admire the success of Premier Mussolini "in disciplining the nation." He did not use the word Ethiopia, but he told a dinner audience that "today a new Italian Empire faces the future and takes up its responsibilities as the guardian and administrator of an alien backward nation of 10,000,000 souls."[7]

When Mussolini wrote his autobiography he did so at the instance and prodding of one of his most devoted admirers, the United States Ambassador to Italy, the late Richard Washburn Child, who had been in Italy during a considerable part of the whole fascist episode and knew it at first hand.[8] When the book appeared it contained a fulsome preface by the Ambassador, just as another book by Count Volpi, Mussolini's Finance Minister, on the glories of Italian fascist finance, carried a complimentary preface by Mr. Thomas W. Lamont.[9]

Mr. Sol Bloom, now chairman of the Foreign Relations Committee of the House of Representatives, said on the floor of the House January 14, 1926:

> He [Mussolini] is something new and vital in the sluggish old veins of European politics. It will be a great thing not only for Italy but for all of us if he succeeds.
>
> It is his inspiration, his determination, his constant toil that has literally rejuvenated Italy and given her a second, a modern, Renaissance.
>
> He has taken nothing for himself, neither titles, money, palaces, nor social position for his family. His salary is only . . . about $1,000 in American money.
>
> I can only compare Mussolini and his men to what would have happened if the American Legion, led by a flaming hero, had become sick and weary of trusts, of graft, of incompetence, of stupidity, and, feeling their youth, their intelligence, and their patriotism bursting within them, had organized to demand the right to try their ideas of a sane and strict administration.
>
> Although bloodless, Mussolini's "revolution" has changed Italy for the better.
>
> You do not find any violence there and you do not find any strikes.

[7]New York *Times*, November 6, 1936.
[8]*My Autobiography*, by Benito Mussolini, Scribner, New York, 1928.
[9]*The Financial Reconstruction of Italy*, by Count Volpi and Bonaldo Stringher, Italian Historical Society, New York, 1927.

The world-wide interest in Italy today is undoubtedly due to the career and the achievements of her great Premier, Benito Mussolini, who, crashing out of obscurity three years ago, has remained the most powerful personality in Europe ever since.[10]

Mr. Churchill was not the only one to see another Cromwell in Mussolini. Dr. Nicholas Murray Butler said "that it was safe to predict that just as Cromwell made modern England, so Mussolini could make modern Italy." He boasted of his friendship for Mussolini, who covered him with decorations, and he described "fascism as a form of government of the very first order of excellence," and insisted that "we should look to Italy to show us what its experience and insight have to teach in the crisis confronting the twentieth century."

Dr. Gaetano Salvemini, who preserves these choice examples of applause for the Duce in his recent book *What to Do with Italy*, also favors us with one from the late Mr. Otto Kahn, who spoke before the faculty of Wesleyan University, November 15, 1923:

> The credit for having brought about this great change in Italy and without bloodshed belongs to a great man, beloved and revered in his own country, a self-made man, setting out with nothing but the genius of his brain. To him not only his own country but the world at large owes a debt of gratitude.
> Mussolini was far from fomenting class hatred or using class animosities or divergencies for political purposes.
> He is neither a demagogue nor a reactionary. He is neither a chauvinist nor a bull in the china shop of Europe. He is no enemy of liberty. He is no dictator in the generally understood sense of the word.
> Mussolini is far too wise and right-minded a man to lead his people into hazardous foreign adventures.
> His government is following the policy of taking the state out of business as much as possible and of avoiding bureaucratic or political interference with the delicate machinery of trade, commerce, and finance.
> Mussolini is particularly desirous for close and active co-operation with the United States. I feel certain that American capital invested in Italy will find safety, encouragement, opportunity, and reward.

[10] *Congressional Record*, January 14, 1926, 69th Cong., 1st Session.

The great fascist evangelist did not fail to excite the admiration of some of those American foreign correspondents who are now proclaiming themselves the most ardent lovers of democracy and flinging around their venom upon men who were denouncing Mussolini's fascist dominion when they were extolling it. Mr. Herbert Matthews, of the New York *Times*, in *The Fruits of Fascism*, tells us that he was for long "an enthusiastic admirer of fascism" and intimates that he was converted only when he saw the fascist airmen raining bombs on Spain in 1938. Eleanor and Reynolds Packard, United Press correspondents, in their book written after their expulsion from Italy, assure us that historians will divide Mussolini's dictatorship into two parts and that the first, covering twelve years of his collaboration with the democratic powers, was marked by a social program that was good, despite his oppressions, and that is being copied now by democratic countries. To Mr. Matthews there was a time when Mussolini was the "one man who seemed sane in a mad world."[11]

I recall these testimonials here merely because of their bearing on American and British opinion upon what happened in Italy. We cannot count on all good people in America rejecting fascist ideas. To many the pursuit of the hated Red justified the elements of violence in the episode. To others the imperious need of meeting the challenge of labor justified the cudgels. Mussolini was all right as long as he played along with the democratic powers. "I do not deny," said Mr. Churchill as late as December 1940, in a speech in the House, "that he is a very great man. But he became a criminal *when he attacked England.*" Mussolini's crime lay not in all the oppressions he had committed upon his own people, not in his trampling down of liberty in Italy, in attacking Ethiopia or Spain, but in "attacking England." It is precisely in this tolerance of ordinarily decent people for the performances of such a man that the terrible menace of fascism lies for all peoples.

[11]*The Fruits of Fascism*, by Herbert L. Matthews, Harcourt, Brace & Co., New York, 1943. *Balcony Empire*, by Eleanor and Reynolds Packard, Oxford University Press, 1942.

PART TWO

THE BAD FASCISM: GERMANY

I · The Impartial Microbe

ONE FRUITFUL ORIGIN of much of the confusion about fascism in Germany arises out of the variety of people who hate it. Each hates it for some special reason. And while most people here abhor it for its brutal assaults upon the substance and implements of free government, there are many whose hatred is inspired by some special personal or group indignity or injustice suffered at the hands of the Führer. Thus Hitler is execrated by some who are themselves fascists—as, for instance, those fascist dictators whose regimes have rolled under his tanks equally with their democratic neighbors, or some of those former colleagues who were squeezed out of his congregation, or some of those disillusioned businessmen who gambled with him and lost.

A great many books have appeared, written either by these liquidated disciples or religious and political groups ruthlessly oppressed by him. It is a fair statement, however just their deep sense of wrong, that such books have reflected their flaming hatreds rather than their sound intellectual judgments. They have explained fascism in terms of their hatreds. These volumes have had a powerful influence here. They have gone far toward implanting the belief that fascism in Germany is the product of extraordinarily able yet evil men or that it is due to some demoniac possession of the German people themselves.

For the American honestly in search of the seeds of fascism no analyses could be more misleading than these. If fascism is the work of a handful of brutal and lawless men, we need have no fear of it here. We are never without leaders both able and corrupt. But they are not sufficiently numerous and powerful to make very much headway against the peculiar structure of our government. If the phenomenon is merely a manifestation of the paranoid mentality of the German people then certainly we are in no danger of infection unless we, too, are a little demented.

But alas, the most terrifying aspect of the whole fascist episode is the dark fact that most of its poisons are generated not by evil men or evil peoples, but by quite ordinary men in search of an answer to the baffling problems that beset every society. Nothing could have been further from the minds of most of them than the final brutish and obscene result. The gangster comes upon the stage only when the scene has been made ready for him by his blundering precursors.

Writers like Mr. Herbert Agar lash themselves into a luminous fever of righteousness as they survey the world. Those phenomena in social life they do not like they write down as the fruit of barbarism. And barbarism is just another name for Germany, just as the same word turns out to be a synonym for Russia with others. To Mr. Agar the world suffers from the "German disease," which contaminates the earth. Germany "has remained outside the stream of Latin culture."[1]

One recent writer sees Germany as a "thousand-year conspiracy against Greco-Christian civilization" while still another, an eminent psychiatrist, announces that the German people suffer from a paranoid condition, that they are mildly insane, that fascism and the war are therefore the work of crazy men who are incapable of maintaining a stable order.[2] The doctor thinks the problem is one for psychiatric medicine, while still another writer[3] thinks the solution should be entrusted to the surgeons who, by detailing 20,000 of their number, could sterilize all male Germans in one month and all female Germans in three years. One wants to purge the dis-

---

[1] *A Time for Greatness*, by Herbert Agar, Little, Brown, New York, 1942.
[2] *The Thousand-Year Conspiracy*, by Paul Winkler, Scribner, New York, 1943. *Is Germany Incurable?* by Richard M. Bricker, M.D., Lippincott, New York, 1943.
[3] *Germany Must Perish*, by Theodore N. Kaufman, Argyle Press, Newark, 1941.

ease out of the Germans, the other wants to purge the Germans out of the world.

But the explanation is not quite so simple. Germany is not the only country where fascism has appeared. It took power in Italy a decade before it ruled in Germany. It was in Turkey as soon as it attacked Italy. Indeed in the first days of his fascist adventure Mussolini liked to refer to himself as "the Mustapha Kemel of a Milanese Angora." If Germany was "outside the stream of Latin culture," surely this cannot be true of Italy. The fascist microbe has played no favorites. It has penetrated through Protestant Germany, Catholic Spain, Orthodox Greece, and Mohammedan Turkey. In each such country dictators have popped up fitting perfectly into the national background.

It would be impossible to find races of people in Europe differing more widely in history, culture, tradition, and tastes than Germany, Italy, Portugal, and Turkey, nor dictators more sharply distinguished from each other than Hitler, Mussolini, Metaxas, Salazar, and Kemel Pasha. In Italy, Mussolini supported the monarchy; in Germany, Hitler abominates it. In Spain, Franco allies himself devoutly with the Church; in Italy, Mussolini used the Church; in Germany, Hitler castigates it. The German Führer makes anti-Semitism an article of Nazi faith. The Duce ignored it save as a gesture of politeness to the Führer after the alliance. Fascism has made its appearance not only in Italy, Spain, Germany, Greece, Portugal, and Turkey, but likewise in Yugoslavia, Rumania, Poland, and other European countries, with a wide swing to South America and Asia.

It is fatuous to look upon fascism as a growth indigenous to any particular country. And it is equally false to say that it would not have arisen save as the work of Hitler or Mussolini. We cannot escape the significance of the fact that in each of these numerous countries a fascist tyrant sprang up at the right moment and all within a very brief period. It is true that in each case the country itself, its history, manners, culture, tradition, political system have greatly colored the external trappings of its fascism, and in each case the peculiar character of the leader has had an important effect upon the form, practices, techniques, slogans, and rituals of the movement. Had fascism entered Germany in the hands of some other leader than Hitler it would probably have worn different clothes, sung different songs, shouted different oaths, carried different banners and, perhaps, killed different people. But the essence of it would be the same. It is this essence we are trying to discover and identify.

There are other elements of confusion. Fascism is essentially a dictatorship. But dictatorship is not the only feature of the structure. All dictatorships are not fascist dictatorships—as, for instance, the Russian proletarian monstrosity. The economic ingredient of Russian communism is utterly unlike that of fascist Germany. It is a mistake, therefore, to define fascism as a dictatorship, just as it would be a mistake to define an automobile as a vehicle with four wheels. The other ingredients must also be considered. It is these we wish to discover. This emphasis on the dictatorship element in fascism is the cause of endless misapprehension. The dictatorship leads to all the ugly episodes, the brutal, overt acts that make up the daily news of fascist countries. The minds of Americans have been kept busy with the external drama, the shirted troopers, the putsches, the scandals, the obscenities, the assassinations and riots, the personal histories of the unpleasant heroes of the drama. The other and deeper essential elements—the elements which preceded the dictatorships and made them possible—are ignored. For these elements are humdrum and unworthy of the pens of reporters who are in search of action, incidents, drama. In some countries, where the drama has been less vivid, where the dictator is a Salazar rather than a Hitler, and where the amount of bloodletting has been very little, the fascist order has come in for a good deal of very friendly attention from Americans. We are already in danger of drawing a distinction between good fascists and bad fascists, just as we once did between good trusts and bad ones.

One peculiar weakness of the human mind seems to be that it cannot hate the object of its dislike without exaggerating or at least changing the form of the wickedness. Fascism in Germany and in Italy, looked at frankly, seems to me sufficiently hateful as a form of life. Taking it for what it is ought to exhaust the resources of aversion. But apparently fascism as it is seems not nearly ugly enough to satisfy the tastes of some of its more voluble critics. In order to hate it they feel bound to import into it evils it does not possess. This is silly. Because in this deformed and exaggerated shape it is not nearly so frightful because it does not exist. If I find myself in a wilderness I can be intelligently afraid of lions and tigers and reptiles as they are. The man who comes to me with the alarm about approaching man-eating cats and boa constrictors and who describes them to me as they are will fill me with a reasoned fear and induce me to take measures for safety. But the wild-eyed alarmist who rushes up with descriptions of dragons with flames pouring from their nostrils, swallowing two and three men at a gulp, will not excite me at all. I will not believe that such beasts will come upon me. I am afraid of such a beast as fascism just as it is because I know it can exist, that it flourishes not only in some distant jungle but seems to be at home in almost any kind of woods and climate and may actually put in an appearance here. I fear it because I know it may arise in America, taking on the coloration of the American jungle. Let us see, therefore, if we can isolate the real elements of fascism in Germany as a preliminary to searching for them in our own midst.

II · Resetting the Scene

THERE IS a generally held assumption that the German people have always lived under a highly centralized, autocratic government only thinly veneered with parliamentary forms and that therefore they were singularly open to the designs of a fascist regime.

As a matter of history it is a fact that the two peoples of Europe who resisted longest any attempt to bring them under a central, unitary government were Italy and Germany. Many years ago Dr. Edward Preissig called attention to the fact that Germans, one of the most numerous racial groups in Europe, "remained for centuries the most divided nation of Europe."[1] More recently two

[1] *Political Institutions of the Old World*, by Edward Preissig, Ph.D., Putnam and Sons, New York, 1906.

younger critics and victims of Hitler, Erika and Klaus Mann, observed that "the German people do not take to centralization. Germany's structure is regional. The Germans do not care to, and do not actually, accept dictation from Berlin."[2] The annotator of the Reynal and Hitchcock American translation of *Mein Kampf* notes this fact. "Manifestly," he observes, "the Germans have tended to break into groups, and most efforts to keep them together have failed or succeeded only in part. Doubtless the major reason for this divergence is not racial but religious. . . . After the war Germany very nearly disintegrated again. Movements favoring an independent Rhineland, an independent Silesia, an independent Bavaria gained considerable momentum. Many Germans will tell you that if the Hitler movement should fail, a new breakup of Germany would follow."[3]

I mention this not as expressing any special virtues among either Italians or Germans but as a fact completely at variance with some popularly accepted notions of these histories. England, France, Russia, Spain long before—centuries in some cases—had been drawn together into national, unitary bonds. Until the middle of the last century Italy remained a land of eight small states, Germany a collection of some thirty-nine separate units.

When, following the Franco-Prussian War, the Germans united in a single state, the new nation was erected not into a single central political unit, but rather into a federal union of many states. The constitution lodged certain very limited powers with the federal government—the empire—and reserved the remainder to the states. The central government had jurisdiction over foreign relations, the army and navy, imports and exports, the postal, telephone, and telegraph system, and nothing else. Even the administration of the federal laws was committed not to federal officials, as with us, but to the several states. Far from being an autocrat, the Kaiser presided over a federal government which actually possessed less powers than the United States federal government.

Its power of taxation was severely limited. It depended for its revenues on import and export duties, excise taxes and stamps on

---

[2] *The Other Germany*, by Erika and Klaus Mann, Modern Age Books, New York, 1940.
[3] *Mein Kampf*, edited by Dr. George N. Shuster and others, Reynal & Hitchcock, New York, 1940.

documents, and inheritance taxes—the last a questionable stretching of its powers. Excise taxes could be levied only on sugar, tobacco, spirits, and beer. It could impose no income taxes. The revenues thus collected were never sufficient for the empire. It was forced to depend, therefore, upon another source of funds; namely, the matricular contribution. That is, when the taxes levied by the central government were insufficient to meet its requirements, it could call upon the several states to contribute on the basis of population. But apparently it had no effective means of enforcing these contributions for many of the states remained habitually in arrears. This is a very different picture from that despotic state which is popularly envisioned as the creation of Bismarck.

For forty years after the founding of the empire, the central government made futile efforts to expand its powers. These were forcefully resisted by the several states until after the World War. The states of the German federal government were far more jealous of their sovereign powers than the states of our union.

The inadequacy of empire revenues drove Bismarck frequently to attempt purchase of all the German railroads to get their profits for the central government. The states resisted this until after the Great War. They said that with an annual revenue of 800,000,000 marks from the roads Bismarck could tyrannize over the parliament, the stock market, and the states.[4] He tried to erect state monopolies of tobacco to eke out with its profits the state deficits but was balked.[5]

It would not be true to say that the empire enjoyed parliamentary government in the unrestricted sense of that word. There was an empire parliament composed of a popular assembly, the Reichstag, and the Bundesrath, representing the states. The Reichstag was not so potent an instrument of popular government as the British House of Commons because the Chancellor was named by and responsible, not to it, but to the Emperor. The Chancellor, however, had to do business with the Reichstag since all money bills had to be voted by it and it frequently resisted his demands.

The socialist membership in the Reichstag increased steadily. Bismarck sought to force repressive laws against it but for long

[4]*Prince Bismarck,* by Charles Lowe, Cassell & Co., New York, 1886.
[5]*Cambridge Modern History,* Vol. XII.

without success. Even after an attempt on the life of the King, his proposal for a law to restrict the socialists was defeated by a large majority. It was not until a second attempt to kill the King was made that Bismarck got his law. The Reichstag just before the World War had 100 socialist members, in addition to many liberal groups. It is not difficult to imagine the pious mutterings of horror from our conservatives if our House of Representatives were invaded by a hundred socialist members.

The only purpose of noting these facts about the old German imperial state is to fix in the reader's mind that the German people up to 1914, while by no means enjoying the fullest measure of political freedom, were far from being an empire ruled by an autocrat. There was a spirit—and a growing one—of resistance to arbitrary tendencies. The Germany that dropped helpless into the arms of Hitler in 1932 did not begin its march to that ignoble destiny from a condition of highly absolutist government such as Russia or even Austria or their Balkan neighbors, but as a civilized community accustomed to many of the techniques of representative government operating on the parliamentary form and exercising many restraints on the executive.

III · The Revolt of the Masses

GERMANY was a society in which the instruments of producing and distributing goods was of the capitalist order. By this I mean that Germany operated under a system in which the tools of production were owned by private individuals or groups, who produced goods and distributed them for profit within the framework of a money economy.

The German states held investments in numerous enterprises—railroads, power companies, municipal transport, mines, forests, and some industrial enterprises. This has led to the impression that the empire had diluted its capitalism with a good deal of socialism. The empire had but little of these enterprises. They were held by the several states. But even here it was not socialism but rather state capitalism, if such a term is permissible. The German states made a point of operating their enterprises for profit as a source of state revenue. It was in no sense an experiment in production "for use" in a classless society. Moreover, while in bulk these enterprises were considerable, they formed only a small fraction of the whole economy. Nevertheless, they did accustom the German mind to the intrusion of the state into enterprise as a normal function of government.

Whatever its shortcomings it remains a fact that Germany between 1870 and 1914 was the most prosperous large country on the continent. But despite this fact, it is equally true that its economic system, in common with that of other countries, was beset by grave difficulties. These may be classified as (a) chronic inability to provide subsistence for a large part of the population and (b) recurring periods of depression.

This brings us to say what is of the utmost importance to this whole subject; namely, that in this system of private capitalism there is an organic flaw of some sort which tends to break it down at intervals and to infect it with a heavy dilution of poverty at all times. I do not say that this defect is irremediable. And obviously no one will say that poverty has increased under the capitalist system. Even so unfriendly a witness as Karl Marx said in 1848, before the greatest creations of capitalism had been produced:

> The bourgeoisie during its rule of scarcely one hundred years has created more massive and colossal productive forces than all the preceding generations together. Subjection of nature's forces to man, machinery, application of chemistry to industry and agriculture, steam navigation, railways, electric telegraphs, clearing of whole continents for cultivation, canalization of rivers, whole populations conjured out of the ground—what earlier century had even a presentiment that such productive forces slumbered in the lap of social labor?[1]

In the years after Marx wrote that paragraph Germany became the most prosperous nation on the continent. But despite this the two great problems—persisting poverty and cyclical depression—

[1] Quoted by Robert Hunter in *Revolution—Why, How, and When?* Harper Bros., New York, 1940.

grew in virulence as a social irritant. What we see in Germany, therefore, was an economic order that functioned better than in any continental country but which failed to produce enough purchasing power to provide all her people with the means of obtaining a decent share of that production while the system bore within its body some little-understood organism which at intervals brought the whole community to distress. There was nothing new about this. The history of the present economic system in any form is a history of recurring crises. But it is a fact that in the last fifty years, as the capacity to produce rose and the well-being of the people improved and the problem of production seemed almost solved, the problem of crises became more acute.

What is the explanation of this? The economic system of the present century differs from its more rudimentary form in an earlier century in this: (1) It has developed amazingly the power of the machine to produce; (2) it has extended in an extraordinary degree the mechanisms of credit; (3) it has elaborated equally the institutions of organization through the corporation; (4) it has fostered huge organization of mass control through trade associations, labor unions, cartels; (5) it has seen an intricate spread of social control over many of the processes of the economic system.

Whether these forces, while expanding the power to produce, have also contributed to the mechanistic difficulties of the system is a matter to be considered.

This condition is common to the whole capitalist economic world. Germany, even before World War I, was fast in the grip of this difficulty. But what is the explanation of the psychological reaction of the people of Germany to this condition? Grave as it was, the problem was not new. The answer must be looked for in another social rather than purely economic phenomenon. The force behind the great ferment in Germany finds its explanation in what Ortega y Gasset has called the *Revolt of the Masses*. This he describes as follows:

> Whereas in past times life for the average man meant finding all around him difficulties, dangers, want, limitations of his destiny, dependence, the new world appears as a sphere of practically limitless possibilities, safe and independent of anyone. Based on this primary and lasting impression, the

mind of every contemporary man will be formed, just as previous minds were formed on the opposite impression. For that basic impression becomes an interior voice which ceaselessly utters certain words in the depths of each individual, and tenaciously suggests to him a definition of life which is, at the same time, a moral imperative. And if the traditional sentiment whispered: "To live is to feel oneself limited, and therefore to have to count with that which limits us," the newest voice shouts: "To live is to meet with no limitation whatever and, consequently, nothing is impossible, nothing is dangerous, and, in principle, nobody is superior to anybody." This basic experience completely modifies the traditional, persistent structure of the mass-man. For the latter always felt himself, by his nature, confronted with material limitations and higher social powers. Such, in his eyes, was life. If he succeeded in improving his situation, if he climbed the social ladder, he attributed this to a piece of fortune which was favorable to him in particular. And if not to this, then to an enormous effort, of which he knew well what it had cost him. In both cases it was a question of an exception to the general character of life and the world; an exception which, as such, was due to some very special cause.[2]

Ortega then goes on to point out that the traditional mass-man of the past would not have accepted authority external to himself had not his surroundings violently forced him to do so. His surroundings do not violently force him to do so now and so he considers himself the lord of his own existence. This mass-man in Germany, as elsewhere—but of all continental countries, most in Germany—saw what modern life could do for him. He saw poverty banished from among many of his neighbors who were once condemned to it as a normal state of life. Means of transport had enabled his neighbors to move away more easily. He heard of a world of abundance that had appeared beyond his narrow frontiers. The school taught him to read. The newspaper brought him the opinions of many men and the story of the world's progress. He began to feel that his age-old poverty need not be his inevitable lot. He began to demand more from life and occasionally to taste its sweetness. He got to looking upon the government as an instrument to provide these things and, in Germany, this was a government of most limited powers. There was an impatience with disorder, hunger, depression. Men turned to the government as an agent of the people to correct these ancient

[2]*The Revolt of the Masses*, by José Ortega y Gasset, W. W. Norton, New York, 1932.

evils. What, actually, had happened was that the popular tolerance of poverty and crises was gone.

Ortega is not talking about that kind of proletarian revolt which flamed up so many times in Europe under the pressure of unendurable oppressions. The common people had risen in England under Cromwell, the Russian serfs had poured into the streets under Catherine II as well as Nicholas to be mowed down by grapeshot. The populace of Paris had stormed palace and barricade not only under Louis XVI but in the days of the Commune. In every country and in every age the masses, goaded to desperation, have on occasion rushed upon their oppressors. But this revolt of which Ortega speaks was of a different nature. It was a state of mind that did not necessarily involve force. It was a repudiation of age-old assumption, a new conviction of right and of power. And it took the form not of violent insurrection against the government, but of relentless demands upon the government.

The most powerful organized agency of this revolt was the Socialist party. Germany more than any other country became the center of radical economic explorations and propaganda. Its philosophy permeated the labor movement and percolated into the thinking of all political parties. Grave questionings of the assumed permanence of the capitalist system had gotten about. While the socialists offered their own substitute system, every variety of reformer appeared with all sorts of proposals for the repair of the capitalist society itself. The influence of the old Junker groups waned. The socialists had more than a hundred members of the Reichstag in the year when war was declared. But equally important was the change that had come over the composition of the non-socialist members of that body. Jules Cambon, French Ambassador to Berlin in 1913, warning France of the state of affairs in Germany, wrote: "In the Reichstag for 1878 out of 397 members, 162 belonged to the aristocracy; in 1898, 83; in 1912, 57. Out of this number 27 alone belong to the Right, 14 to the Center, 7 to the Left, and one sits with the Socialists."

As the shadows of the coming war of 1914 lengthened over Europe, Germany was feeling the effect of one of those economic depressions which then darkened the skies of all Europe and

85

America. The problem of the creaking economic society was reaching the crisis stage. The militant radical elements at the height of their power, the complaining yet not so militant liberal elements joining socialists in halfway reform measures, the conservatives bewildered and angry were ready for an epic struggle for power. Always for the distressed and baffled government in the presence of this threat there is one door open and offering at least momentary escape—war. The imperial government rushed through that door—and to its doom.

The old imperial Germany was a capitalist society governed under a constitutional monarchy on the federal principle with the central government severely restricted. For many years this society exhibited all the characteristics of the capitalist order. It enjoyed a degree of material progress exceeding that of any other continental country, but also it was subject to the appearance, at intervals, of economic depressions and to the presence at all times of poverty in its industrial areas.

As in most countries, the misfortunes of the poor had been looked upon as the province of private charity. But with the rising tide of popular discontent, social welfare, which had been the peculiar property of private philanthropy, became an institution of political activity. The socialists had taught that poverty was the fruit of the system but that pending the recasting of the system it was the duty of the state to mitigate the lot of the poor by various devices. After the second attempt on the Kaiser's life, Bismarck succeeded in putting into effect his repressive measures against the socialists. But the bitter resistance to these measures and the generally bad impression left in the popular mind brought forcibly to his attention the necessity of doing something himself for the neediest elements of the people. He saw the political benefits he could collect from a program of social welfare to counteract the agitations of the socialists and their fellow travelers. As a result we see added to the German picture the institution of state philanthropy—state social welfare—instituted by the old Junker Bismarck. Beginning in 1883 he put through the first social-insurance law, compensation insurance, and finally, in 1889, the old-age pension and sickness-insurance system. Thus he established the principle in Germany that the state must make itself responsible for those members of society who through physical or economic adversity could not take care of themselves.

IV · Old Devil Budget

SOCIAL-WELFARE MEASURES took some care of the aged, the sick, and the idle. But social-welfare measures will not make an economic system function. If 20 per cent of the people are the victims of want, the remaining 80 per cent must be enabled to continue producing both goods and income for themselves and the victims. Just as social-security and welfare measures became a fixed institution of the Reich to aid the underprivileged, public spending of borrowed funds became gradually an institution of the German capitalist system to keep the functional portion of society alive.

The German empire set up for business in 1871. It began under peculiarly happy circumstances. It was born out of a short, victorious war that paid for itself and made a profit. Bismarck extracted from France an indemnity of 4,467,096,402 marks. This was enough to enable the empire and the separate states to pay off all their war bonds and have a comfortable balance. The big French indemnity became the parent of a vigorous boom in a new nation which set up for business debt free. One would suppose that this vigorous state, with an industrious and thrifty people devoted to orderliness and discipline, with a passion for good public housekeeping, a large surplus in its hands, and a brilliant and forceful statesman at its head, would have continued to pay its way if that were possible. Yet the empire which began debt free in 1871 was by 1875 going to the moneylenders. The central government's capacity to tax was limited. It could never collect enough to pay all its bills. The budget was chronically out of balance. Reichstag after Reichstag quarreled with the government about the budget. So that by 1876 Bismarck resumed state borrowing.[1] Despite repeated deficits

[1] "Financial Reform in Germany," by Gustav Cohn, University of Göttingen, *Yale Review*, Vol. 18, November 1909.

government spending rose and with it government borrowing and debt. The debt history up to World War I may be stated briefly in round figures thus:

Year	Debt
1871	0 Marks
1885	410,000,000 "
1897	2,317,000,000 "
1909	4,233,000,000 "
1913	4,897,000,000 "

The several states and municipalities also rolled up large debts. The total for all was:

Federal government	4,233,000,000	Marks
States	14,262,000,000	"
Municipalities	5,295,000,000	"
Total	23,790,000,000	Marks

Thus for fifty years the practice of state borrowing was also an institution of state policy. People of all parties continually grumbled about it, but the practice was tolerated by all. However, the public debt became one of the incessant irritants of public life. The speeches of public men and the writings of leading publicists for twenty years preceding World War I complained of Germany's impossible fiscal policy. By 1908 we find the German imperial Finance Minister writing that "the vital question of Germany's finances must be solved *now*" and that "the stability of the empire is exposed to risk."[2] Yet the Reichstag refused to supply by means of taxes the revenues needed by the Reich. The practice became embedded in the traditional finance techniques of the empire. It was bad but it had popular acquiescence. No one, however, defended it as a scientific arrangement for the purpose of absorbing public savings and creating national income as the economists of the republic did later on and as Hitler's economists do now.

The policy had another very serious consequence. Oddly conservative Germany, dominated by Junkers and industrialists, be-

[2] "Germany's Serious Financial Dilemma," by Herr Reinhold Sydow, in the *Deutsche Rundschau*, summarized in the American *Review of Reviews*, Vol. 38, December 1908.

came the paradise of state-owned enterprises. This is referred to generally, along with the social-welfare measures, as an example of German state socialism. It was, however, in no sense a surrender to socialist ideas. It was the policy of very hardheaded, pragmatic administrators. The central government and the states, in need of funds and finding the taxpayer reluctant, turned to state enterprise. The various German states owned and operated public utilities, railroads, mines, forests, telegraph and telephone systems, and certain industrial enterprises as a means of making profits for the governments to supplement the inadequate tax revenues. Bismarck made a number of efforts to buy up all the railroads for the central government to solve its revenue problem but was balked by the states. He admitted he was aiming at a monopoly of tobacco and spirits production for the empire as a means of swelling empire revenues. Unable to get the railroads for the central government, he succeeded in having the Prussian state government take them. He did this by issuing government bonds—60 billion marks—for the shares of the private companies.[3]

The extent to which the German federal and state governments had come to depend on the profits of their enterprises to pay their bills may be seen from the following figures compiled by *Le Figaro* (which explains the use of francs instead of marks) in 1909. This estimate includes the revenue of the empire and the states, which was 9,656,000,000 francs. Of this sum only 3,887,000,000 was collected in taxes. The balance—5,769,000,000—was derived from railroads, mines, post offices and wire systems, forests, and other enterprises. Only 40 per cent of the public revenues was received from taxes.[4]

It must be said here, of course, that a good deal of the public debt arose from public investments in revenue-producing enterprises. This applies chiefly to the debt of the states. Most of the debt of the central government arose out of non-revenue-producing expenditures. It was dead-weight debt.[5]

[3] *Prince Bismarck,* by Charles Lowe, Cassell & Co., New York, 1886.
[4] "The Secret of Germany's Budget," translated from *Le Figaro's* reports, *Harper's Weekly,* Vol. 53, January 2, 1909.
[5] Various reasons have been assigned for World War I. The causes of that were doubtless many. But the fiscal policies of the Imperial government may well bear their full share. It

When Germany declared war in 1914, she proceeded to do on a colossal scale what she had been doing on a smaller scale for fifty years. She borrowed to pay the war bills. In 1900 she had financed the "East Asiatic Expedition"—her share of the Chinese Boxer invasion—amounting to 276,000,000 marks, wholly with borrowed funds, which obligation along with all her other debts was still due as she prepared to invade France in 1914. Her World War I expenditures were as follows. The 1913 budget, for purposes of comparison, was 3,848,000,000 marks:[6]

	1914	6,936,000,000	Marks
	1915	23,909,000,000	"
	1916	24,739,000,000	"
	1917	42,188,000,000	"
	1918	33,928,000,000	"
Carried forward from	1918	32,599,000,000	"
	Total	164,299,000,000	Marks

cannot be said that Germany went to war to escape her fiscal difficulties. It is never so simple as that. But governments have a way of getting themselves into financial jams from which they see no escape, while those very financial troubles are in turn generating other pressures. Statesmen find themselves utterly bewildered in the center of these clamoring problems. The door of war is ajar and beckons as an escape. With the aid of a convenient conscience, they may find some good reason for sinking through its inviting opening. In the light of these observations it is interesting to find M. Jules Cambon, French Ambassador at Berlin, writing to his government in 1913 and offering the following dark prophecy, at a time when the government, pressed for funds, proposed heavy death duties:

"The country squires represented in the Reichstag by the Conservative party want at all costs to escape the death duties which are bound to come if peace continues. [A last resort of the government to meet its fiscal needs. Author's note.] In the last sitting of the session which has just closed, the Reichstag agreed to these duties in principle. It is a serious attack on the interests and the privileges of the landed gentry. On the other hand, this aristocracy is military in character, and it is instructive to compare the army list with the Yearbook of the Nobility. War alone can prolong its prestige and support its family interest. During the discussion on the Army Bill a Conservative speaker put forward the need for promotion among officers as an argument in its favor. Finally, this social class, which forms a hierarchy with the King of Prussia as its supreme head, realizes with dread the democratization of Germany and the increasing power of the Socialist party, and considers its own days numbered. Not only does a formidable movement hostile to agrarian protection threaten its material interests, but in addition the number of its political representatives decreases with each legislative period. In the Reichstag for 1878, out of 397 members, 162 belonged to the aristocracy; in 1898, 83; in 1912, 57. Out of this number 27 alone belong to the Right, 14 to the Center, 7 to the Left, and one sits with the Socialists." Quoted in *Democracy after the War*, by J. A. Hobson, London, 1918.

[6] *German Economy*, by Gustav Stolper, Reynal & Hitchcock, New York, 1940.

Of this amount 96,929,000,000, or 60 per cent, was borrowed in nine war loans. This was piled on top of the accumulated indebtedness of fifty years.

When the war ended, the republic came into being. It would not be fair to apply to this government between 1920 and 1923 the ordinary rules of fiscal criticism. As it faced its heroic task Germany was best described in the words of Hitler's former colleague, Otto Strasser: "The past was in ruins, the present shattered, the future without hope."

To the vast internal war debt was added the fantastic external debt—the reparations penalties, not yet fixed but looming at a figure no nation in the world could have paid. With fifty years of precedent by the rich and prosperous empire, it would have been strange indeed if the bankrupt new republic, with only a half-hearted tolerance of the people behind it, could have escaped a continuation of the debt policy. The figures speak for themselves. From 1920 to 1923 the receipts and expenditures were as follows:[7]

	Receipts	Expenditures	Deficits
	(In gold marks)		
1920	1,895,000,000	7,034,000,000	5,139,000,000
1921	3,750,000,000	7,821,000,000	4,071,000,000
1922	1,889,000,000	3,847,000,000	1,958,000,000
1923	1,241,000,000	8,462,000,000	7,221,000,000

These inadequate receipts were supplemented by the issuance of a floating debt as follows:

1921	2,313,000,000	Marks
1922	4,685,000,000	"
1923	6,955,000,000,000	"

This brought Germany to that fantastic episode of inflation which ended by literally extinguishing all debts save the reparations due to her conquerors. While this inflation had wiped out the savings of everyone, had ruined the middle class, extinguished insurance policies, bankrupted all sorts of industries and their creditors, and

[7] *The Recovery of Germany*, by James W. Angell, Oxford University Press, 1929, 1932.

dislocated all the machinery of production and distribution, it had freed the nation from internal debt.[8]

With the collapse Germany went into a profound crisis—unemployment, paralysis of industry, bankruptcy, bewilderment. Gustav Stresemann became Premier. Hjalmar Schacht, president of the Reichsbank, stopped the printing presses, invented a new currency unit—the *Rentenmark* (equal to a trillion inflation marks)—the Dawes Plan was adopted, and in October 1924 a foreign loan of 800,000,000 gold marks was made to the Reich. Thereupon the country, thus crushed by defeat and inflation, proceeded to stage one of the most spectacular recoveries in the history of business. At the end of the last war America suffered her own moderate-sized depression from 1920 to 1923. At that point we began that amazing upward flight known as the Coolidge Boom or the New Era. Oddly the vanquished Germany, starting almost from scratch just a year later, put on a recovery in many respects even more remarkable than ours, and one which lasted almost the same length of time—until 1929—and ended, as ours did, in a disastrous economic crash.

Germany had lost by the war and the treaty 13 per cent of her territories, 14 per cent of her arable land, 74 per cent of her iron ore, 68 per cent of her zinc ore, 26 per cent of her coal production. She had lost the railways, potash mines, and textile industries of Alsace-Lorraine. She had been compelled to deliver to her enemies all her merchant ships over 1,600 tons and much of the rest, a quarter of her fishing fleet, 5,000 locomotives, 150,000 railway cars, 5,000 motor trucks. She had seen her foreign investments confiscated and had been subjected to a huge reparations bill in money and kind.[9] Yet in the five years from 1924 to 1929 she had built up her industrial production to a point greater than in 1913. In 1927

---

[8] It is well to recall that this inflation was produced not by "printing" government currency but by printing government bonds. Germany borrowed this grotesque inflation money on treasury notes and bills from the Reichsbank, accepting Reichsbank notes in payment which the government proceeded to spend, just as if the United States were to borrow money on bonds from the Federal Reserve Bank accepting Reserve currency for its bonds. The whole inflation was accomplished by an ever-widening and extending use of the policy of borrowing from the banks. The printing consisted in the government printing bonds or notes and the Reichsbank printing currency.

[9] *German Economy*, by Gustav Stolper, Reynal & Hitchcock, New York, 1940.

steel production was back to the prewar figure, railroads and rolling stock were superior to prewar days, her merchant tonnage had increased from 400,000 tons to 3,738,000 tons—all new. Her commercial bank deposits rose from $342,000,000 to $1,657,000,000.[10] Her savings deposits, wiped out by the inflation, had risen to 24,000,000,000 marks.[11] She had regained, says Dr. James W. Angell, a large part of the world leadership she had lost during the war.[12]

Where did the money for all this come from? How was it created? What was the secret of this magical increase that appeared so wonderful until the bubble burst? The answer must be that it was accomplished by the use of that same fatal instrument for creating national income—government borrowing. The nation that had been drawn toward a great war by a combination of forces, one of which was its fiscal sins, that saw itself pillaged after that war by one of the most grotesque fiscal disasters in history, now turned once again to the same dangerous weapon. But this time the politicians were supplied with a new theory of national debt by the professors. In the past bewildered ministries had taken refuge in deficits under political pressure. People demand increased spending. Politicians are eager to comply. More expenditures mean heavier taxes. But people resist more taxes. Here are contradictory streams of public desire. Both must be followed. People call on the government to spend while denouncing it for doing so. They cry out for economy but are unwilling to do without the benefits of extravagance. So citizens subscribe to the general virtue of economy and politicians solve the problem of spending more without taxing more. They resort to borrowing. But these old offenders never made any defense of the policy save political necessity. At most they defended it merely as the lesser of two evils.

But after the war, when the republican government came into power, that peculiar creation—the German professor of economics—inserted himself into the scene. He proceeded to unfold a new theory that fell like manna from above into the bewildered treasury. The old-fashioned fear of national debt, they assured the politicos,

---

[10]*Europe Since 1914*, by F. Lee Benns, Crofts Co., New York, 1935.
[11]*German Economy*, by Gustav Stolper, Reynal & Hitchcock, New York, 1940.
[12]*The Recovery of Germany*, by James W. Angell, Oxford University Press, 1929, 1932.

was one of the superstitions of "orthodox" economics. The "new" economics had its own fresh theory. Public debt must be sharply distinguished from private debt. Public debt can be expanded almost indefinitely provided it is internally held. In fact, where a government owes merely an internal debt it can be said to be debt free. Of course debts call for interest payments. But the taxpayers merely pay the interest to themselves.[13]

The idea was not new for we find Renatus in his *Twelfth Hour of Capitalism*, before Hitler came into power, complaining that the idea that internal debt, where the "money remains in the country," is not dangerous had been used by the old empire government to make the war loans more palatable.[14] That was pressure propaganda during a war to unload mountains of securities. But now economists who believed that principle dominated government thinking. And the theory became an extraordinarily convenient one.

Between 1926 and 1931 the republican government built up another 6,813,000,000 marks of debt and the various state governments had accumulated a new deficit of 13,988,000,000 marks.[15]

Here was a combined federal and state deficit over just these five years of 20,801,000,000 marks. Playgrounds, swimming pools, schools, hospitals, and health projects were built and carried on by states and cities with the aid of government financing. Roads—the time-honored extravagance of governments in search of means of spending—were built profusely. Heavy subsidies were paid to

[13] Sigmund Neumann in *Permanent Revolution* (Harper's, 1942) says: "Nazi fiscal policies have been a challenge to nineteenth century ideas. Running into debt no doubt spelled certain ruin for a government because it indicated that the state was living beyond its means, i.e., its capacity to be taxed. In a period of expanding economy it had become axiomatic that it was private industry which provided all the opportunity for the investment of savings and guaranteed the natural flow of capital. Twentieth-century economics soon realized the limitation of such an automatic self-regulation in a contracting society. It reconsidered, therefore, the essential place of the state in the direction of productive forces through active state interference. It commenced to view 'national debt' in a different way. The real concern of modern capitalist society must be whether its total financial wealth, including the national debt, is large enough to permit the production of the national income that its fiscal capacity affords. Such considerations probably opened the way to some kind of financial double morality that conceived of different standards in individual household and state bookkeeping."

[14] *Twelfth Hour of Capitalism*, by Kuno Renatus, Alfred A. Knopf, New York 1932.

[15] The figures for these deficits are as follows. They are taken from the Basle Report on German Finances made by the Young Plan Advisory Committee, December 23, 1931, and approved by the Bank for International Settlements, which is reported in full in *Current*

agriculture, and great sums were spent on rural resettlement and rehabilitation. States and cities flocked to Berlin with their appeals for funds to restore and overhaul every sort of public and semi-public edifice from museums to post offices.

Arthur Rosenberg in his *History of the German Republic* (London, 1936) says:

After 1924 the officials lost all sense of the value of money and seemed to believe that money would always be available at any time and in the quantity that was needed for any purpose. Thus it came about that all possible kinds of new buildings and undertakings were embarked upon that were useful and defensible in themselves but were out of keeping with the true economic situation of Germany. In consequence of the general prosperity the Reich government largely increased the salaries of its officials and the state governments and municipalities naturally could not lag far behind.

Rosenberg quotes from a letter written by Gustav Stresemann on November 24, 1927, to Dr. Jarres, chief burgomaster of Duisberg:

I make no secret of the fact that it is above all the policy of the individual states and the municipalities that causes me grave anxiety in the field of foreign affairs. Time and again I have said in my public speeches that it is necessary to distinguish more clearly between reality and appearance. I have no doubt that the will to work in a proper fashion does exist. Nevertheless certain measures have given rise to impressions that do us incalculable harm. The fact that the Prussian state has granted fourteen million marks for rebuilding of the Berlin Opera House and will perhaps make a grant of

History, Vol. 35, February 1932. The receipts recorded here for the central government include only the taxes retained for its own use:

Year	Receipts	Expenditures	Deficits	
(Central Government)
1926–27	5,312,000,000	6,561,000,000	1,249,000,000	Marks
1927–28	6,357,000,000	7,154,000,000	797,000,000	"
1928–29	6,568,000,000	8,375,000,000	1,807,000,000	"
1929–30	6,686,000,000	7,987,000,000	1,301,000,000	"
1930–31	6,534,000,000	8,193,000,000	1,659,000,000	"
(State Governments)
1926–27	6,363,000,000	10,639,000,000	4,276,000,000	Marks
1927–28	7,189,000,000	1,674,000,000	+5,515,000,000	"
1928–29	7,730,000,000	12,426,000,000	4,696,000,000	"
1929–30	7,593,000,000	12,836,000,000	5,243,000,000	"
1930–31	7,482,000,000	12,770,000,000	5,288,000,000	"

more than twenty millions in all, creates the impression in the world at large that we are rolling in money. Not a single one of the victorious states has embarked upon such an undertaking. That Herr Adenauer (chief burgomaster of Cologne) has built a marvelous hall, and boasts that it contains the greatest organ in the world, produces the same effect. . . . The Press Exhibition in Cologne was regarded as the most luxurious affair of its kind that had ever been organized. Frankfort-on-Main was left with a deficit of two and a half million marks as a result of its Music Exhibition. Dresden builds a Museum of Hygiene with the help of a Reich subsidy. . . . Please tell me what I am to say to the representatives of foreign powers when they tell me of these things awakening the impression that Germany won rather than lost the war. I have no longer any answer to give to these reproaches.

This government spending stimulated private enterprise. And private corporations began to borrow too. Industrial plants, modern stores, mining properties, railroads and utilities, all were built or modernized with funds loaned by the banks. But the banks became overextended. The ratio of bank capital to deposits, which before the war had been four or five to one, became fifteen and twenty to one. Nevertheless, to the outside world here was the spectacle of a resurgent Germany astonishing her neighbors with the swiftness of her recovery. After all, the debt theory was working. Many now forget that while rich America was rollicking in the lush glory of the Coolidge New Era, Germany was basking in the sunlight of her republican new deal.

The magic of the "new economics" worked for a little while—for five years. But in the end the whole thing cracked up. But the apostles of the new economics said their theory had not had a sound test. The trouble lay, they said, with the great external debt imposed by reparations. In a sense this is true. Germany was forced to pay heavy reparation sums to her conquerors. But actually little if any of it came out of her internal revenues. From September 1924 to July 1931 she paid out 10,821,000,000 marks. But the money to make these payments she borrowed from abroad. Loans from abroad totaled, according to Dr. Stolper, some 20 billion marks, or about 18 billions, according to Dr. Angell. In addition around five billion additional marks were invested in German industry by foreigners. It was these foreign loans which became the basis of the credits extended to German industry by the German banks. But the government's credit at home began to fade as early as 1928 when it was forced to pay 8 per cent for money. But the outside world scarcely dreamed of the extent to which the government was operating in the red.

This fact was concealed by a device that has not failed to inspire its champions in this country in recent years—namely, the double budget, actually a fake budget. The Germans separated so-called "ordinary" items from "extraordinary" items. The extraordinary items included outlays for "productive" purposes, sometimes euphemistically called "investments." The chief purpose of this device is to deceive the people and hide the deficits of the government. The first warning the outside world had of the situation came in 1928, when S. Parker Gilbert, Agent General of Reparations, gave the alarm in a paper published in the "Advocate of Peace through Justice."[16] Gilbert pointed out that while the government borrowed to meet expenses it had increased salaries by 1,250,000,000 marks. There was much agreement within Germany with Gilbert's apprehensions. But there was also wide approval of the government's fiscal policy. But government debts are due, not by the people, but by that organized entity known as the government. It can pay its debt charges only when it can get money from the people to do so. And the people can and frequently do refuse to disgorge the necessary funds. When that time comes the ability of the government to borrow is sadly impaired. By 1930 Chancellor Hermann Müller was having difficulty extracting any further taxes from the citizens. He then hit upon a shabby expedient. He began to talk about *more social security*. Under cover of this pretense he proposed to raise the rates. But what he really had in mind was to greatly increase charges for social security much beyond its cost in order that the government might "borrow" the surplus to meet its expenses. This palpable fraud exposed Müller's ministry to such violent attack that he was forced to resign.

By this time the country was launched on a full-scale depression with all the familiar scenes and circumstances. Unemployment

[16] Quoted in the American *Review of Reviews*, Vol. FF, January 1928.

began to increase. Industries closed their doors and many failed. The banks, which had loaned their short-term deposits on long-term securities to these industries, began to fail. There was a banking crisis. The government declared a banking holiday. It guaranteed the deposits of the great Darmstadter bank, financed its reorganization, and finally forced all banks to become state institutions in fact though remaining private in name. The government forced bank consolidations. As the banks controlled large-scale industry, the nationalization of the banks actually put private industry at the mercy of the government. Dr. Heinrich Bruening, able and incorruptible leader of the Center, became Chancellor. He had inveighed against the irresponsible fiscal policies of the government. But it was too late. Actually it is possible to suggest several courses that would have saved the situation *if* they had been followed. But it is that fatal *if* that cannot be expunged from the picture. The courses were not followed because the power of decision to take such courses was wanting. The edifice of republican Germany was crumbling. In two years Hitler would be in power.

The significance of all this lies in its exhibition of the practice of all German governments to use public debt as an instrument of state policy until finally the government which preceded Hitler actually adopted it as a means of creating national income. This it did with the consent and approval of the controlling groups in the society. So that we may say, in view of the surrender of all types of government to this inevitable policy, that it represents a definite stream of opinion and desire in the community—a stream too strong for purely political ministries interested primarily in remaining in power to resist.

V · The Supreme Project

WE NOW COME to another powerful stream of thought. Probably one of the most completely misunderstood of all modern institutions is militarism. While military organizations take their origin in man's lust for war, militarism is something more than a mere war machine. By militarism I mean that institution in which the nation maintains large national armies and navies in time of peace, usually raised on the principle of conscription. It cannot be too much emphasized that you do not have militarism until you have the principle of universal military service or some form of conscription *in time of peace as a permanent institution* of national policy.

To think of militarism as a purely military business is to miss completely the gravest aspect of this utterly evil thing in modern society. Alfred Vagts, in his history of the rise and spread of militarism, correctly observes that it "presents a vast array of customs, interest, prestige, actions, and thought associated with armies and wars and yet transcending true military purpose."[1]

Over the past seventy years reformers have fought militarism on the following grounds: (1) that it involves a crushing economic burden; (2) that it draws from the producing mechanisms of the nation great numbers who might be adding to its wealth; (3) that it is an instrument of tyranny; (4) that it is a breeding ground of war.

To the last two propositions there is no answer. But the first two are based on almost complete misconceptions of the most powerful motives back of militarism.

There is another illusion that needs to be dispelled. It is that militarism was the invention and darling of the old Junkers—the Prussian nobles. We will greatly underestimate the danger of militarism if we persist in this error. It has drawn its support from all sorts of social groups. There have been times when it found its chief supporters among the liberals, with the old Junkers actually resisting its expansion. Even socialists have toyed with the idea of militarism. All this will, I am sure, fall upon incredulous ears accustomed to some of the popular perversions of European history.

The revolutionists in France called it into being when their country was beset by the armies of the aroused monarchs of Europe. The weapon thus forged for the defense of liberty quickly fell into the hands of the tyrant who used it from 1804 to Waterloo as an instrument of conquest. This led to a demand for its use in Prussia by Blücher as a defense against Napoleon. The chief opposition came

[1] *The History of Militarism*, by Alfred Vagts, W. W. Norton, New York, 1937.

from the Junkers. They did not oppose military power. Yet they did not relish this monstrous child of republican France. But they had more substantial reasons. They were interested not so much in conquest as in the preservation of their class. They thought of the army as a weapon in the hands of the monarch against internal attack. Conscription created a mass army of proletarians into whose hands weapons would be placed that might be turned against the throne and the nobility. Moreover, the idea of a mass army was incompatible, they said, with the institution of monarchy. That institution is based on rank. The army provided the means of preserving their rank through the officers' corps. A great national army would create the need for a far larger number of officers than the nobles could supply. They would have to be recruited from among the middle classes. This was repugnant to the Junker mind. It had to yield, however, because of the imperious necessity of armies so large that only the masses could supply them. The Bourbons ended conscription on the fall of Napoleon for this very reason, and it was not revived until Napoleon III came to power in 1848. From this point on Germany, France, Italy, and Russia contended with each other in the race for conscript armies. But Germany never pressed into service as large a part of her population as France. In 1913 France had 2.10 per cent of her population with the colors while Germany had only 1.2 per cent.[2] As late as 1913, when the military men asked for three more corps, the Prussian Minister of War objected that it would mean "a larger number of officers drawn from circles hardly fit," and this "aside from other dangers would expose the officers' corps to democratization." The Junkers were not against the army. It was their darling and they wished to keep it so.

Liberals must bear their full share of responsibility for the growth of this institution. The parliamentarians of 1848, promulgating the essentials of a constitution, along with freedom of speech and press, equality before the law, removal of social ranks, right of assembly, trial by jury, and other basic rights, called for *general military service*.[3] In 1861, when liberals formed the German Progress party

[2] *The History of Militarism*, by Alfred Vagts, W. W. Norton, New York, 1937.
[3] *Roots of National Socialism*, by Rohan D'O. Butler, E. P. Dutton, New York, 1942.

and were called "democrats," they produced a crisis by demanding parliamentary control of army budgets which brought the strong hand of Bismarck to the helm to resist them. This episode is frequently described as a growing revolt against a great army. Nothing could be further from the truth. The King wanted a bigger army and three-year enlistments instead of two. The liberals opposed the three-year enlistment. But they were willing to give him as big an army as he wished. Ludwig, in his *Life of Bismarck,* confirms this, and Vagts says that the liberals asked the German generals if they were sure the army was big enough.

I recall these facts because of their bearing on the important phenomenon which seems to involve liberals along with the reactionaries in some of the most reactionary and suppressive devices of central governments. Those old liberals belonged to the Manchester school. They were for parliamentary government and checks upon the Crown. But they were also for building foreign trade, and they saw the value of military weapons in the event of collision with other economic imperialist empires. To the old Junkers the army had a different meaning. It was an institution to furnish berths to their sons and to preserve the monarchy. "It was the liberals," says Vagts, and not the conservatives, "who pursued the dreams of the German empire yet to come. It was a Prussian liberal to whom it occurred in 1836 that Holland ought to become Prussian because it was rather a necessity for Prussia and would be a benefit to Holland. It was the same liberal (who said) 'It might come about that we would demand Alsace and Lorraine from France, the Baltic countries from Russia.' "[4] Even the socialists, who had persistently opposed militarism and its handmaiden imperialism, at times toyed with the alluring drug. They could not wholly resist the fascination of the idea that militarism, bad as it was, did in fact put weapons into the hands of the proletarians which might be turned in the right direction when the day of revolt arrived. Jaurès, the French socialist leader, thought the conscript army was to be preferred to the professional army. Engels had advised his colleagues that in the event of hostilities "everyone should be drawn into the service and that the armed nation should assume control over domestic and

†*The History of Militarism,* by Alfred Vagts, W. W. Norton, New York, 1937.

foreign policies." I do not wish to say that socialists as a party persistently favored the militarism of Germany. I merely wish to point up the very disturbing fact that people of all sorts and for quite different reasons could see some special virtue in this thing. In maintaining the institution of militarism the imperial government knew that it was running safely with an approved current of thought and desire among the people. And, however men differed for special group reasons in supporting militarism, at bottom the chief reason that paralyzed any strong opposition to it was economic. The institution begins with those who love military power, the expression of national might, and those nationalist groups who yearn for imperialist aggression. But it ends by finding its broadest support in the influence it exerted upon the economic system.

The plain truth is that militarism became Germany's greatest single industry. It played a role as prop of the economic system as great, if not greater than, let us say, the automobile industry in America. Critics have directed their fire against Krupp and his fellow munitions makers. But it would be a great mistake to suppose that it was Krupp and his colleagues who made militarism possible. It was something more deeply rooted than the interests of the war profiteers. Others have complained of the insupportable burden of armaments. In England increased grants for soldiers were fought on the ground that enlarging the army resulted in withdrawing more men from industry and the production of wealth in the labor market. Mr. Herbert Perris[5] has calculated that while the German Army cost 67 million pounds a year there was a far greater social loss in drawing so many men from productive pursuits who could have earned 100 pounds each had they remained in civil life, and that this loss must be added to the money cost of the army. All this is based on the theory that had these men remained in civil life they would be at work raising crops and producing goods. But, alas, they would have, at most times, merely added to the number of the unemployed. The English critics were right in saying that the army took men out of the labor market. But it was a market glutted with labor. It took the unusable surplus labor. And the problem of government to find work for these men

[5]*Germany and the German Emperor*, by Herbert Perris, Henry Holt, New York, 1912.

was far more poignant and imperious than the problem of their lost production—when in fact they would have been producing nothing. Actually the employment of hundreds of thousands in the army and of many more hundreds of thousands in the industries which supplied these armies, all paid for by the government with funds partly created by going into debt, had the effect of making work for those who were not in the army and thus increasing the national produce, at least for a time.

As time wore on and a great industry grew up around it, the relation of this institution to the economic life of the country became obvious. We have noticed the growing demand upon the government from the indigent and the unemployed and from the swiftly returning crises in industry. And we have seen how the institution of social welfare and the spending of money on all sorts of enterprises enabled the government, by borrowing money, to create income. This income, infused into the blood stream of the nation, vivified industry generally and acted as a stimulant and support of the economic system. But this stratagem, while supplying a temporary stimulus, had the effect of creating a national debt that excited the fears and, finally, the bitter resistance of the taxpaying and investing groups. They will always interpose an impassable opposition to continued public deficits for purely civil enterprises. But they will not object to spending money on armies for national defense. Governments were confronted with this curious paradox; namely, that the most vociferous enemies of unbalanced budgets were also the most willing supporters of expenditures for military power. Statesmen in Germany—and in every European country—found after a while that it was possible to get taxes up to a certain point and borrow funds beyond that for military purposes. And they understood also that money spent on military projects was just as effective in providing supplementary energy to the economic system as funds spent on any other kind of public project. It was those deficits created by vast military expenditures which did for the German economic system what our deficits over the last ten years have done for ours—kept the organization of private business in motion.

The importance of this industry may be judged from the following facts. In 1907 there were 600,000 men in the German Army and 33,000 in the Navy. In addition to these there were about 1,800,000 men in the materials industries, such as mining and metals and forestry and in commerce and trade, whose employment was dependent wholly on the army and naval orders of the German Government. This leaves out of account the number employed in agriculture to feed such persons and the number employed to clothe and house them. Instead of being a burden, therefore, militarism was a great Public Works Administration and Work Projects Administration rolled into one which, with public funds, provided work for a vast army of military men and industrial workers.

It is not to be supposed that this fundamental fact was not known to German politicians but was only discovered recently by discerning Americans. One has but to look through the pages of German public history during the past seventy years to see how it weighed on the consciousness of her political and industrial leaders. The matter was endlessly debated. To critics of army budgets, militarists pointed out that a third of the army expenditures were returned to the taxpayers in some form. The estimate is a modest one. The government industriously cultivated the good will of the farmers from whom they bought vast quantities of hay and grain. But also they made it a special point of good-will policy to pay farmers the most liberal damages for injuries to fields during maneuvers.

Military men, when confronted with the mutterings of disaffected taxpayers, always pointed out how good these government military expenditures were for business. Stumm could imagine no expenditure more productive for the community than those for armies. Schlieffen said, when military economies were discussed: "The national economy, the machine with its thousand wheels, through which millions find a living, cannot stand still for long."[6] One of the German delegates to the 1898 Peace Conference, Colonel Schwarzhoff, declared that "armies were not impoverishing the peoples and the military service is not a burden." He said his country owed its prosperity to military service.[7] The German people believed this. Professor Snyder observes that: "In spite of the fact that millions

[6]*The History of Militarism*, by Alfred Vagts, W. W. Norton, New York, 1937.
[7]*Ibid*.

in taxes were required in order to maintain this rapidly increasing naval power, the public in general was pleased with the new navalism. People associated prosperity and 'good times' with monarchy and its militaristic props, the army and navy, and they seemed to be convinced that this prosperity would continue if the fighting forces of the nation were continually modernized."[8] It is interesting to note that in our own country this theory of industrial stimulus was accepted by many, for we find Samuel Colt, as far back as 1837, during the depression of that period, suggesting that it might be overcome by large appropriations for armaments.[9]

The funds which the German imperial government was borrowing were used almost entirely for military outlays. Without such immense appropriations for the army the government might have avoided borrowing. But without these appropriations a million and a half men would have been out of work. To abandon militarism would have meant demobilizing the greatest industry in the land.[10]

Mr. Arthur Guy Enock has made a carefully adjusted table of total defense expenditures by Germany and a parallel table of increase in the national debt by years. It shows that from 1900 to 1920 the military expenditures increased steadily and that the national debt increased every year save two. It also reveals that the army and navy appropriations were greater than the corresponding contemporary increase in national debt.[11] It follows that the increase in debt was necessitated wholly by the armament outlays. Increase in debt could have been eliminated by paring armament payments by the amount of the new debt. In some years as much as half of all military outlays were provided for by borrowing. During the war, of course, the entire military budget was borrowed. These findings are corroborated by Dr. Adolph Wagner, professor of political science in the University of Berlin, who said in 1902 that the loans of the government were due chiefly to the extra outlays

[8] *From Bismarck to Hitler,* by Louis L. Snyder, Bayard Press, Williamsport, Pa., 1935.
[9] *The History of Militarism,* by Alfred Vagts, W. W. Norton, New York, 1937.
[10] In 1907 the army and navy budget was 1,198,000,000 marks. This was more than enough to pay directly the wages of 1,800,000 men, leaving out of account the secondary effects on wages of these payments.
[11] *The Problem of Armaments,* by Arthur Guy Enock, Macmillan, New York, 1923, Appendix.

for the army and navy and strategic subsidies for the states for the same purpose.[12] Mr. Alfred Vagts makes a very pregnant observation on this point. "The people," he says, "became inclined to believe in a superior kind of planning which the crisis-beset capitalism did not know how to provide, but which seemed to be inherent in successful military institutions."[13] In other words militarism, without being designed to do so, came to provide Germany with that instrument which the later-day planners have been demanding—a means of increasing national income by public expenditures through borrowed funds. In truth militarism had become the great accepted and universally tolerated Public Works Administration of Europe. Had it been a mere burden to the peoples by reason of its tax exactions it would never have survived. It was because the tax burden was at least temporarily offset by the increase in national income provided through maintaining with public funds Germany's biggest industry that it was permitted to continue.

This helps in understanding how utterly futile were those feeble appeals for disarmament that preceded the World War, in 1898 and 1907, as well as those made habitually by peace groups since. At these conferences delegates gathered to discuss whether or not Germany and France and Russia—but particularly Germany and France—should dismantle the largest single industry within their borders. The politicians understood this and so did the people, if the simple-minded reformers did not. In 1898, when the proposal for a disarmament conference was sent to the Kaiser, it came back to the Foreign Office with this notation written in the margin: "How will Krupp pay his men?"

Mr. Edward Hallett Carr, who writes with such intelligence of the world's present dilemma, perceives this. He says: "The economic consequences of the production of armaments are no different from the economic consequences of the production of a pair of silk stockings. . . . The special features of the demand for armaments which have enabled it to be used for a solution of the unemployment problem are two. In the first place the demand, being unlimited

---
[12]"National Debt of the German Empire," by Dr. Adolph Wagner, *North American Review*, Vol. 174, June 1902.
[13]*The History of Militarism*, by Alfred Vagts, W. W. Norton, New York, 1937.

in extent, imposes a system, not merely of planned production, but of planned consumption. Secondly, the plan of consumption is not determined by considerations of price and profit."[14] All this being so, he thinks we must find a substitute for armaments in the world of planned production and consumption when the demand for armaments has passed away.

Mr. Carr omits the third and most important reason why armament production became the instrument of income production. Peace projects would have served as well. There is always a powerful resistance to public spending and even public borrowing. But it was possible for the statesmen of Europe to break down this resistance when the spending was for armaments. Militarism is a burden as well as a stimulant. But the burdens fell upon unorganized individuals. The benefits fell upon organized groups. And even in a democratic society the unorganized individual is no match for the organized producer. And so unorganized individuals who have to serve in the army and pay taxes had no chance against the organized groups whose very existence was based on militarism—the military caste, the politicians in power, the industries and agriculture which supplied the army and navy, including more than a million workers who owed their jobs to it, the communities which drew sustenance from those industries and the army camps, the farmers who sold hay and grain and food to the armies, and industrialists. Moreover, those who bore only the burden were intimidated by the fear of industrial collapse which would attend the liquidation of militarism and engulf all in its disaster. Over and beyond this was the great opiate of national defense applied to all dissenters. Europe had enmeshed itself in a whole web of slumbering feuds. When a nation embarks upon militarism as a means of supporting its economic life then powerful, active, and vicious external enemies become an economic necessity. The nation must be kept sharply aware of its dangers. War scares are an essential part of the technique of promotion. With these psychological weapons statesmen can extract from their terrified citizens or subjects consent for military outlays when it would be utterly impossible to do so for peacetime enterprises however worthy. And best of all, the most powerful and vocal of all

[14] *Conditions of Peace*, by Edward H. Carr, Macmillan, New York, 1942.

enemies of public spending—the conservative groups—can be drugged with the fears of external—and internal—aggression.

VI · The Planned Society

GERMANY, like Italy, did not content herself with social-welfare and government spending to buttress her economic society. More perhaps than any other European nation, Germany was the breeding ground for philosophies concerned with planning and managing refractory human nature and its disordered economic machines. Almost one hundred and fifty years ago Johann Gottlieb Fichte built a schematic social philosophy in which the part of each man was arranged for him with the state as the general manager of the works. To escape "commercial anarchy" the society should be "enclosed," isolated, in order to bring its parts under management. This is autarchy, and enclosure is essential to its aims. You can manage only that portion of society to which your authority extends. Hence if you propose to manage your own society you must exclude the producers and distributors of other societies to whom you cannot apply your arrangements. Each citizen, said Fichte, should be "installed in the possessions suitable to him." The state alone can do this and unite a number of persons "in a totality." The citizen should be licensed to engage in that occupation which he desires, but if the occupation is already crowded, this will be denied him. The state will supervise production and trade. Each farmer will be given a quota to cultivate. When he exceeds his quota the state will impound his surplus, issuing him a certificate for it which he may use at some other time. Here was an almost complete outline of autarchy.[1] Fichte proposed a system of foreign trade by barter, with volume, quota, and types of goods designed for export fixed by the state, each district receiving its assigned share and all conducted, not by private exporters and importers, but by the

[1] An illuminating discussion of this will be found in Rohan D'O. Butler's recent book *Roots of National Socialism*, E. P. Dutton, New York, 1942.

state. To cap it all he emphasized the necessity of the state including within its walls such territories as it might need to render it self-sufficient. Dr. Butler, summing up Fichte's system as set out in his *The Closed Commercial State*, says that Fichte argued for a planned economy, total national autarchy, quota systems, artificial production substitutes, intensive armaments, living space, forcible unresisted occupation of territory, complete co-ordination of such territories, transfer of populations, and cultivation of nationalism. This materialistic social organism he supplied with a spiritual stimulant, the spirit of the German *Volk*, on the principle that the Germans alone preserved in their purity among all the Teuton peoples the original German blood and language. Long before Fichte, of course, the Cameralists, as the Prussian mercantilists were called, had insisted on the idea of the enclosed state. But it was from different motives and theories than those which moved Fichte, nor did they go so far in an all-out regimentation as he. However, Fichte was merely taking another step in a direction in which German, as well as French, thought had been moving. Thus the root concepts of the modern state that we have seen flower in Germany and Italy and other continental countries were kicking around in the German mind for nearly two centuries.

For years employers in pre-Hitler Germany fretted in the harrowing illusion that they produced too much, that they competed too savagely, that they cut one another's throats, and that overproduction wrecked them all. They devised various ways of combining to eliminate these evils as well as to present a united front against their rapacious workmen. In Germany, as in Italy, combinations were regulated and legalized. The cartel, which originated in Germany, was nothing more than a trade agreement between business rivals to control prices, production, sales policies, quotas, territorial rights. Dr. Gustav Stolper quotes Professor Kleinwächter, an Austrian economist, as saying that the cartel was the "pioneer foundation of a state-controlled economy." The cartel was an attempt by producers to plan the economy as it affected their product. It could be but a step to substituting the state-organized and supervised cartel for the private one.

The German banks did their bit. The German bank was not precisely like the American. It used its deposits to buy outright shares in industrial and utility corporations. It was a combination bank and investment company. As these banks accumulated vast blocks of shares they became in fact holding companies. As banks amalgamated, their power over industry widened, and their capacity to control and plan it was increased. The German states also owned mines, forests, railroads, power plants, utilities, industrial enterprises. Thus the whole fabric of German enterprise was enmeshed in numerous mechanisms of control—some by the state, some by banks, some by cartels.

Labor, of course, subjected industry to its controls through organized pressure. In Germany, as in Italy, labor and socialism were closely intertwined. And here, too, socialists were deeply implicated in the doctrines of syndicalism. The official party program did not countenance it but, just as in Italy and France, the idea of the syndicalist society as distinguished from state socialism was making headway among the rank and file of the party. In substance the syndicalist believed what the cartelists believed—that the industrial group must be subjected to government and to government of the producers. The cartelists looked upon the employers as the producers; the syndicalists looked upon the workers as the producers. Both shied away from government of industry by the state; both believed in self-government in industry. But were they, in fact, so irrevocably far apart? What was the owner interested in? The security of his investment, the permanence of his profits, continuous operation free from depressions, protection from excessive production and cutthroat competition. What was the worker primarily interested in? The security of his job, the permanence of his employment, and a full share in the product of his labor. Both believed that the producing industry should be a monopoly. Was it wholly unthinkable that men who held these views among employers and workers, under stress of calamitous economic disturbances, might not find a common meeting ground?

This suspicion was making its way into the minds of a good many radicals—socialists or syndicalists—who, tiring of their bleak proletarian socialist dreams, began to toy with the idea of adapting the doctrines of syndicalism to the capitalist system. This, perhaps, is one of the most destructive intellectual phenomena that appeared in Europe. Socialism and even syndicalism, with all its renunciations of commonplace morality, made a body of beliefs that could be defended as coherent and logical systems. But when the socialist and, even more, the syndicalist, began to propose his nostrums as medicine for the capitalist system, there appeared a diseased and corrupted form of socialism which found its neophytes in the oddest quarters. The famous Dr. Stöcker, the Kaiser's court preacher, became the center of one of these hybrid schools of imperial socialism, and his equally famous disciple, Friedrich Naumann, tried his hand at establishing a party on these theories which, oddly enough, he called the National Socialist party. Walter Rathenau, a leading industrialist, played with these alluring theories too. Naumann, in a burst of spiritual elation at the universal appeal of his philosophy, said: "We hardly knew that fundamentally we all wanted the same thing: the regulated labor of the second capitalistic period, which can be described as the transition from private capitalism to socialism provided only that the word socialism is not taken to mean the phenomenon of purely proletarian big business, but is broadly understood as folk-ordering with the object of increasing the common profit of all for all."[2]

Mixed up with all this was a concept of government equally decadent, since it represented the struggle of the baffled capitalist pragmatist to save a part of his capitalist target by amalgamating it with the socialist torpedo. Just as the pinks attempted to unite socialism and capitalism in a companionate marriage, men like Walter Rathenau, Foreign Minister in the republican government, toyed with the idea of uniting autocracy and democracy. There must be a democratic base to society. That is, somewhere down at the bottom, spread out as the ultimate but remote power, is the people. But the superstructure of government built on this proletarian mass must be an autocratic administration, built on the principle of hierarchy. The instrument of this aristocratic autocracy would be an elite. Rathenau had undoubtedly been fiddling with Pareto's idea of the circulating elite. The elite would run the show—supply the officers of the social hierarchy as it did to the military hierarchy.

[2] *Roots of National Socialism*, by Rohan D'O. Butler, E. P. Dutton, New York, 1942.

The masses would be shorn of their power by this political elite just as the army of businessmen would be shorn of their power by the intellectual bureaucracy that would relieve them of the drudgery of making decisions about their affairs.

Wherever these new socialist-capitalist intellectuals bobbed up with their remedies, these took the form of what they called planning. The very word "planning" is blown full with double meanings. No intelligent mind can suggest a reasonable objection to planning for any human institution, including the capitalist system. To one this will mean that the reasonable man will look over that system, locate its faults, ask what are the special factors of life in the system, where and what are the glands which supply it with its vitality, what exhausts and enervates them at one time and surcharges them with unhealthy energy at another. Having answered these questions, he will ask what arrangements ought to be made to make this system function at its highest possible capacity for human good. But this is not the meaning in the idea of "planning" as the word is used by the new school of national socialist planners. With them planning is a continuous function of government. It means blueprinting the structure of every man's business, charting the course of every industry, centering in great government bureaucracies the initiation and direction of every economic mechanism, making decisions about the behavior of every businessman and every business group flow across a desk in the capital.

Bruck, in his *Social and Economic History of Germany*, expresses the opinion that the first step toward the final disaster was made by Walter Rathenau. Rathenau was head of the *Allgemeine-Elektrizitäts-Gesellschaft*, the leading electrical company of Germany, and was given to philosophical rumination on the economic condition of his country. When the war began he was put in charge of the organization of Germany's industrial front. He began his work in a small room in the War Office where he and his colleagues began to group the various economic categories essential to the war effort. They began with iron and steel, and little by little almost every important branch of industry was formed into organized bodies under the supervision of the government. Complete compulsory cartels were created. The organization, beginning in a little office, quickly proliferated, spread out until it occupied whole blocks of buildings. Here was a comprehensive cartelization of industry regulating prices, competition, products, qualities, territory—every phase of production and distribution. Here, in fact, was the planned economy actually in effect. It was, therefore, no longer a question whether Germany would have such a thing. She had it. The question was whether she would cease to have it when the war ended. And when the war ended, Rathenau, a leader of the conservatives, wrote:

> From the ruins will arise neither a Communist State nor a system allowing free play to the economic forces. In enterprise the individual will not be given greater latitude; on the other hand individualistic activity will be consciously accorded a part in an economic structure working for Society as a whole; it will be infused with a spirit of communal responsibility and commonweal.
>
> A more equal distribution of possessions and income is a commandment of ethics and economy. Only one in the State is allowed to be immeasurably rich: that is the State itself.[3]

When the old imperial government collapsed with Germany's defeat, the republic was established after a brief interval with the adoption of the Weimar republic. And now we find the republican socialists and liberals toying with these same ideas. The constitution itself, though the socialists did not have a majority in the Weimar assembly, had a socialist tinge. And the new government began straightway to try its hand at some experiments in planning. It amounted to a legalization of the principle of cartelization which had always been strong.

In the disorder following the collapse of the imperial government, workmen's councils operated in Germany. Under their influence the constitution recognized this institution as a permanent sector of business. Wage earners were entitled to be represented in workers' councils organized in each local enterprise as well as in district councils in each economic area, all united in national workers' councils. These workers' councils were to meet representatives of employers in similar groups. Here was an organization of industry into shop, district, and national councils, with employers and employees

[3]Quoted in *Social and Economic History of Germany*, by Werner Friedrich Bruck, London, 1938.

represented, under the supervision of the government. Drafts of laws touching social and economic policy had to be submitted by the government to the national economic council before such laws were introduced into the Reichstag. Moreover, the council could itself propose laws to the Reichstag. Benns, commenting on this, observes:

> It was a recognition that the old type of political legislature gave at best only a haphazard and scrappy representation of the economic interests of the people. According to this scheme, the political legislature would continue to represent the people as individuals and to ensure to them individual liberty; but the functional parliament would represent the great economic groups and corporations. This plan for a separate functional representative body was expected to be "the most original contribution of the German revolution to political thought."[4]

Here was the principle of syndicalism grafted upon a capitalist society. This is what Mussolini was talking about several years later when he proceeded with his corporative state idea. Mussolini then talked the same language as these German republicans because Mussolini was a syndicalist and these German socialists and left-wing liberals were deeply touched with the philosophy of syndicalism. This was the beginning of organizing the society along craft lines rather than geographical lines or at least to provide a double type of parliament—one an economic and the other a political parliament. The radical groups put into writing in the constitution what the conservative Rathenau was talking about in vague phrases.

Rathenau, however, made a substantial contribution to this development. As chief of the War Raw Materials Office, he founded a series of mixed companies—that is corporations in which the government and private industry were partners. These mixed public-private partnerships were permitted to continue after the war. Fritz Thyssen, later to become a financial backer of Hitler, speaks with approval of a kind of industry found in the Rhenish-Westphalian electric works, where the shares were owned partly by private capital and partly by the communes which took their power from these companies, but where the management was in private hands,

[4] *Europe Since 1914*, by F. Lee Benns, Crofts & Co., New York, 1935.

with the community represented on the directorate. Thyssen, steel magnate and ultra-conservative, says of this:

> The result is that a kind of sparring match takes place between the private economic interests on the one hand and the communal interests of the cities and villages on the other. The object is precisely this: to ensure that the private economic interests must not injure the commonweal. The final supervision is, of course, the business of the government.[5]

One argument in later years for this system was that this gave the state all the advantages of ownership without the dangers of management of many industries which would result in the creation of a vast state bureaucracy. The Hitler regime was especially attracted by this scheme and it became an integral part of its whole economic policy. Like everything else it did, however, the whole system and all its techniques were forged for it by that strange collaboration of conservatives and radicals, which must ever remain one of the most singular phenomena of these times.

The experiments in state ownership, state control, state partnerships were numerous. One example was the coal industry. A Reich Coal Council was organized, which applied the principle of planning to the coal industry. The same thing was done for the potash industry. This was done in 1919 but continued to flourish all through the Weimar regime.[6]

The Weimar republic invaded the banking field. It organized the *Reichskreditgesellschaft*. It operated on the same model as the private banks and quickly rose to the rank of the Big Four and finally gave the state dominant position in the banking field. The government owned, as a legacy of the war, enterprises of various kinds. These were transferred to government-owned corporations in which the government held stock through a great government-owned holding company known as *Viag* (*Vereinigte Industrie Aktiengesellschaft*) with which was combined the *Reichskreditgesellschaft* to finance them. By 1926 it is estimated there were 1,200 cartels operating in the Reich. The government was struggling to create a balance between industrial and farm prices—parity—and to this

---

[5] *I Paid Hitler*, by Fritz Thyssen, Farrar & Rinehart, New York, 1941.
[6] *German Economy*, by Gustav Stolper, Reynal & Hitchcock, New York, 1940.

end adopted import and export quotas and embargoes, state monopoly of corn, state purchase of farm supplies, and many other types of regulations of agricultural credits.

Labor laws followed much the same pattern. The republic organized mediation in labor disputes and shop councils. Before the war labor contracts were private. Under the Weimar republic collective bargaining was recognized as an institution in the public interest. Free unions were distinguished from yellow unions (yellow unions being company affairs). Finally, mediators could intervene to force compromise and could issue decisions which, if accepted by one party, were binding on both. This, begun in the interest of the worker, became more and more the rule, gradually breaking down collective bargaining, which remained largely as a fiction. Stolper observes:

> There is a tragic irony in the historical development by which the German Revolution first greatly enhanced the importance, strength, and authority of the German unions, only to land them at the end of this period almost in the position of administrative organs of the state, consequently deprived of their real function of constituting a powerful body of workers to face the power of the entrepreneurs.[7]

Private industry suffered much the same fate. For years the German Government had been slowly evolving as the superintendent of a state-coerced industrial system. Dr. Angell points out that at first the capitalist entrepreneur controlled. Then the bank, a powerful central agency acting for large masses of capital, exercised control. With the war the government took over this function and the Weimar regime embedded the principle in the institutional structure of the state. The politicians became preoccupied with the problems presented by big business on one hand and labor on the other—and the little businessman got lost in the shuffle.

The aim in which Bismarck had failed was accomplished almost at a stroke in the Weimar Constitution—the subordination of the individual states to the federal state. The old imperial state had to depend on the constituent states to provide it with a part of its funds. Now this was altered, and the central government of the

[7] *German Economy*, by Gustav Stolper, Reynal & Hitchcock, New York, 1940.

republic became the great imposer and collector of taxes, paying to the states each a share. Slowly the central government absorbed the powers of the states. The problems of the individual states and communities, the problems of business groups and social groups were all brought to Berlin. The republican Reichstag, unlike its imperial predecessor, was now charged with the vast duty of managing almost every energy of the social and economic life of the republic. German states were always filled with bureaus, so that long before World War I travelers referred to the "bureaucratic tyrannies" of the empire. But now the bureaus became great centralized organisms of the federal government dealing with the multitude of problems which the Reichstag was completely incapable of handling. Quickly the actual function of governing leaked out of the parliament into the hands of the bureaucrats. The German republic became a paradise of bureaucracy on a scale which the old imperial government never knew. The state, with its powers enhanced by the acquisition of immense economic powers and those powers brought to the center of government and lodged in the executive, was slowly becoming, notwithstanding its republican appearance, a totalitarian state that was almost unlimited in its powers.

Germany, under the republic, was not moving toward the socialist idea of state ownership, but rather toward the syndicalist idea of the organization of society into economic provinces, with property privately owned and regulated tightly by private cartels—in a few of which labor was represented—but all under the paternal supervision of the government. But it was under the supervision of the political state which the old syndicalists abhorred. The state, as Sorel had predicted, with its powers enhanced by the acquisition of immense economic powers, was becoming a totalitarian or despotic state.

VII · Machiavelli's Men

IN ALL that has preceded this the economic factors have, perhaps, been unduly emphasized. This is owing to the fact that in the last two years the tendency has been to ascribe all that has happened in Europe to an explosion of human wickedness, and it has seemed necessary to bring the economic factors back to their place in the picture. Many diverse forces, of course, influence the course of human events. In other periods of social change different social energies have in turn exerted a dominating influence—religion, politics, dynastic ambitions, waves of moral disease or resurgence. In the present era doubtless it has been the economic disorder which has been predominant. But it is not the only one. This era may perhaps be compared to the long period that marked the end of feudalism and the rise of capitalism. Society seems to be struggling toward some new form of economic organization. Whether or not modern capitalism is in its death throes, as so many assure us, I do not undertake to decide. But certainly the economic society which we somewhat loosely term capitalism is passing through a crisis now which may be the culminating crisis in a long series of convulsions of increasing intensity. It may, in a sense, be described as a period of economic decay, presenting all the symptoms of anemia and general debility. Such a period makes a rich breeding ground for other parasitic diseases of the spirit, which have nothing essentially to do with economics, but which thrive in the soil of economic distress.

I have already referred to Ortega's theory of the revolt of the masses. The nineteenth century, he maintains, had produced a new man and infused into him formidable appetites and growing means of satisfying them. These include social, political, economic, and technical instruments that armed him with a new efficiency in his struggle with nature. His inability to use these instruments as successfully as he hoped has produced in him a quality of "indocility." Docility and indocility—these are the words which describe the difference between the masses of the eighteenth and those of the twentieth century.

Against these expectations of the masses, the failure of their organized societies to realize them stands in dark and menacing contrast. The unwillingness of the masses to submit to this failure led to a serious loosening of their adhesion to the political principles of government on which these societies were based. Impatience grew to exasperation and to a search for some other instruments of social control better adapted to their appetites. Losing faith in an order of society which had once seemed everlasting and which had promised such rich harvests, they have lost faith in many other ideas and doctrines to which, in their former docility, they clung. The minds of men are now open to all sorts of doctrinaires, promisers, evangelists of the good life. There has been a weakening of the normal and routine inhibitions of the old order.

It has been suggested that we are witnessing a revolt against culture. I am not prepared to admit that there has been a revolt against culture. There is at present, it is true, a vast social upheaval which is the result of the failure not of our culture, but of the arrangements we have made for managing our society.

In societies great masses of men are moved by a deeply rooted desire for quiet, orderliness, routine, the undisturbed round of the day's duties and distractions, the habits of the seasons, the succession of feasts, and for security. Generally they want to be left alone, whence arises the seemingly paradoxical surrender to public disciplines on what might be called the whole range of traffic. This they look upon not so much as coercion of themselves as a restraint upon others. Having no wish to walk on the grass or drive to the left or to offend against any of the generally accepted understandings that enable large numbers of people to live in a limited space without bothering one another unduly, they are willing that the law should restrain those who itch to defy these arrangements. This trait is found in all urban populations and, of course, nowhere so much as in Germany. There some apologists have explained the German's tolerance of the ubiquitous *verboten* sign as a form of the German's peculiar desire for freedom, for these disciplines leave all who are willing to follow them free from annoyance by the minority that would rebel against the rules. There is something to be said for this. But it can become too much a habit of the spirit, a rule of behavior that after a while may subdue the mind to excessive regulation. When, therefore, governments extend too far their disciplines or fail in the generally accepted objectives of government, the mass of men will remain docile for a long time. However, in Germany their docility was deeply ruffled. This yearning for order restrained them for a long time from overt acts of resistance. The revolt was a revolt of the spirit. It roused their minds against the government, not their hands. It took the form of a slow but progressive loss of tolerance and a deepening suspicion of existing institutions.

Moreover, the war had wrought darkly upon the minds and hearts of many. Sigmund Neumann, pursuing his thesis of permanent revolution, sees the basic faith of the era of liberalism in the ultimate goodness and improvement of mankind profoundly shaken by the war. Four years of war had bred the cult of violence. The heroic virtues became popular. Moral anarchy reigned. Why not? The so-called Christian virtues of humility, love, charity, personal freedom, the strong prohibitions against violence, murder, stealing, lying, cruelty—all these are washed away by war. The greatest hero is the one who kills the most people. Glamorous exploits in successful lying and mass stealing and heroic vengeance are rewarded with decorations and public acclaim. You cannot, when the war is proclaimed, pull a switch and shift the community from the moral code of peace to that of war and then, when the armistice is signed, pull another switch and reconnect the whole society with its old moral regulations again. Thousands of people of all ranks who have found a relish in the morals of war come back to you with these rudimentary instincts controlling their behavior while thousands of others, trapped in a sort of no man's land between these two moralities, come back to you poisoned by cynicism.

These economic and human disturbances set the stage for several types of men. The notion that all the immoral or amoral performances that are exhibited in such times of stress as followed Germany's defeat proceed from the hearts of wicked men is far from the truth. There is a sort of person who is well named by Ortega the "excellent man," as distinguished from the common man. This excellent man is "one who makes great demands upon himself and for whom life has no savor unless he makes it consist in something transcendental. He does not look upon the necessity of serving as an oppression. When, by chance, such necessity is lacking, he grows restless and invents some new standard, more difficult, more exigent, with which to coerce himself. This is life lived as a discipline."[1]

These are the men who are the living and active disciples of the

[1] *The Revolt of the Masses,* by José Ortega y Gasset, W. W. Norton, New York, 1932.

German romantic school of philosophy. A few such men, endowed beyond their fellows with sense as well as inspiration, have made the most benign contributions to the world's progress. But unfortunately there are too many of them, and there is no rule that will guarantee that all of them will know what they are about. In fact, there is a principle that almost guarantees most of them will be wrong. For, like Nietzsche, most of them are enemies of rationalism. They are romanticist first and always. As Josiah Royce puts it, when defining Schiller's philosophy, their motto is "Trust your genius; follow your noble heart; change your doctrine whenever your heart changes, and change your heart often. . . . The world is essentially what men of genius make it. Let us then be men of genius and make it what we choose."[2]

One finds numerous men of this stamp among the rank of the endowed—the academicians, the sons of the rich, the eternal secretaries of foundations and institutes. Removed from the sordid details of money-getting, with leisure to ponder the woes and dreams of the world, holding themselves above and apart from the hard, pragmatic necessities of balancing either a commercial or a community budget, they come to think of themselves as the excellent men of the world, as having a peculiarly enlightened insight into its ways. They develop the itch for world-remolding and work endlessly at the job. In periods of distress they come forward to replace the practical men, who, knowing little of the anatomy of society and the mind, move as complete pragmatists. In moments of crises they go tumbling to the centers of power with their doctrines, their formulae, their programs, blueprints, and all. They swarmed to Berlin when the last war began, and they remained to take over the vast bankruptcy that was left when it ended. Never in history have they been basking in such a paradise as now.

But it is not only the excellent men who come running to the center of things when mischief is afoot. There are what Spengler calls the cosmic men—wholly different from the ideologues. They are a breed upon whom the harness of civilized life sits with discomfort. They are men who, as Spengler says, are "tired to death of money economy." Such men "hope for salvation from somewhere or

[2] *The Spirit of Modern Philosophy*, by Josiah Royce, Houghton, Mifflin, New York, 1892.

other, for some real thing of honor or chivalry, of inward nobility, of unselfishness and duty." All the grand events in history are carried forward by beings of the cosmic order. Roll the war drum and every soul among them thrills, just as every A string on a harp vibrates when you sound the tuning fork. D'Annunzio inflamed the minds of the Italian youth as he flung incendiary slogans at their restless minds and summoned them to repeat the glories of antique Rome. Germany was well supplied with men of this stripe—so numerous that they need not be named—who lamented more than any other damage done to the fatherland the extinction of the army and the end of that channel to glory. Germany nurtured these types in the disordered years up to 1924. They went into temporary eclipse during the great boom up to 1929. As soon as the bones of the state carcass began to show again, they appeared once more full of the noblest sentiments and the most ardent philosophies and the most glamorous plans for updoing the world and re-creating the glories of Germany. They were, in fact, more numerous than ever, for a whole new generation was back from the battlefields heartbroken at the humiliation of the fatherland and now had planted in their hearts the dream of glorious revenge—of the day when Germany's great legions would march again and would turn upon her enemies and re-establish her ancient glory.

They believed that war is the natural condition of men, that militarism is the perfect institution because it is the framework of the knightly life, and that imperialism is the natural enterprise of great spirits and the logical basis and occasion of war. Without war men will rot. All they ask is that the war shall have a noble purpose. It may be the spread of religion, the white man's burden, the nation's honor or, by a peculiar paradox, war to end war—a noble and glorious and righteous and civilizing war to end that evil institution of war without which men will rot. No matter what the cause, even though it be to conquer with tanks and planes and modern artillery some defenseless black population, there will be no lack of poets and preachers and essayists and philosophers to invent the necessary reasons and gild the infamy with righteousness. To this righteousness there is, of course, never an adequate reply. Thus a war to end poverty becomes an unanswerable enterprise. For who can decently be for poverty? To even debate whether the war will end poverty becomes an exhibition of ugly pragmatism and the sign of an ignoble mind.

Germany had her squadrons of poets and philosophers and professors to perform this service. And they would not seem, if you were to meet them, very different from the tribe anywhere else in the world—scholarly, full of the milk of human kindness and reasonableness, love of order, and concern for the basic virtues of civilization. In England it could be such a soul as John Ruskin, endlessly weeping over the sufferings of the poor while summoning the young men of Oxford to go forth and conquer all the lands they could lay their hands on. Or it could be so great a lover of order as the London *Times* which, before the last war, bemoaned the long peace. "This nation," it said, "is a good deal enervated by the long peace, by easy habits of intercourse, by peace societies and false economies (on the army). It wants more romantic action to revive the knightly principle." In Italy the doctrine would find its evangelists among literary men by the score, and these would include her two foremost scholars and her foremost poet.

There is another batch, not so numerous, but more dangerous perhaps. They are the men who yearn for power. The opportunity for them to attain power is not always present. And the conditions favorable to one man may not suit the peculiar talents of another. Always there are men of the Mussolini or Hitler stripe present in all societies. But they require the proper conditions for their emergence. It is entirely possible that neither Hitler nor Mussolini would have reached to more than local eminence, and then as public nuisances, had there been no World War I. The cultivation of this evil crop of lawless hunters after power has been ascribed in large measure to the spadework of men like Machiavelli, Nietzsche, and Spengler, especially Machiavelli, who is hailed as the founder of an ever-growing school. But the importance of the Florentine philosopher—as well as the German authors of *Zarathustra* and *Decline of the West*—is a good deal exaggerated. The power-hunters did not need Machiavelli or Nietzsche to tell them there was a moral code for the herd and another one for them. Corrupt leaders in New York, Chicago, Kansas City, or Philadelphia in our own day—and throughout history—

most of whom never heard of Machiavelli, operate on this principle. They do not recognize the moral law as binding on them. They lie, cheat at elections, graft, bribe voters, and employ violence wherever it will produce results, and feel no need to hold down their heads while doing so. What is more, the people clothe their behavior with a kind of tolerance. They are welcomed in the most respectable circles, sit in the front pews at church, are fawned upon by pastors, and collect for themselves rich majorities at successive elections. Had Machiavelli never lived and Nietzsche been consigned earlier in life to the asylum before he invented the myth of the superman, these ward lords in America and war lords in Europe would have gone their several ways.

It is beyond doubt that Mussolini must have read with glowing pleasure, as indeed he did, the philosophies of Machiavelli and Nietzsche which ran so perfectly with his own concepts of virtue. As for Hitler, he doubtless never read either. There had been going on for a long time a slow erosion of morals, and it may well have been that the frank avowals of the Machiavellis and Nietzsches encouraged the devotees of the new laxity. It must have fallen like a stimulating balm upon the dreams of many a moral outlaw in search of power at some level of the hierarchy to discover that a great Italian savant and a distinguished German philosopher and poet had taught that there was a separate and convenient morality for them as distinguished from the herd.

VIII · War

MY AIM has been to show that Germany, like most European countries, had been for forty-four years preceding the war subject to certain defects seemingly inherent in the economic system; that during those years the nation grew in prosperity and wealth but, despite this, poverty remained in large areas and the whole system was subjected to depressions at frequent intervals. Coincident with this was a growing revolt of the masses which consisted, not in any revolutionary episodes, but in a spiritual discontent and a questioning of the wisdom of leaders and the soundness of the parliamentary structure. Throughout this period ministry after ministry, struggling with the economic and political problems growing out of these conditions, fell into the practice of following certain settled principles of action, and these principles of action were arrived at by a long period of acquiescence in the demands or tolerances of the people. These we have described during the period of the old imperial government as follows:

1. The policy of state debt and spending to supplement the income of the nation and create purchasing power, done haltingly and with misgivings. No matter what kind of ministry was in power all followed this practice because, despite the misgiving, the public demanded results which could be obtained in no other way and was willing to tolerate the practice.

2. There was a settled approval of the policy of the philanthropic state which undertook to quiet the opposition of the indigent through measures of social welfare. No government could have existed that had cut the social-welfare services or those other government services made possible by government borrowing. Hence ministries which did these things ran with and not against the stream.

3. Originating in the aristocratic support of the military caste, pushed further by the general situation in Europe and the demand of the business world for armed might as an ally of foreign relations and by the dreams of the devotees of the knightly spirit, militarism became the greatest economic prop of the existing order, the great and glamorous public-works project of the empire, which withdrew great numbers from the unassimilable labor pools and supported a gigantic industry with public funds. Because of a variety of interests, but chiefly because of the economic interest, militarism had the support of the nation.

4. The old Bismarckian policy of an integrated German empire in Central Europe and an avoidance of the institution of colonial adventure was forced to give way before the growing ambitions of the empire. Militarism could be supported only by a continuous propaganda based on fear and on glory.

5. Next was the widespread demand from every section of the populace for regimentation and control of the economic system, including the principle that control should be exercised by producers in the interest of producers. This led to a widespread belief in, or tolerance for, the idea of corporativism.

6. Along with this went the rising loss of faith in the parliamentary government. This did not comprehend the whole mass of the people but infected large and influential portions of them.

As the years 1913 and 1914 came down on the empire, it was facing the consequences of these policies and opinions—the debts had risen to critical proportions, the demands of the poorer groups were becoming louder, the need for more conservative spending policies was evident, yet this was impossible because the necessity for a great military establishment had been embedded in the popular mind by propaganda, while any cut in military expenditures would have meant an increase in unemployment. The gathering difficulties of industry were pushing the country in the direction of still more extensive efforts at control. War in the Balkans had unsettled affairs in Europe. Great shortages of capital resulted in a disastrous decrease in new enterprises. Government bonds could find no buyers. Bavarian and Westphalian manufacturers were discharging their workmen, unemployment was spreading, and living costs were rising. All the problems of forty years—debt, the capital-labor struggle, the demands of the indigent, unemployment, the cost of militarism, and the ambitions of the imperialists were at climactic levels. Into this disorder—which could have been paralleled in every continental country—a Serbian patriot fired a revolver and set in motion a series of swift events which ended with the Great War and the final defeat of Germany in November 1918.

The war over, a republican government succeeded the imperial one. Thereafter the same forces went to work—the old debts, the struggle between labor and capital, the unemployment, poverty—all many times multiplied by the war. And then the republican government proceeded to do what the old imperial government had done —continued in debt until the vast bubble burst, after which, starting out free of internal debts, it proceeded to create more deficits and debts to create national income, to install more extensive social-welfare institutions, and to extend the mechanisms of regimentation and control to the economic system.

Militarism—not merely Germany's greatest industry but the industry that was the medium for government spending—was banned by the Treaty of Versailles, which also ended her policies of imperial aggression, though it did not liquidate all the dreamers. The republic did create more democracy rather than less and established an authentic parliamentary government which, alone of its policies, ran counter to a very large section of public opinion. In short, the great streams of opinion and desire remained unchanged by the war save that they were intensified and the effort of the government to comply with them was also intensified.

IX · Hitler

WE ARE NOW ARRIVED at the point at which Adolf Hitler makes his appearance on the crest of those deeply running streams we have been describing. Hitler began his career as a political leader in 1919. What was his philosophy? What were his aims? What statement of principles is available as he began?

A national assembly had met at Weimar in February and framed a republican constitution. The socialists had twice as many in the convention as any other party, but they did not control the assembly. They did, however, impart a socialist tinge to that document. They elected a socialist, Friedrich Ebert, as President. In the midst of this Kurt Eisner, socialist Bavarian Premier, was assassinated by a nationalist officer, a Soviet government was proclaimed in Bavaria and put down by the conservative Free Corps, the constitution was accepted by all of Germany, and a socialist, Bauer, was named Chancellor of the republic. The Red terror was frightening the souls of the conservative groups of Germany. Bela Kun headed a Red government in Hungary, the communists were organizing, plotting, threatening everywhere. Munich, after Eisner's murder, came into the hands of the conservatives and the city became thereafter the center of reactionary activities. It was, however, ablaze with agitation. Unemployment was widespread, food scarce, prices high. Little groups of all shades of opinion were meeting in beer halls and haranguing listeners on street corners. The Free Corps—volunteer roving bands of soldiers under adventurers of various sorts—were numerous, combining military and political ambitions. At this point Hitler began. Stationed just outside Munich with his regiment, he was assigned to collect information about several of these groups. He ended by joining one of them. It consisted of a handful of men who met in a little beer hall and called themselves the German Workers' party. The first seeds of this agitation, which was one day to split the world, were planted, with a strange irony, by an organization known as the Association for the Promotion of Peace. Thus sponsored, a branch was formed in Munich in 1918 by a locksmith named Anton Drexler. It did not go far, and on January 5, 1919, while communists in Berlin were rioting to overthrow the Ebert provisional government, Drexler reorganized his group into the German Workers' party. The chief figures in this diminutive movement were Drexler, an engineer named Gottfried Feder, a professor named Dr. Johannes Dingfelder, a journalist named Karl Harrer, and a young reporter named Hermann Esser. Hitler was the sixth man to become a member. With the exception of young Esser there was nothing vicious about these men. Oddly enough there was no very tight agreement among them on doctrine. Each seemed intent on his own brand of social medicine and willing to go along with the others provided they did the same by him. Drexler was a more or less futile, confused person, whose chief fixation was a hatred of labor unions because they had inflicted some injustice on him. Feder, an engineer, had come to the conclusion that the woes of capitalism were traceable to the institution of interest. He expounded the theory that there were two kinds of capital—productive and speculative. To all who would listen he would preach the gospel of "breaking the bond slavery of interest which is the steel axle around which everything turns!" His grand remedy was to nationalize the banks, institute state ownership of land, and substitute the German for the Roman law, and he worked out a theory of money—which was inevitable—a kind of printing-press currency that came to be known later as *Federgeld*—feather money. He was the precise duplicate of innumerable men of the same stripe and character who may be found in this country at any time.

Dr. Dingfelder was a gloomy philosopher who foresaw nothing less than the downfall of human nature through the failure of production and who was fond of picturing in dark colors the final dreadful catastrophe when Nature herself would go on strike, her fruits growing less and the rest devoured by vermin.

Karl Harrer, the journalist, was a moderate man, who did not like the talk he heard against the Jews. Hermann Esser, on the other hand, a precocious philosopher, was a valiant Jew-hater and harangued small groups on street corners with a confused mixture of anti-Semitism and socialism. Here was a nondescript flock which, with no common philosophy and, while neither wicked nor deranged, was quite as dangerous because of its ignorance. Its members were the type usually described in this country as crackpots. They mustered recruits. There was a definite socialist tinge to their councils and the recruits were mostly socialists or ex-socialists or syndicalists in search of some similar banner. The group could have been duplicated in a score of other spots in Munich. There was no man so poor that he might not found, like Anton Drexler, the locksmith, a political party. The others, however, lacked what the German Workers' party had, and that was Adolf Hitler.

What was Hitler's contribution of doctrine to all this? It amounted literally to nothing. His social program might be summed up as follows: That the socialists were scoundrels, the Jews scoundrels, the German race is the greatest race, the Versailles Treaty must be destroyed, Germany's army must be restored, the Social Democrats must be driven from power.

But all this has little to do with social organization or solving the problems of Germany at that time. It is doubtful if he had any other views than such as might pop up from time to time. In *Mein Kampf* he confesses that he had rather liked social democracy. "The fact that it finally endeavored to raise the standard of living of the working class—in those days my innocent mind was foolish enough to believe this—seemed to speak rather in its favor."[1] But it is clear

---

[1] *Mein Kampf*. Reynal & Hitchcock American translation, 1940.

that he did not associate Marxism and socialism and really knew little of either. His mind was preoccupied with the reconstruction of the German Army, which he worshiped and which he described as that "army whose organization and leadership was the most colossal affair which the earth has ever seen so far."[2] In the defeat of that wondrous instrument of power he had beheld the impossible and his mind, overpowered by the catastrophe, was filled with hatred of those who had done it. And he believed that the job had been done by the people at home led by socialists and Jews. He drew from the miscellaneous army of people around him his first faltering conviction—Feder's "interest-bondage" theory, the nationalization of the banks, and state ownership of land. In time the German Workers' party decided to change its name to the National Socialist German Workers' party. Its leaders drew up a program of principles which became the famous Twenty-Five Points, a meeting was held, and Hitler read these points to the small crowd. These "points" remained for a number of years the official program of the National Socialist party. It is very important to examine them and to perceive how little resemblance they bear to the ultimate policies of that party.

The points included in this program may be divided into three categories—political, military, economic. They are presented here not in their original order but in the groups named:

Political— Abrogation of the Treaty of Versailles.
All Germans must be included in the same state.
Citizenship in the state for Germans only.
No further admission of non-Germans.
Forcible emigration of all newcomers since August 1914.
Living space for the German people.
The rights of all citizens shall be the same.
A stronger central government—under control of the central parliament.

Military— Return of a national instead of a professional army.

Economic—Confiscation of war profits.
Taking over of all trusts by the state.
Abolition of all unearned incomes.

[2]*Mein Kampf.* Reynal & Hitchcock American translation, 1940.

> State share in profits of all large industries.
> Confiscation of lands for all purposes without compensation.
> Relentless measures against usurers and profiteers.
> Bigger and better old-age pensions.

In the political section of this program there was nothing in violent collision with the widely held views of many powerful groups—particularly the nationalists and conservatives—and these views the National Socialist party continued to hold to the end, save the right of all citizens to equal rights and the institution of parliament as the agency of central control. Hitler substituted the idea of the elite and the idea of the hierarchial leader for the principles of equality and parliamentary government. The ideal of a German national army again also had deep roots in Germany and represented no departure from traditional thought. The economic section of the platform, however, was predominantly socialist and, despite the character of the new constitution and the semi-socialist regime then in power, could not have been adopted without a tremendous struggle against the opinions of several powerful minorities —too powerful to be overthrown.

At this period Hitler was a mere amateur in revolutionary technique as compared with Mussolini when he began. While he adopted the platform, his interest was not in its doctrines so much as in the instrument that had come into his hands as a means to power, which distinguished him from his colleagues who were wrapped up in their doctrines. But he did not yet understand how he should or would shape his course in that pursuit. He denounced German parties for cooking up platforms to suit all sorts of people and announced boastfully that he was always ready to make a front against public opinion and that the National Socialist party "would never become a bailiff of public opinion but its ruler." This, however, is precisely what the National Socialist party did.

New and more capable converts to the party began to arrive and to shoulder out of the way the smaller persons like Feder and Drexler—men like Roehm, Gregor Strasser, Hess, Julius Streicher, Rosenberg, Goering and Goebbels. Strasser, Roehm, and Streicher were socialists. Goebbels had a pet peeve—the war profiteers. Goering was a pure adventurer and nationalist. Hence for a while the party kept to its socialist trend. But Hitler was not too pleased with this. He was himself no socialist. And so, as he sought support from the conservative and military groups, he offered his definition of the word "socialist" as used in the party's name. "Whoever," he said in *Mein Kampf*, "is prepared to make the national cause his own to such an extent that he knows no higher ideal than the welfare of the nation, whoever in addition has understood our great national anthem, *Deutschland, Deutschland, über alles* to mean that nothing in the wide world surpasses this Germany, people and land, land and people—that man is called a socialist."

In 1923 he was jailed for his part in his ill-starred beer-hall *Putsch*. He had plenty of time to think things over and to discuss affairs with fresh recruits. Otto Strasser says that when Hitler emerged from jail he was a changed man. Originally dedicated to the idea of violent revolution, he now determined to proceed by strictly legal means. And then also he began to cultivate closer relations with conservative groups. Dissension began to boil up among his diverse groups of supporters. Otto Strasser asked him what he would do about Krupp's if he attained power—would he leave it alone or not. "Of course I should leave it alone," he replied. "Do you think I am crazy enough to ruin Germany's greatest industry?" The word "socialist" in the party name made it possible for many old social democrats to transfer their allegiance to Hitler without seeming to betray too much their old cause. But now the Social Democrats were no longer exercising so large a share in the government. Germany was on the way back to prosperity. Hitler became aware that he must find his strength somewhere else. Fellows like Feder and other Nazis in the Reichstag were offering bills about "the bond slavery of interest," etc., but no one seemed to pay any attention to this. Indeed this is a remarkable feature of the whole course of these democratic revolutionary movements. The items of the program seem to count little. The general promises and the party stratagems and the show put on by the leaders count more. Giolitti said he owed it to Mussolini not to be too much concerned with the programs of such leaders as with their tactics. Hitler found that the fight on the Jews had brought him some very influential elements. Erika and

Klaus Mann observe that "there was something frightening at the swiftness with which the bar and the medical societies recast themselves to exclude Jews."[3] His relentless battle on all that was summed up in the word "Versailles" was bringing to his side great numbers of businessmen. Germany had gone through the inflation and was now prosperous, but great numbers of businessmen believed that the reparations burden would ruin Germany again. Big business finally moved over to his side. But it was the last convert. Fritz Thyssen made up his mind to back Hitler. He came to this conclusion when the Young Plan was before the country. He tells us he was convinced of the necessity of uniting all parties of the Right against it. And it is interesting to find him classifying national socialism, filled as it was with old socialists like Strasser, Kock, and Streicher, as a party of the Right. With the collapse of business, the Young Plan, according to Thyssen, was the principal cause of the upsurgence of nationalists. And Hitler rode that wave vigorously. Thyssen advanced money to buy the Brown House—the Nazi headquarters—and later contributed a million marks to the party. He introduced Hitler to the entire body of Rhenish-Westphalian industrialists. All the old theories about confiscation of war profits, taking over trusts, ending unearned incomes, confiscation of lands, state sharing of profits of big corporations, were discarded. National socialism had become precisely what fascism was in Italy—a full-fledged organism for preserving and maintaining the system of modern capitalism. Despite all Hitler's talk about molding public opinion, public opinion had molded him. He did what the old parliamentary leaders of Italy and Germany had done. He searched out the great streams of opinion and desire and demand in Germany and he ran with them, not against them. He ended by getting power when Hindenburg summoned him to be Chancellor of Germany on January 25, 1933.

Once Hitler was in power the moment for mere promises was over. He had to deliver. He had denounced Bruening for the rising unemployment and the whole republican regime for its spending and debts. Now he had to end unemployment. But he had no plan. He had to resort at once to the time-worn device that had been used by Pericles, Augustus Caesar, Louis XIV, Bismarck, Giolitti, and the

[3] *The Other Germany*, by Erika and Klaus Mann, Modern Age, 1940.

republican parliament of the Reich. He had to spend money and borrow what he spent. And he had to pretend that all this was quite new and novel.

He spent vast sums on all sorts of things. He outdistanced his neighbors in looking after the submerged tenth. He launched projects to create work. He spent money on projects to increase the birth rate, improve health and reduce crime, on schools, roads, railways, playgrounds, house-building projects, home repairs, farm subsidies, and even on his widely publicized scheme to enable Germans to enjoy at low rates excursions of all sorts. Then after 1935 he launched his grandiose schemes of militarism with the restoration of conscription and a great program of armament building. Some of the money was raised, of course, by heavy taxation. But most of it was obtained by the use of government credit. All this meant unbalanced budgets, just as in Italy and in America. It is very difficult to get reliable budget figures, particularly after 1936. The budget for 1936 was computed by a German economist for a writer in *Harper's*[4] and this estimate shows 9 billion collected in taxes of which 2½ billion were delivered to the states, leaving 6½ billion to spend. The government spent 12 billion, thus having a deficit for the year of 5½ billion.

I have not been able to find any satisfactory figure of the national debt in this period. Gustav Stolper says the best figure he can arrive at is that the debt rose from 11,700,000,000 marks in 1933 to 40,000,000,000 or more in 1938. But a special dispatch to the New York *Times* from Berlin dated November 6, 1936—two years earlier—puts the public debt at something more than 50 or 55 billion marks. A dispatch to the New York *Herald Tribune,* September 1, 1941, fixes the debt as of September 1, 1939, at 107,000,000,000 marks. The data are unsatisfactory and, in each case, probably underestimate the truth. Since the war the debt has risen to 203,000,000,000 marks, according to a report from Berne based on computations of the Reich Ministry of Finance (New York *Times,* February 23, 1943).

These vast sums were borrowed from the people to as great an extent as propaganda appeals and compulsion could induce them to

[4] "Germany's Hidden Crisis," by Willson Woodside, *Harper's Magazine,* February 1937.

lend. But the mainstay of borrowing in Germany, as here, despite all the fancy tales told of new and ingenious fiscal inventions by Schacht, were the banks. There has been a good deal of admiration in this country among the devotees of public spending and debt of the so-called magical stratagems of Dr. Hjalmar Schacht. Generally Schacht tried as far as possible to do two things: he tried to keep Germany's state bonds and treasury paper out of the banks, and he tried to compel private individuals to supply the funds for state enterprises without involving the government in avoidable debt.

For instance, the Treasury would borrow a large sum from the banks. It would give the banks its short-term notes. The banks would give it a deposit. This is an inflationary proceeding. The next step would be to get the whole transaction out of the banks. Schacht would then go to the large steel or munitions or finance companies and "request" them to buy the bonds from the banks out of their profits as a patriotic duty. Thus the bonds would be removed from the banking system and go into the hands of private investors.

He also put into effect a regulation that in any given field of industry or finance—the steel industry, the arms industry, the motor industry, the insurance companies, etc.—when the surplus of cash funds exceeded a certain amount these funds should be invested in government securities. However, Schacht would then go to the industry and inform them that the government had ordered the construction of a large power plant or a great steel works or a huge plane factory. The plant would be built by a private corporation formed at the order of the government or it would be built by an existing private corporation. In this country this method has been followed. But our government borrows the money and lends it to the private corporation. Thus the government has a liability on its bonds, takes the risks and borrows its funds at the bank, thus adding to inflation. In Germany, Schacht would go to these large private steel or finance or other corporations and "request" them to buy the bonds of the private corporation building the new industry. Thus the government's credit was kept out of the transaction. Billions of dollars have been utilized in this way. However, these devices do not suffice for the immense sums required by the government for its vast enterprises in road and swimming-pool and school and playground and armament building. The banks are gorged with government paper just as in Italy and in America, despite all the highly advertised cleverness of Schacht.

Still another method was to issue promissory notes to contractors, much as Mussolini did, which were not negotiable at the banks for three months, after which time they could be turned in at the banks as collateral, the government extending them automatically every three months. Much cash was obtained by confiscating the property of the Jews, by seizing the funds of trade-unions, as well as the gold reserve accumulated by the republican government and the hundreds of millions of shares owned by government combines and banks. But nothing could save the government from constantly resorting in the end to outright borrowing from individuals and banks, chiefly the latter.

This, of course, was using a very old device. But the German Nazi economists explained very patiently in words of five and six syllables that all this was perfectly in accordance with sound national socialist finance. The old-time fear of state debt was just a silly superstition, the making of these great loans by the state was actually a "dynamic use of public securities" to create greater national income, government debt need never be paid as long as the interest is met, and the interest was not a burden since it was paid by German taxpayers to German bondholders—it was an internal debt and therefore in fact no debt at all. Germany, they explained, had been freed from the shackles of finance. One American writer at least said of it with almost boundless admiration: "The program required money, and *Hitler declared the financial obstacles were not to bar the way.*"

The beautiful part of this was that it worked—or seemed to. And certain American political financiers pointed out that by this means Hitler had solved Germany's problems and had created "full-blast employment." "They have attained what economists call full-blast employment and they are not headed for the financial rocks no matter how ardently we may hope and believe that such a fate must be their end," said Mr. Dal Hitchcock in *Harper's*.[5] How could anyone doubt the success of this "new" system of finance? The national

---

[5] "The German Financial Revolution," by Dal Hitchcock, *Harper's Magazine*, February 1941.

income rose from 45 billion in 1933, when Hitler took power, to 76 billion in 1938. There were 6,000,000 unemployed in 1932, 3,745,000 in 1933, and only 164,000 in 1938. Later no one was unemployed and laborers were being imported from all the surrounding countries.[6]

Of course there is no trick to this at all. Any government can do it. As long as it is able to borrow and spend it can create employment. But no free government can keep this up indefinitely. The old parliamentary Italian government and the old German imperial government borrowed and spent for many years. But they did it on a very moderate scale compared with this and just enough to barely keep out of too much hot water. In the end even these timid debt policies landed them in trouble. But no free government can keep up the massive debt policy of Hitler. The reason is obvious. A time comes, and that soon, when the burdens begin to outweigh the benefits and when the burdens fall not only on the most powerful elements in the community but on all elements. Banks shy away from taking any more bonds. Private investors refuse them altogether. The cost of servicing the debt becomes immense and calls for tax levies, not to create employment, but to pay interest, and those who hold the bonds constitute only a small minority of the community. The people, with the power of life over the personnel of the government, will throw out of office the party guilty of the offense. The state is in desperate fiscal trouble and the vast debt makes the use of further borrowing as an escape impossible. But in a despotic government, where neither people nor banks have anything to say, the dictator may impose his will to continue this practice for a longer time. In the end, however, it is an impossible system

---

[6] Egon Ranshoven-Wertheimer in *Victory Is Not Enough*, W. W. Norton, New York, 1942, says:

"The almost complete disappearance of unemployment prior to the outbreak of the war has certainly supported the Nazi arguments of 'practical socialism' in the eyes of hundreds of thousands of workingmen. They had seen their own representatives in the past helplessly grappling with the employment problem and could not help comparing their situation with a past in which they had been condemned to the moral misery of the 'dole.' While this has not converted the majority of the industrial workers of Germany, it has made them apprehensive lest the downfall of Hitler might restore, with their political liberties, the liberty of seeking non-existent employment. Such a critical attitude would have been entirely impossible had their own socialist movement bequeathed a record of accomplishment instead of a memory of disappointment."

of national existence, and even Hitler could not harness his people with it indefinitely save by invoking the patriotic motif and engulfing his nation in war. In such a situation war becomes the only escape even for a dictatorial government.

The policy has had one important consequence. Inevitably it puts the government in complete control of the fiscal department of industry. The government decides what industries are needed and either provides the funds or arranges for them by compulsion. It becomes the universal banker, investment broker, biggest bondholder, and, in many cases, shareholder. *Business remains in private hands, but investment becomes socialized.* This is what has happened in Germany.

When Hitler came to power he was confronted with his promises to establish the corporative system. Thyssen says that Hitler entrusted to him this task. But when Thyssen began, he discovered, to his dismay, that the Nazi leaders were interested in other matters. The old socialist wing of the party was preoccupied with economic matters and the nationalist element, led by Hugenberg, was equally bent upon bringing the economic system under management. But men like Hitler and Goering and Goebbels and Roehm and their ilk were bent chiefly on power and the multitude of arrangements under way to that end. Thyssen saw that the Nazi leaders had no plans—above all no economic plan. Everything was improvisation. The last visitor with the most attractive and imaginative and sensational drug to be shot into the arm of society was apt to command the Führer's assent. Otto Strasser, from the Left, and Rauschning confirm this statement. Thyssen says that Hitler was not interested in economics, that he agreed with everybody. Hitler himself confirms the criticism about his attitude toward economic matters. In *Mein Kampf* he had said that the intelligentsia looked upon the German collapse as of economic origin. But economics, he insisted, was only of second or third importance. "The political, ethical-moral as well as factors of blood and race are of the first importance." However, a Supreme Economic Council was formed to be the center of planning. It met once and never met again, and Thyssen's dream of a tightly organized system based on the old guild idea under the command of Germany's greatest industrialist came to an end.

However, it would not be true to say that the corporative idea was wholly liquidated. There was a pretense of organizing business into craft and professional categories, with the employing groups and workers formed into syndicates in corresponding districts. There is no need to go into the details of these arrangements. They ended, not in the structure of so-called self-governing corporativism, but in a series of organizations which became merely an apparatus for control in the hands of the state. At the head of each employing and each worker group was a leader named by the state whose decisions were absolute. What has emerged is a completely planned economy, planned by the state in an absolute autarchy. In Italy there is an elaborate organization of industry, agriculture, finance, and professions into so-called self-governing guilds. Dr. Salvemini insists, probably with full justification, that in Italy, too, this intricate and detailed fabric of self-governing industry is a fiction and that in fact it, too, is merely an instrument for state control in which the leaders are chosen by the state and dominated wholly by it. My own belief is that this is inevitable in any such system, that any political or economic society must function according to its nature, and that in the nature of things, whatever the original purpose or pretense, the system of industrial self-government in a capitalistic society must end—and swiftly—in complete state control.

The word "corporativism," therefore, may well lead us astray in forming a judgment of this aspect of fascism. Inevitably economic society, if organized at all, must be organized in economic categories —which means some form of the syndicate or trade association. For many decades, as we have seen, businessmen, labor leaders, conservative political leaders like Hugenberg and radical leaders influenced by the syndicalists, have moved steadily toward the theory that the economic society must be planned and managed, and that the planning and management must be done by the producing groups under the supervision of the state. And it was this theory that drew to Hitler's side the erstwhile socialists imbued with the syndicalist philosophy and itching for a chance to remodel capitalism in the socialist image, as well as the great industrialists who wanted to complete the cartelization of Germany. And this is what they got, but only after it had passed through the mental processing machine of the Nazi party leaders who composed it all to become purely an adjunct of that organization's achievement of absolute power. But it is a government-planned and government-managed autarchy, just as Italy is, and just as any fascist state is, since this is one of the essential and characteristic elements of the fascist state.

Planning had come in for much advertisement through the Russian model, but it was, in fact, a pet theme with German philosophers and economists for over a century. But the essential difference between planning in a communist country and planning in a capitalist country was lost on these schemers. A corporation, like the United States Steel Corporation, can, and must of necessity, plan its operations. It can plan because it owns outright all its plants and is complete master of its decisions. It can and must decide what products it will make, what production processes it will use, what its financial policies will be, over what areas it will extend its operations, what its sales and promotion and price policies will be. It must assume the risk involved in these plans. A communist society is, like the United States Steel Corporation, a gigantic holding company, for it owns its steel mills, its railroads, its banks, and every other agency of production and distribution. The production, employment, wage, distribution, price, and promotion policies of this immense holding company—the Soviet Government—must be laid out by that government. But in a capitalist state the government does not own either the production, distribution, or financial organizations. When, therefore, it proposes to plan, the plans are for industries and organizations it does not own. Planning for such a government becomes a wholly different process, unless the government is bent on telling every enterpriser what he must produce, how and when, what and to whom he shall sell, and at what price. The great difference between the communist state and the fascist state is that in the communist state the government plans for the industries of the nation which it owns and in the fascist state the government plans for industries which are owned by private persons.

This means incessant, comprehensive intrusion into the affairs of every business enterprise. This can be accomplished in several ways. The enterprises may be organized into guild or corporative groups that make plans under the supervision of the government and subject to its interference and control and final decision, or the government may make the plans directly, using the guilds or corporatives or trade associations as mere advisory bodies. In theory Mussolini adopted the first method and Hitler the second. Actually, the tendency of this planning, however it begins, is to drift toward the second method and that is what happened in Italy. Accordingly, what emerges in the end is a multitude of colossal bureaus which take over the direction and supervision of all industry and trade and which gradually absorb all the decisions of industry and trade.

It is in this that the true significance of the word "bureaucracy" takes its origin. When government confined itself to managing its own affairs, policing society, managing its armed forces, furnishing a judiciary to society, protecting the health and persons of its people, it operated through agencies which were called bureaus and those who manned them were called bureaucrats. But the modern government bureaus and their bureaucratic managers in the national socialist state are something quite different. The vastness of the modern state, the multitude of human situations it undertakes to regulate and care for, the extension of its directing hand to the affairs of every business unit are such that the bureaucrats participate in the formulation of the policies and making of the decisions of private life. The bureaus are no longer behaving as the servants of the state rendering services to the people as citizens. They are now engaged in managing and operating the private affairs of the people. And while the whole tendency of European states has been in this direction, it has remained for the fascists to adopt the practice as an institution of government upon a general—or to use its favored word—a totalitarian scale.

Of course the first necessity when this is attempted is to have an enclosed state. The government cannot plan for the shoe industry and make its plans stick for any part of it save that part which it can reach with its decrees—that is, that part located in its country. Hence the plans for the shoe industry are necessarily limited to the domestic shoe industry. Those plans include production schedules, qualities, prices, wages, labor terms, forms of organization, conditions and standards of work and of competition. Obviously no government can enforce these conditions against producers of shoes in a foreign country. It will permit no domestic shoe producer to compete unless he conforms to all the conditions. And of course it cannot permit a foreign shoe producer to compete with the domestic producers when he is immune from all these directive regulations. Hence the foreigner must be excluded. It is for this reason that the planned state, the autarchial state, is necessarily an enclosed state. Hitler, Mussolini, and Stalin are the great exemplars of autarchy in our world.

Along with the devices of autarchy and public debt, Hitler of course reintroduced militarism and with it the inevitable plunge toward imperialism. That phase of his program is too well known to call for any additional comment here. The Great War had done to Germany what it did to no other country—it had not merely defeated her and wrecked her economic system but had extinguished completely her greatest industry, militarism. Like other nations she could, as well as she was able, turn to rehabilitating all her other enterprises. But unlike them she was forbidden by the terms of the Treaty from reviving her greatest enterprise and the one she knew most about managing and whose effectiveness as a great job- and income-producing public project she had reason to know so well.

With six million people out of work, with the great Ruhr heavy industries restored, only a great army was needed to absorb large sections of the unemployed as soldiers and as workers in the armament and other industries. Rauschning, who was associated with the Nazi movement at the time, describes the impatience of all hands to get armament quickly under way in order to deal with the unemployment problem. In time the restoration of militarism, supported by a flood of government-created purchasing power, wiped out unemployment in the Reich and made some very deeply disturbed statesmen in the democratic countries look with envy and admiration upon its complete success.

Autarchy or the planned economy, planned consumption or the debt economy, militarism and imperialism—these became the essential elements of Hitler's brand of fascism, as they did of Mussolini's. But of course to this was added the fifth element of dictatorship. For all the other ingredients there was ample precedent in Germany and, indeed, the republican government which preceded Hitler had fully developed the two most important—the planned economy and debt. Militarism and imperialism were impossible in republican Germany under the Versailles Treaty, but these ancient evils were deeply rooted in German history. But what of the dictatorship? How was that developed? What preparatory arrangements were to be found in the republic for what Hitler did on that front? The answer must be that before Hitler came into power the dictatorship was already fairly complete. It was far from fixed and rested rather upon the name, the vanishing fame, and the whim of an aged man, President von Hindenburg, who stood upon the edge of the grave. But the fact of dictatorship, however unsteady, had been established. Once in power, the completion of that job was a simple one for Hitler—far simpler for him than for Mussolini.

Article 48 of the Weimar Constitution provided that the President, in an emergency, could govern by decree. The emergency envisaged by the constitution-makers was one growing out of military or other forms of violence. It was never intended that a Chancellor who could not get a majority behind him in the Reichstag could ignore that body and govern independently of it through presidential directives. In the state of party government in Germany it was difficult for a Chancellor to gather a majority. Conservatives, liberals, and radicals were split into several parties. When, in 1930, Heinrich Bruening was named Chancellor in the midst of the new depression and the sweep of the Nazis to public support, he could not get a coalition of parties sufficient to make up a majority. He urged and persuaded President von Hindenburg to govern by decrees under Article 48. This was certainly an abrogation of the democratic process. It is fair to say that the situation was grave, that the Hitler storm troopers were expressing themselves in the technique of thuggery in city streets, and that efforts were being made by several groups to unite with the Nazis to form a government. The shadow of Hitler hung over everything. What Bruening did certainly was to set up a form of dictatorship, and this is none the less true because Bruening was an honest and patriotic man and in no sense a seeker after personal power. This was the first step on the road to the liquidation of the Weimar republic, though it was undertaken with a different objective.

Here we see at work that dread erosion that devours institutions and particularly free institutions. Bruening had a precedent for what he did, and a precedent created by the very people who denounced him most lustily. Dr. Luther, as Chancellor, to make matters easier for the government during the stabilization episode, had invoked Article 48 of the constitution. He knew the article was not intended for such a use. He wrote later: "It must be admitted that at the time these clauses were drafted the author only had in view police or other measures for public safety. In reality *this article proved extremely useful* in terms of urgent necessity in rendering possible the enforcement of economic measures, especially taxation."[7]

Here is the spectacle of a Minister of State justifying the unconstitutional use of a power designed for police purposes to enforce economic and taxation measures on the ground that it was "extremely useful." Having been done once by upright and patriotic men, it could be done again for some other purpose by equally upright and patriotic men. Bruening, therefore, invoked it to govern without the Reichstag. A motion was made in the Reichstag to force withdrawal of the Bruening decrees and passed by 236 to 225 votes. Bruening therefore advised Hindenburg to dissolve the Reichstag and call new elections. They were held September 14, 1930. They resulted in an enormous gain for Hitler, who polled for his candidates six and a half million votes compared with only 800,000 in the last election, and brought him 107 seats in the Reichstag instead of twelve. In these circumstances Bruening continued to govern by decree, and the Reichstag slid into a kind of feeble acquiescence by referring the constitutional question to a commission.

Luther who began it and Bruening who repeated this stratagem were not evil men. The result of the precedent was all the more damaging for the very reason that Bruening was a man of unimpeachable integrity. He was doubtless the ablest German statesman of the whole period, save perhaps Stresemann, and even that exception may not stand. He was a man of singular probity of life, a devout Catholic, a deeply patriotic, patient, prudent, and courageous intellectual. He had devoted much of his life to editing and leading the Catholic Trade Union movement in Germany. As Chancellor

[7]*Hindenburg*, by Emil Ludwig, John C. Winston Co., Philadelphia, Pa., 1935.

he lived with becoming modesty in a few rooms of the chancellery, using the public taxi instead of an imposing limousine, conducted himself with exacting frugality as an example of high citizenship in a period that called for sacrifices from everyone, and gave numerous exhibitions of his purity and strength of character. He of course believed that he could save Germany from the danger that hung over her. Yet in the end the desperate measure he adopted merely made the oncoming absolutism easier.

Bruening attempted to call Germany away from the madness of the policies she had been pursuing. By 1930 the country was launched full upon a depression. Unemployment, which was 2,000,000 in 1929, rose to 3,000,000 in 1930 and would be 6,000,000 in two years. Germany could no longer borrow abroad and the central government could no longer borrow at home. Tax revenues declined everywhere. He told Germany she was pursuing an impossible course. Her great external debt required that she should build her export trade. Yet every policy pursued was in the direction of raising prices and labor costs. Desirable as higher wages and good prices were, they had the effect of destroying Germany's foreign trade at the same time that the state had stabilized the mark at prewar levels. He told Germans they must sacrifice. Yet what chance had this grim counsel, built on reality, against the irresponsible promises of Hitler who, while denouncing the debt policies of the republic, told Germans he would give them security from the cradle to the grave and ensure to them the good life? When in power he would establish systems of compulsory civil service which would find jobs for millions. He promised to build 400,000 houses a year. He held up the vision of a great program of road, street, sidewalk, swimming-pool, and public-edifice building along with painting, plastering, and repairing on a vast scale. Hitler had no notion how he would do this save by pursuing the very policy he denounced—borrowing and spending. Bruening's policy enraged the Social Democrats, the farmers, the small businessmen—all of that population poisoned by the privations of the depression, the past benefices of the republican ministries, and the hopelessness of more years of sacrifice. In the end he was dismissed by Hindenburg through the machinations of General von Schleicher and Von Papen, and Von Papen was made Chancellor. Von Papen was named without any reference to the Reichstag. His position was wholly illegal from the start. He took the next logical step. He proceeded to govern by decree and to seize the government of Prussia, consolidating the state and federal government under his hand. He dissolved the Reichstag and called new elections. Hitler, who had gotten six and a half million votes in 1930, now got fourteen million for his candidates with 230 seats in the Reichstag instead of 107. At this point, however, the republican government was at an end. It was now a question of what these adventurers would do with the apparatus of government that remained. Hindenburg was a dictator—old, feeble, vacillating, pulled and hauled by a palace cabal headed by his son, Von Papen, and Von Schleicher, and with no fast hold upon the dictatorship. Von Papen became Chancellor in June. He was let out in November to make room for Von Schleicher.

Then in January 1933, on the advice of Von Papen, Von Schleicher was ousted and Hitler called to power by Hindenburg after an election in which his vote was reduced from fourteen million to eleven and a half million. How vain and meaningless it must have been for men in Germany who still clung to the shreds of the tattered democracy to talk against Hitler's climb to power because of the fear of dictatorship when the men he was to replace had themselves already built the foundations and the superstructure of dictatorship! Hitler had merely to complete the job by ridding himself of reliance on the decrepit Hindenburg. He dissolved the Reichstag, called an election in which his party got seventeen million votes, gained control of the Reichstag, got a vote from the compliant majority giving him full power to rule by decree, suppressed all labor unions and all other parties, and when, sometime later, Hindenburg died, had the office of Chancellor and President consolidated into one. The whole armory of fascism was complete for Hitler when he arrived at the chancellery. The work had been done for him by the men who preceded him and most of all by the men of the republic. For fascism, as it turned out in Germany, as in Italy, bore no resemblance to the heterogeneous collection of principles enunciated by the National Socialists as they set out to capture the German state.

Hitler's national socialist program of confiscating war profits, taking over all trusts by the state, abolition of all unearned incomes, state share in the profits of all large industries, confiscation of lands without compensation, relentless measures against makers of profits, the right of all citizens to equal rights, and a strong central government dominated by the parliament—all this was swept aside and forgotten. Instead he took over the policies and principles enunciated and practiced by his various precursors—autarchy or the planned economy, government-created purchasing power through debt from the republican government, and militarism and imperialism from the old empire. The dictatorship was all neatly set up for him. Even the destruction of the power of the individual states was well advanced. Under the old Germany the federal government had to depend on the states for part of its revenues. Under republican Germany the states became the mendicants of the central government. In the end the government of Prussia as an independent entity free of the federal state was liquidated. Hitler, instead of molding the new German state in his own mold, permitted the powerful minorities of that state to mold his government. And that German state even presented him with the only instrument that can make an autarchy supported by government debt work—if only for a while—the dictatorship.

On the question of the dictatorship Hitler was a completely practical man. This was a point he had thought about. He proceeded to do all that was necessary to nail it down and perpetuate it in his person. But a dictatorship founded in a modern state that has tinkered with the processes of democracy, particularly a dictatorship that is achieved by demagogic means, must root itself in the tolerance and acquiescence, if not the outright approval, of the people. Hence Hitler adopted a group of devices—the one-party system, the principle of the elite, the military party, the suppression of all opposition of party, press, book, or speech, and the intensified employment of propaganda on the positive side to sell to Germans the aims of the Nazi party through radio, newspapers and movies, schools and colleges. These entailed persecution, the jail, the concentration camp, exile, violence in various forms, and the brutalities that are common to all dictatorships. It is these performances of force that have commanded the attention of the writers and commentators who have denounced Hitler. Yet it is not these that distinguish Hitler from other dictators. It is the dictatorship along with the establishment of an autarchial, militaristic imperialism supported by public debt which makes fascism.

Was Hitler inevitable? He had generated an immense disorder and rendered himself a colossal nuisance. But he moved through a series of crises in each one of which his fate was in the hands of some hostile power that might have crushed him—but did not. What if Bruening had used the power of the state—police and army—to suppress him? To do that Bruening, first of all, would have had to be something other than Bruening. To do that Bruening would have had to be himself a man of violence. And if in addition to his use of the executive decree to legislate and rule he had hunted down and liquidated by violence his most serious political opposition, we would have had then in Bruening the very phenomenon which Hitler symbolized—dictatorship by force. Bruening would have been the dictator instead of Hitler. What if Hugenberg had not made the preposterous mistake of supposing that he could use Hitler? Hugenberg was a leader of the nationalists, dispenser of their war chest, and it was he who decided to bring the nationalist support to Hitler's party and who persuaded Fritz Thyssen to finance Hitler. What if General von Schleicher, a confirmed nationalist Junker, close to Hindenburg, had not decided he could play a game with Hitler and tie the so-called national socialist energy to his fortunes when he became Chancellor? What if Von Papen had not in turn advised Hindenburg to sack Von Schleicher and make Hitler Chancellor? It is possible that either Von Schleicher or Von Papen might have liquidated Hitler or that Thyssen might have left him and his party to struggle hopelessly without funds. And in this case Hitler could have been barred from power. But none of these "ifs," had they materialized as facts, would have saved Germany from Hitlerism, by which I mean fascism. And this for the simple reason that had Von Schleicher or Von Papen done this they would have taken Germany into fascism quite as swiftly as Hitler. It might have been different in its scenes, its national episodes, its cast of characters, its tempo, and other characteristics. For those who are pleased with the distinction between good fascism and bad fascism, there might have been a difference. Von Papen was toying with the idea of a great revival of the guild state. Hugenberg was convinced that parliamentary government was done for and that governmental structure must be recast on the model of big business—the model of hierarchy.

I do not mean that Germany could not have been saved from fascism. This is a point that must remain unresolved in history. To maintain such a thesis would be no less than holding that man is the helpless victim of invincible forces in the hands of fate. I do not believe this. Yet it is difficult to escape the conviction that if the great currents of economic and other social forces that push men on are not resisted in time, the moment comes when the decisions are taken out of the hands either of individuals or society. There is good ground for believing that this moment had arrived in Germany when Bruening came to power. The nation was now caught in a flood of forces—unemployment on the increase, the economic system slowing down, a vast internal debt and tax structure weighing down worker and employer alike and paralyzing enterprise, an external debt which imposed an exhausting drain. People were not willing to consider the hard, sacrificial journey toward which Bruening beckoned. Neither orthodox capitalism nor social democracy nor any form of representative government had any friends left. No system had any support save such as embodied in one form or another the several central ingredients of national socialism—autarchy and government debt spending. If Hitler had not come to power someone else would have done so—Roehm or Gregor Strasser or Von Papen or Von Schleicher or some general or statesman selected by the nationalists and Junkers or, conceivably, Germany might have been swept by another Red wave. But the destruction of representative government and private capitalism of the old school was complete when Hitler came to power. He had contributed mightily to the final result by his ceaseless labors to create chaos. But when he stepped into the chancellery all the ingredients of national socialist dictatorship were there ready to his hand.

It will not do to dismiss the Hitler episode in Germany as an upsurge of gangsterism or as the victory of wicked men or the work of soulless big business. That there are evil men in the lead in national socialism and that the weapons and methods of the gangster played a part in bringing them to power are evident. But to isolate these disreputable characters and interpret national socialism wholly in terms of them is gravely misleading. Otto D. Tolischus, long New York *Times* correspondent in Germany, writes:

> Hitler was no mere gangster leader, as mistaken propaganda pictures him. Gangsters do not carry great nations with them. There is a better clue to the Hitlerian strength in Germany than the too simple explanation that Germany is ruled by a gang with guns.[8]

Louis P. Lochner, Associated Press representative in Berlin from 1924 to 1941, says: "Hitler is convinced of the divine origin of his mission, convinced that he is commissioned by divine Providence to acquire for Germany the leadership of Europe for a thousand years."[9]

Hermann Rauschning, who was president of the Danzig Senate until he broke with the party and whose books contain the most scathing repudiations of its behavior, says of the old party members that there was an honest belief among them that they were laboring in the cause of their country. Otto Strasser, brother of Gregor, leader of the socialist wing of the movement until murdered by Hitler, says that when Hitler began he was not an unprincipled demagogue but was genuinely convinced of the righteousness of his cause.

We cannot afford in so serious a matter to take our estimates of this movement from the caricaturists who make hideous pictures of the German leaders. History at the cartoon level isolates only the unpleasant features and events and then exaggerates them to gain its effect. There are men of dark and sinister character in national socialism—a burning and scornful nihilist like Goebbels, a predatory sybarite like Goering, ruthless and sadistic beings like Himmler, Ley, and Streicher. But there were great numbers of men who were, if not good men, at least no worse than certain important politicians to be found in this and other countries. The first apostles—Feder, Drexler, Harrer, and Dingfelder—were the common or garden variety of crackpot which flourishes in this country, where we have some precious specimens at this moment in positions of great in-

[8] *They Wanted War*, by Otto D. Tolischus, Reynal & Hitchcock, New York, 1942.
[9] *What About Germany?* by Louis P. Lochner, Dodd, Mead & Co., New York, 1942.

fluence. The stronger leaders who came later—Gregor Strasser and Kock, socialists, Darré, Frick, and Schacht, Thyssen, Hugenberg, were men representing special theories or powerful groups differing no whit from the type found here. There was that mixture of good, bad, and indifferent men, burning zealots of social theories, practical politicians, industrial, labor, farm, and class leaders of all sorts, approving or winking at acts of violence and sinister deals under the influence of the loose morals of revolutionaries. We are not unfamiliar with this phenomenon in America, where the most respectable citizens in the interest of party solidarity and victory do not draw away from collaboration with such persons as Jimmy Hines of New York, Pendergast of Kansas City, Frank Hague of New Jersey, and that precious collection of statesmen who rule Chicago.

We are accustomed now to look at the men who made national socialism possible through the medium of two monstrous acts—the European war and the persecution of the Jews. Here we have been trying to determine the political and economic content of national socialism and the forces that brought it to power. We are not examining the roots of the World War or the guilt of the attack on Czechoslovakia, Poland, and Russia. In a sense these aggressions were the inevitable consequence of the policy of militarism which national socialism adopted for various reasons and which leads always to war, so that had it not culminated in these attacks it would have struck its blows in some other direction. But it was not the war which brought national socialism to power. It was the policy of Hitler when he came to power rather which produced the war. There were large numbers of leaders and great masses of people who supported the national socialists who did not envisage this war as one of their policies or inescapable results. Fritz Thyssen, who had been close to Hitler and who helped finance him, says:

> The German people will experience a great disillusionment with its god, Hitler, who has made war not by reason of his genius, but because he slithered into it. War, in the last analysis, came because nobody knew any longer what to do. Hitler believed he could impress the German people with his attack on Poland and so force them to renewed admiration of their god.[10]

[10] *I Paid Hitler*, by Fritz Thyssen, Farrar & Rinehart, New York, 1941.

Dr. Egon Ranshoven-Wertheimer makes this statement:

As far as I am aware, not a single foreign observer who was resident in Germany between Hitler's rise to power and the outbreak of the second World War has ever suggested that the German nation had any active desire for war. Hitler, who was aware of this mood, assured the nation that he wanted peace and that he was resolved to maintain it. The support of Hitler's foreign policy (up to the seizure of Prague), even outside the ranks of adherents, rested upon a reluctant admiration for a man who seemed to be able to get so much for Germany without involving her in war. He knew how to create the great myth of being the great redeemer who would stop short of war.[11]

Rauschning tells of an able and patriotic Jew genuinely devoted to his fatherland and brokenhearted by his expulsion from Germany. He said to Rauschning with a tinge of bitterness: "Really, but for the persecution of the Jews and the war on Christianity, this Nazi movement might have gained the world."

There is no end of testimony for this same attitude toward both Hitler and Mussolini. The crime of which they are held guilty by so many is not the establishment of national socialism or fascism or their doctrines, but the launching of the European war and the persecution of the Jews in the case of Hitler and the desertion of the Western powers in the case of Mussolini. National socialism or fascism itself, divested of these crimes, did not excite that universal execration either in Britain or America or France which it deserved.

Hitler in his unsuccessful race for the presidency had polled fourteen million votes before he became Premier and got possession of the instruments of state coercion. It was not the Junkers and industrialists who were responsible for Hitler. These gentlemen—the Von Schleichers, Von Papens, Thyssens, and Hugenbergs—came in at the eleventh hour when they saw this seemingly irresistible force and foolishly supposed they could seize and use it. In a country that had been humiliated and ruined by war, devastated by inflation, crushed by an impossible external debt, and finally betrayed by a republican regime which could not save it from another depression, it was the little man, the unemployed, the

[11]*Victory Is Not Enough*, by Egon Ranshoven-Wertheimer, W. W. Norton, New York, 1942.

indigent, the many former socialists who had lost faith in their party, plus the great numbers of young and old army men, who formed the backbone of the movement. To these people, of course, the evangel of national socialism was presented in very different terms from those used by its critics here. In America it was described only in its darkest colors. To Germans it was offered as a flaming crusade for liberation and righteousness. Rauschning has made a vivid description of this terrible gospel which I quote:

It was the seduction of liberation! Young and old men and women were suddenly lifted out of their narrow conceptions, out of the pettiness and limitations of their aspirations. A great world, a world of great appetites and passions, was spread before their eyes. This Nazism made them dizzy with the unprecedented opportunities it revealed to them. Satisfaction of ambition, undreamed-of pleasures and freedoms, the strangest and most intoxicating prospects opened before them. Chances grew up in front of them like magic flowers in enchanted meadows. They had only to wish. The blue flower of romance that had satisfied the wishful dreams of earlier generations through the pleasures of the imagination had become a fruit of paradise—a position, a job, that carried a pension, at an unheard-of salary, a post of command.

In Germany as in Italy, in a country that had been for nearly twenty years, save for the brief interval of a crazy boom, ridden by war and depression, it was the day of the promissory evangelists. The unemployed would be put to work, the poor released from their hovels, the little man made secure in his shop, the aged provided with pensions, while youth would own the world; the mortgage-ridden farm and home owner would escape the bond slavery of interest. "We are the standard-bearers for the great struggle for the liberation of mankind," cried Dr. Ley in Berlin. "The high-spirited effort of the worker to win equality of rights with the middle class was defeated by the materialism and selfishness of the intellectuals who were his false leaders. It has been left to us to assure the worker of his place in our commonweal. No class rule from below, also none from above, but the true classless society of the eternal people, which no longer recognizes parties or special interests, but only duties and rights in relation to the people as a whole." And Hitler said: "We shall banish want. We shall banish fear. The essence of National Socialism is human welfare. There must be cheap Volkswagen for workers to ride in, broad Reich Autobahns for the Volkswagen. National Socialism is the Revolution of the Common Man. Rooted in a fuller life for every German from childhood to old age, National Socialism means a new day of abundance at home and a Better World Order abroad."[12]

Of course they had no key to the secret of abundance save the old, well-rusted keys which all their predecessors had used—spending of borrowed money by the government, plunging it hopelessly into debt, the planned autarchial society in which private business and labor would fall under the iron hand of the bureaucratic state, vast armies to consume the unusable labor of the young, and a huge armaments industry to provide work for the others. It was all a fraud—a fraud these men could perpetrate a bit better than their republican and parliamentarian predecessors because with their dictatorship they could silence the grumbler at taxes and regimentation. It was a fraud, alas, to the soundness of which some of the most eminent and respected persons in Germany had testified in the best manner of their polysyllabic profundity.

Of course the element of fascism that makes it odious to the more sober observers in this country is its hatred of democracy. But there are whole legions of writers and pundits in America ceaselessly vocal in their devotion to democracy who nevertheless are committed to the theory of the autarchial planned state and the principle of the consumptive economy effected by national debt, who like at least a little militarism and do not run away from a little righteous imperialism, but who balk at the war on democracy which the fascists, with more consistency than themselves, carry on. But after all neither Hitler nor Mussolini invented the theory of the circulating elite, the hierarchial government, and the absolute leader which are essential to fascism. A whole series of writers over several generations—German as well as British and French—had given full rein to their scorn of democracy. I do not refer merely to men like Nietzsche and Spengler and Keyserling, the latter of whom

[12]Quoted in *Men in Motion*, by Henry J. Taylor, Doubleday, Doran & Co., Inc., New York, 1943.

when he toured this country was received and entertained with the greatest consideration by many of the same people who now stand aghast at the flowering of the dark philosophy he preached. Nor do I refer merely to men like Houston Stewart Chamberlain, the Britisher, and Gobineau, the Frenchman, and their kind. I have in mind rather some of those men whose names are uttered with the greatest respect and even affection at the present time, some of whom now wear the crown of martyrdom as refugees at the hands of the present German exemplars of the folk and the elite. Walter Rathenau, who was Foreign Minister in the republican cabinet in 1922 and who dreamed of a new guild society or corporative state, said:

> Rule everywhere should be autocratic. Every government save the autocratic is powerless and incompetent. Autocracy and democracy are not antitheses which exclude each other. On the contrary, they can only become operative through union. It is only upon a democratic basis that autocratic rule can and should rest; democracy is only justified when it has an autocratic superstructure.

This is precisely what Hitler has provided Germany with—though it doesn't look so pretty when it crawls out of the doctrinaire's study and takes over in the citadel of power. Thomas Mann, who is now one of our most petted refugees, was one of those Germans who venerated Kultur with a capital K—as he put it himself. He was an admirer of Nietzsche and in a tract in 1918—*Betrachtungen eines Unpolitischen*—he produced for his country what he called an "anti-democratic polemic." In the preface to that work he wrote: "I record my deep conviction that the German people will never be able to love political democracy ... that the much decried authoritarian state is the form of state most suitable to the German people." He saw the last war as the eternal struggle between this German Kultur with a capital K and the democratic intellectualism of the West for which he did not conceal his dislike. The German idea of culture, he said, "must reject and make war upon the democratic-republican form of state as being something alien to land and folk." What else has Hitler done? He has produced the planned society of the liberal Rathenau and has created the elite as the basis of the autocratic state and the guardian of the folk. But when it is produced—since it takes an act of violence to produce it, which implies the services of violent men—Mr. Mann does not like it and is now here in flight from the terrible fruit of his teachings. And he is covered with the sympathies of some of those who like to believe that Hitler invented all this wickedness and that it sprang out of the evil souls of a handful of fellows who are the enemies of that civilization which Mr. Mann himself once said was the mortal enemy of German culture.

Hitler did not invent national socialism any more than Mussolini invented fascism, which is the same thing. None of the numerous scholars credited with the dark fame—neither Othmar Spann of Vienna, nor Werner Sombart, nor Pareto—invented it. The whole content of fascism has been suggested from time to time either piecemeal or in large doses even before Fichte. It represents few of the ideas with which either Hitler or Mussolini started their movements. Hitler liked to think that he was "making a front against the entire public opinion" and that national socialism must never become the bailiff of public opinion, never its slave but its ruler. But actually Hitler was forever feeling around for the pulse of the great controlling minorities. He played with them all, coddled them all, promised all, and lied to everyone. He courted the old nationalist Hugenberg while he pampered the socialist Gregor Strasser. He cajoled his old comrade Feder, the enemy of the "bond slavery of interest," while he made terms with Schacht the banker. He made ambiguous promises to labor while he dealt with Thyssen for funds. He sent Goering to Rome to assure the Vatican that national socialism was rooted in Christianity while Rosenberg attacked religion and preached his weird forms of paganism. He played every card, worked every side of every street until he was able to put his finger on what may be called the great mass pulse and say: here lies power. Until he came into power he sought diligently to locate the great streams of public thought.

These streams or drifts are not necessarily to be found in organized form. A single thought or desire or a single deeply rooted impression or belief or hope or superstition finds a home in the minds of many different men—men of different condition in society. They may have widely hostile opinions about many other things, but it is this dominating belief or dream or aversion that will generally determine their public conduct. The idea draws them together into an inchoate and perhaps even indiscernible sub-mass. Or it may be of such a character involving, let us say, an economic interest, which will lead them to organize. But this is not always so. They become many minds all thinking, wishing, moving in the same direction. They constitute a sort of social psychic stream—millions of minds animated by a common expectation or liking or hatred or appetite. Organized or not, they form a compact minority and, according to the importance or intensity of the conviction, a dynamic one. Such a minority will subordinate other beliefs and even strongly rooted mores to this motivating idea. If the idea is not brought into controversy, is not at issue, these many minds may split into numerous groups. But if the controlling idea is invoked in a public way, these minds move together and sweep along to become a powerful current in the stream of life. There are many such, and they run the gamut of economic, racial, religious, cultural, and every form of social energy. To take an obvious example, we have the aged who, for reasons which have been accumulating over many years, have now become the raw material of such a current and a very powerful one. Every politician recognizes this. All seek to run along with that current. But there are others that are not so readily identifiable and which only the astute politician with a nose for such forces can detect.

Spengler noted this phenomenon. He called these sub-masses cosmic forces and the men able to locate and use them he called cosmic men. The term is not precise but is in accordance with Spengler's tendency to overstate or overdramatize ideas. In another place he calls these minorities mass units, having all the feelings and passions of the individual, inaccessible to reasoning, masses of men who cohere on the basis of like purpose, like knowledge, like appetites, like hatreds. Crowds of this order of unity, he says correctly, are seized by storms of enthusiasm or, as readily, by panic.

The astute politician is forever concerned in locating these currents or forces and running with them. It is in this that he differs from the philosopher and the reformer and, above all, the Utopian.

He is not concerned with altering the course of these streams or in abolishing the force but rather with harnessing its power to his own conquest of power. The reformer or philosopher busies himself with outlining projects that run counter to these streams. He wants to change the topography of the country and create new currents running in different directions. This is why his task is so difficult, indeed in any short period impossible, and why he never or seldom comes to power and why the practical politician, instead, takes power when finally, after generations of teaching and exposition and proving by the reformer, the streams of interest and desire begin to run in a new direction. It is chiefly in this that we find the failure of the socialist movement. It ran against all the existing streams, against every vested opinion and interest. It could win great numbers of intellectual supporters and sympathizers but never enough voters. But it would not be true to say that over the years the socialist movement did not finally set up new and powerful streams of thought and appetite which the practical politicians were forced to see and to use. The politician seeking out and using for his own purposes these great streams of interest and desire is irresistible save against another politician who is more successful in locating these currents and harnessing them.

It is not true, however, that this condition makes the future hopeless save as men surrender helplessly to these powerful psychic currents, however sordid or unreasoning. It is not true, as Spengler says, that these mass units are not susceptible to reason. Many of them are created out of the material or economic needs or interests of the individuals who compose them and this is on a level where, not always but sometimes and, in the end, perhaps always, men can be made to see where their interests lie. The hope of the present crisis lies partly in this. And it lies also in the fact that all streams do not run in the same direction. Nor does it even follow that these forces are necessarily moving in the wrong direction and it is possible to make those who compose them see after a while that the leaders who are shouting with them and whipping them on are not necessarily serving their ends. It is possible for men of sound sense, as well as unscrupulous politicians and brainless Utopians, to run with these streams. And intervals of sober re-examination by the people themselves do appear, in which the forces of reason may shape the direction of things.

Hitler and Mussolini were men who perceived these facts—Mussolini consciously, Hitler intuitively. In Germany and Italy scores of movements resembling theirs were started with dynamic and ruthless leaders. But generally they were movements with hard-and-fast programs built on inflexible doctrines, led by men who did not know how to break out of the prison of doctrine and submit their movements to the molding process of popular desire.

The problem of the leader of this type changes when he comes to power. It is one thing to promise employment, security, and bountiful crops, full-blast production, free from the difficulties of competition. These are the things the masses desire. They do not necessarily desire so ardently the regulations by which these blessed yearnings are to be fulfilled. Very soon the leader in power has critics. Then come taxes, the discomforts of regulation, the irritations and even sufferings at the hands of the compliance machinery. It is when the leader takes power that he begins to run against great and powerful currents of opinion. He must enforce compliance with his policies and his decrees. He must, of necessity, be a dictator.

No free society can extort from its people compliance with all the abrasive rules and ravaging taxes, the endless intrusions into their business affairs that grow and multiply, one rule calling for another to correct its repercussions in unexpected quarters, one intrusion the forerunner of countless others. Free men will not endure it. They will, if they retain their freedom, cast it off by driving the leader out and putting another in his place who will now promise them softer and more amiable conditions of life. Hence the leader who rides to power upon the masses' hunger for jobs, for security from the cradle to the grave, for the regulation of business against the evils of overproduction, will quickly enough discover, even if his tastes do not already run in that direction, that he must make an end of criticism, that he must suppress opposition, that he must enforce compliance by the application of force and through a comprehensive attack of positive propaganda. Hence he assumes dictatorial power. He liquidates the critics. He introduces all the time-worn instrumentalities of coercion. But now he has in his hands instruments of positive propaganda such as the world has never known—the radio, the moving-picture projector, and the school. After all, the school, which commands the attendance of all youth at the public expense, is something comparatively new. And there the dictator can take possession of the minds of the oncoming generation.

This is the explanation of Hitler's war not so much upon religion as upon the churches, particularly the Catholic Church. He will endure no competition in the business of indoctrinating the minds of the youth. And this also is the explanation of the cult of adventure and romanticism, the cult of Greatness. For since the dictator, having promised the good life and universal freedom from want and the new kind of freedom implied in this and being forced to exact from his people the most intensive and endless sacrifices, has to hold up before their eyes, particularly the eyes of youth, great super-objectives, glamorous programs of national conquests—conquests of wealth or power or safety—that will distract the mind from the irritations of his system and provide an aim, some grand purpose, some heroic pursuit adequate to the sacrifices demanded. Thus the program which was to give jobs to the unemployed, to put food into the mouths of the poor, provide education and nourishment for all the young, and a niche somewhere in security from want for the old becomes after a while a program in which all, young and old, rich and poor, capitalist and worker, are pouring out their energies and their very lives to achieve the Time for Greatness.

X · Good Fascists and Bad Fascists

WE ARE NOW PREPARED to examine some of the forces that are at work here, some of the streams of thought and desires that run in our own society, and to appraise them in the light of what we have seen in Italy and Germany. Before we do this, however, it is well to be clear upon the central point of the foregoing chapter and to be warned about another danger that stands before us.

First let us restate our definition of fascism. It is, put briefly, a system of social organization in which the political state is a dictatorship supported by a political elite and in which the economic society is an autarchial capitalism, enclosed and planned, in which the government assumes responsibility for creating adequate purchasing power through the instrumentality of national debt and in which militarism is adopted as a great economic project for creating work as well as a great romantic project in the service of the imperialist state.

Broken down, it includes these devices:

1. A government whose powers are unrestrained.

2. A leader who is a dictator, absolute in power but responsible to the party which is a preferred elite.

3. An economic system in which production and distribution are carried on by private owners but in accordance with plans made by the state directly or under its immediate supervision.

4. These plans involve control of all the instruments of production and distribution through great government bureaus which have the power to make regulations or directives with the force of law.

5. They involve also the comprehensive integration of government and private finances, under which investment is directed and regimented by the government, so that while ownership is private and production is carried on by private owners there is a type of socialization of investment, of the financial aspects of production. By this means the state, which by law and by regulation can exercise a powerful control over industry, can enormously expand and complete that control by assuming the role of banker and partner.

6. They involve also the device of creating streams of purchasing power by federal government borrowing and spending as a permanent institution.

7. As a necessary consequence of all this, militarism becomes an inevitable part of the system since it provides the easiest means of draining great numbers annually from the labor market and of creating a tremendous industry for the production of arms for de-

fense, which industry is supported wholly by government borrowing and spending.

8. Imperialism becomes an essential element of such a system where that is possible—particularly in the strong states, since the whole fascist system, despite its promises of abundance, necessitates great financial and personal sacrifices, which people cannot be induced to make in the interest of the ordinary objectives of civil life and which they will submit to only when they are presented with some national crusade or adventure on the heroic model touching deeply the springs of chauvinistic pride, interest, and feeling.

Where these elements are found, there is fascism, by whatever name the system is called. And it now becomes our task to look very briefly into our own society and to see to what extent the seeds of this system are present here and to what degree they are being cultivated and by whom.

In the light of all this we can see how far afield we can be led by those who seek for the roots of fascism by snooping around among those futile crackpot or deliberately subversive groups which flourish feebly under the leadership of various small-bore Führers. Some of these groups are outright anti-American like the Bundists. Such an organization had nothing to do and can have nothing to do with introducing a new system of society into America. Its object was to assist Hitler in so far as it could in his war aims here. It was an enemy organization. And an incredibly foolish one. Then there are various groups that are just anti-communist or anti-communist and anti-Semitic, confusing two things as one, like the Christian Fronters, numbering a few hundred nonentities. There are others that are little different from those old exclusion movements—the Know Nothings, the A.P.A., the Klan—directing their fire against some racial or religious group. They are thoroughly evil things. But they have little and in most cases nothing to do with the introduction of fascism in America. Most of them have no more notion of the content of fascism than the gentlemen who write books about them. It is assumed that because the Nazi movement in Germany and the fascist movement in Italy began with small groups of nobodies led by unimportant people fascism will come in the same way here. It is, of course, possible that the great American fascism may rise thus. We have but to see the flowering of the Ham and Eggs crusade in California and the Townsend movement everywhere to realize the possibilities of a powerful movement organized by unimportant leaders. But when fascism comes it will not be in the form of an anti-American movement or pro-Hitler bund, practicing disloyalty. Nor will it come in the form of a crusade against war. It will appear rather in the luminous robes of flaming patriotism; it will take some genuinely indigenous shape and color, and it will spread only because its leaders, who are not yet visible, will know how to locate the great springs of public opinion and desire and the streams of thought that flow from them and will know how to attract to their banners leaders who can command the support of the controlling minorities in American public life. The danger lies not so much in the would-be Führers who may arise, but in the presence in our midst of certain deeply running currents of hope and appetite and opinion. The war upon fascism must be begun there.

There is one other phenomenon that has appeared which seems to contain some danger of infection. The war has brought us allies. One of them is Russia. And already we have seen how our friendly collaboration in the war enterprise has led to a good deal of nonsense about the Russian government. We are willing to believe that it is no longer anti-religious. There is a notable mitigation of the severity with which we appraised communism and the tolerance with which we have forgiven the purges and brutalities of the Soviet regime. But we also have fascist allies. And not only do we look with indulgence upon their policies because they are our allies but also because instead of being aggressors they are victims of bigger and more powerful fascists. Thus we had a fascist regime in Austria under Dollfuss and later under Schuschnigg. The dictator Dollfuss was pursued by the dictator Hitler but he was the close friend and collaborator of the dictator Mussolini. He had his own record of suppressions, notably that dreadful cannonading of the workers' homes in Vienna. But all this is forgiven and overlooked when Hitler's assassins murder him. Similarly we overlook the fascist structure of Schuschnigg because Schuschnigg was a profoundly religious man and because he, too, was kidnaped and spirited away by the irreligious Hitler. But Austria was a fascist country. There is no doubt about the fact that Schuschnigg was an honest man, a true patriot prepared to sacrifice himself for Austria, and that he was, in addition, a man of deep and genuine religious nature. All of which warns us once again that we must not make the mistake of supposing that the several ingredients of fascism, taken separately, are evil, and that only evil men espouse this new order.

The same can be said for Portugal where the dictator, Salazar, is a man utterly without the offensive personal characteristics of either Mussolini or Hitler; no ranting, posturing, saber-rattling, no pageantry. On the contrary, he is an aesthete, living a life of frugality, a devout Catholic, his office wall adorned with but a single ornament, the crucifix of Christ, at whose feet he is a humble worshiper. The fascist regime of Portugal is a curiosity among the fascist orders of Europe. Its admirers, of which there are great numbers in this country and Europe, like to call it a "Christian Corporativism." This it is, modeled on the old medieval guild form of government so much admired and earnestly urged upon Britain and America by some of her most devout socialist and other leaders, such as Hobson and Cole. The case of Portugal is, however, a very special one, molded by peculiar conditions and saved now by the war and Portugal's alliance with England.

Greece conformed more nearly to the standard pattern of fascist countries, yet because Greece was so cruelly assaulted by Mussolini and made so glorious a defense and because she is now our ally, we do not think of her as essentially wicked because she is fascist. Metaxas, warrior and admirer of the German military system, mounted his cannon in the streets of Athens, liquidated the parliament and the constitution, banished his opponents, branded all opposition as communist, and set himself up as dictator. He put an end to freedom of the press, told editors they "must follow him like soldiers in battle, never consulting, criticizing, or exchanging opinions with him." He instituted a ruthless regimentation of ideas in the schools and told university professors: "I cannot allow any one of you to have ideas different from those of the state." He went into power without any program. He made vague promises of the good life, told the Greeks he was "the first peasant and the first artisan" of Greece, went through all the standard welfare measures, minimum wages, eight-hour laws, pensions, free medical services, etc., accompanied by all the well-known fascist techniques of regimentation. And of course he spent money that he borrowed and made the army the greatest project of all, telling the people that "their turn will come someday."

Many of these dictators had their purges—Kemal Pasha, for instance, to whom we now refer with admiration as "that great man," yet who, when his old colleagues seemed to be getting a little out of hand, had them strung up by the dozens and gave a great ball the night they were being bumped off. What I am driving at is that we are in a way of doing for fascism what we began to do for the trusts in the early 1900s. We began to talk about "bad trusts" and "good trusts." Now we are coming around to recognizing "bad fascism" and "good fascism." A bad fascism is a fascist regime which is against us in the war. A good fascist regime is one that is on our side. Or to repeat what I have already said, a bad fascist regime is one that makes war upon its neighbors and persecutes the Jews; a good fascist regime is one that is jumped on by some stronger fascism and does not alter the long-standing attitude of the country toward either Jews or Christians. And from this beginning there are plenty of Americans who have descanted at length upon the magnificent achievements of Mussolini and the better side of the German regime. And so we flirt a little with the idea that perhaps fascism might be set up without these degrading features, that even if there is to be totalitarian government it is to be just a teeny-weeny bit totalitarian and only a teeny bit militarist and imperialist only on the side of God and democracy.

PART THREE

THE GOOD FASCISM: AMERICA

I · Permanent Crisis in America

ON THE night of October 22, 1929, one of America's most widely known economists addressed a great banquet of credit men. Not only were Wall Street prices not too high, he told his delighted hearers, but we were really only on the threshold of the greatest boom in the nation's history. The prophecy evoked a burst of applause. Next morning, a few minutes after the great bell announced the opening of trading on the Stock Exchange, the storm broke. The greatest economic depression in our history was formally ushered in—though it had been in progress for some time. From this point on, as the country slowly roused itself to a consciousness of the far-spreading crisis, leaders in politics and business repeated with invincible optimism that it was all just a wholesome corrective. After several years a waggish commentator published a little volume called *Oh, Yeah!* It was a sardonic recording of the persistent and unconquerable stream of promises of quickly returning health. There you will find recorded the statements of statesmen, financiers, university professors, leading economists, and editors assuring the people that it was all a blessing in disguise, a corrective phenomenon, that the broad highway to renewed prosperity lay just ahead. All of which proved quite conclusively that these men did not know what they were talking about because they had no understanding of the economic system under which they lived.[1]

Then came the collapse of 1933 on the grand scale—and a resumption of the bright prophecies of happy days. From 1933 to

---

[1] *Oh, Yeah!* compiled by Edmund Angly, Viking Press, New York, 1931.

1937 we beheld the painful ascent up the finicula of government spending and debt. Then, as 1937 ended, came another wave of optimism with predictions of the emergence of the nation into the full sunrise of the greatest boom in our history—this at the very moment when the feeble energy engendered by the emergency alphabetical power units was already spent and we were actually on our way down again into what was called the "recession."

I recall this to illustrate the arresting phenomenon that the idea which refuses most stubbornly to take root in the American mind is the realization of the fact that the economic system is in grave trouble. We are not in just one of those cyclical depressions that have always afflicted us. We are now arrived in that condition that for a good many years characterized the economies of European societies before World War I.

I do not mean that the system is beyond repair and that we must blunder along helplessly until we are sunk in the degrading condition of communism or fascism. What I have in mind to say is that after long years of growth and vigor our system seems to have fallen into a condition of enervation. One thing at least we are aware of—that we have been in a depression for fourteen years. Yet we are not wholly weaned from the vain assumption that, while booms and crises follow each other up and down the business cycle, on the whole our normal condition is one of good times, interrupted at intervals by occasional crises.

The issues before us are too grave for mere assumptions. Let us look, therefore, swiftly at the last fifty years in America. I base the statements which follow on the well-known chart of business activity prepared by General Leonard Ayres, economist of the Cleveland Trust Company. Some objections can be made to this chart. It cannot presume to measure up to scientific accuracy. The same can be said, however, of almost all such charts. But while they may differ, the general results, so far as the point I have in mind is concerned, will correspond. This chart reveals a fluctuating line which represents the rise and fall of business activity. A straight line running through it represents General Ayres's conception of normal activity. When the fluctuating index line rises above the straight line, the country is moving into prosperity. When it sinks below the straight line, the country is falling into depression. If we study this chart in the fifty years from 1892 to 1941 we see that there were twenty-four years below and twenty-four years above normal and two at the normal line. The years of prosperity and depression were equally divided, which certainly does not support the assumption that prosperity was our normal state.

The figures given above represent the duration of booms and depressions in time. Now let us compare them in volume. The data indicate that in bulk the depressions were 15 per cent greater than the booms.

Now let us compare the first 25 years with the second. In the first 25 years the proportion of prosperity to depression was 13.6 years of boom to 10 of depression. In the second 25 years the proportion is reversed—13.5 years of depression to 11.6 of boom. If we compare the volume of boom and crisis in these two periods the picture is far darker. In the first 25 years the proportion of boom to depression was 1.1 to 1. In the second 25 years it is 1 of boom to 3 of depression. Indeed, the depression which began in 1929 is the longest in the history of the country.

I do not lengthen out this description as food for the reader's pessimism. I do it to compel him to look with complete candor on the gravity of the problem which stands before him. If we will examine this chart a little more closely we will become aware of a very sobering fact. In the last twenty-five year period we had two booms. One lasted from 1915 to the middle of 1920. It was a thoroughly unhealthy boom produced altogether by the war inflation. The second was from 1923 to 1929. This was the so-called New Era. Few now make any defense of that. It was generated by a wild, speculative activity that ended in catastrophe. Two booms in twenty-five years and both based on unhealthy phenomena! Is it not time, therefore, that we bring ourselves to complete frankness and realism in the examination of our position? We are now in a crisis which is in no way comparable to those depressions that succeeded booms in a kind of rhythmic fashion. The present crisis is not one of those corrective emergencies in which the infectious elements are washed out by the fever. We are in a condition in which the motor elements in our economic system are definitely enervated.

The sources of power and energy are choked. For fourteen years we have been struggling blindly, not knowing what to do, hoping that in some mysterious way some stroke of luck would boost us out of it. Instead, we have become entangled in a war that will push us deeper in, and we must face again the stark realities of a returning economic crisis. We are now at that point in development, though of course on a different level, reached by Germany and Italy before the last war.

We are, of course, not so deeply mired as these European countries. Our natural endowment is great; theirs was not. Our resources are immense; theirs are not. A combination of circumstances for which we are indebted to a kindly good fortune has set us down in a frame far more hospitable to the ways of democracy. We have enjoyed immense growth in the last fifty years in health, education, economic well-being. Thus while the nation moved fitfully up and down the curves of the business cycle there was a steady advance in the general welfare of the people. And a larger number of people were enjoying these advances.

The trouble lies in this—that while we enjoyed this growth, there was at all times a very large number of people who did not share in it or who did not get as large a share as they believed just, and the whole society was subject with increasing frequency and virulence to the disastrous interruption of its well-being by these growing crises—persisting poverty among so many and deepening crises for all. Now the present crisis is the first in our history of the same general character as European crises.

It is not necessary to review here the incidents of this period. Readers will recall that it evoked a whole train of messiahs with evangels of plenty—Milo Reno and his Farm Holiday, Dr. Townsend and his pensions, Huey Long with his Share-the-Wealth movement, Upton Sinclair and his Epic plan, Major Douglas and social credit, Howard Scott and technocracy, Dr. Warren and his gold-purchase plan, General Johnson and his NRA, Henry Wallace and his plowing under of pigs and grain and, of course, the eternal inflationists. Almost at the same time that republican Germany was drinking the bitter beer of its exploded postwar boom, victorious America was doing the same thing and with much the same episodes and incidental music—rising unemployment, fires going out in factory furnaces, stores closing and banks busting, investment paralyzed, and the masses—the modern masses, conditioned to the better life and dreams of still greater abundance—in revolt against Fate and searching for a savior.

In the end the country did what it always does—threw out the party under whose regime the depression rose and installed the opposition party in power. No comparison, of course, can be made between the Democratic party here and the Fascist and Nazi parties in Italy and Germany. There are resemblances, however, which are striking. They are, indeed, more than striking—they are of the first importance. It will be recalled that the fascists when launching their movement proclaimed a platform of eleven points and that the national socialists did the same, expanding theirs to twenty-five points. It will be remembered, however, that, when they came into power, the most important of these points were dropped and a wholly new and different program inaugurated. In the United States, the Democratic party adopted a platform which conformed at all points with the views of the liberal elements of that party. That platform was brief, crisp, cocksure. Here are its main points:

1. An immediate and drastic reduction of government expenditures by abolishing useless commissions and offices.
2. Maintenance of national credit by a budget annually balanced.
3. A sound currency to be maintained at all hazards and an international economic conference to restore trade.
4. Advance planning of public works and financial help to states for same.
5. Unemployment and old-age pensions *under state laws*.
6. Better financing of farm mortgages and aid to farm co-operatives.
7. Adequate army, but based on facts so that in time of peace the nation may not be burdened with a bill approaching a billion a year.
8. Strict and impartial enforcement of the anti-trust laws.
9. No cancellation of foreign debts, firm foreign policy looking toward peace, etc.
10. Statehood for Puerto Rico and independence for the Philippines.
11. Regulation of investment banking, holding companies, utility companies, and exchanges.
12. More rigid supervision of national banks and other banking reforms.

13. Justice to disabled war veterans.
14. Simplification of legal procedure.
15. Continuous publicity of political contributions.
16. Repeal of the Eighteenth Amendment.

The platform denounced the extravagances of the Hoover Farm Board and the "unsound policy of restricting production" and the resistance of government bureaus to curtailment of expenditures. There were a few other unimportant features.

When the victorious Democrats came into power, the administration did precisely what Mussolini and Hitler did—it threw practically all its important "points" into the wastebasket and adopted a wholly different policy. For this it was roundly criticized by its opponents. But what happened in fact is a phenomenon of far deeper significance than this seeming betrayal by the Democrats. In fact, a wholly different party took power. It called itself the New Deal party. It seized possession of the apparatus of the old Democratic party, substituted an entirely different program utterly hostile to the traditional philosophy of the Democrats and, through certain devices which we shall examine, has continued to operate the political apparatus of the Democratic party to remain in power. It is a singular fact, worthy the attention of future historians, that there is in the Democratic party itself little serious adhesion to the doctrines of the New Deal party. Students of government will have to take note of the fact that under certain circumstances a handful of men can actually manage and navigate a whole political party machine in a direction thoroughly opposite to the well-understood beliefs of its leaders.

Here, however, we perceive nothing more nor less than the familiar phenomenon of government, while talking in brave terms and tones of its grandiose plans, actually dropping into the direction and motion of the prevailing streams of thought running deeply in the great organized and unorganized minorities of the people. The administration proceeded to do, not what it proclaimed as its program in its platform, but those things which the people or rather the influential and controlling minorities wished, however confused they may have been about those wishes. It did precisely what the old democratic regimes of Depretis, Crispi, and Giolitti did in Italy and what Mussolini did later; what the republican regime of Germany did after the war, and what Hitler, after denouncing his predecessors, did later. It denounced the extravagance of the more or less conservative Hoover administration, promised to balance the budget, cut expenditures, reduce military expenditures, etc., and then embarked upon the most amazing program of unrestrained outlays carried on with unbalanced budgets that the world has ever seen.

II · The Good Deficits

THE PRESENCE of the problem of an economic system definitely out of repair did not impress itself on the consciousness of the American public until well after Mr. Roosevelt's administration had had its try at the situation for one term. After that the solemn truth settled only slowly upon our minds. By 1940 there were few who did not feel that there was something definitely out of joint.

However, as in Italy and Germany, our first attack upon our economic disorder, as it appeared in 1930, took the form of government spending and welfare. This was something quite new with us. Before 1914 public spending of borrowed money was a negligible feature of our economy. The expansion that astonished the world in America up to that time had been the product of private enterprise financed by private credit. In 1912, on the eve of World War I, after a century and a half of growth, the debts of our public bodies were as follows:

National	$1,028,564,000
States	345,942,000
Counties	371,528,000
Incorporated places	3,104,426,000
	$4,850,460,000[1]

Most of the national debt was a remnant of the Civil War. The bulk of these debts was municipal, incurred for building city

[1] *Statistical Abstract of the U.S.*, 1929, p. 220.

utilities such as streets, water works, schools, hospitals, and such.

The war of 1917 marked the beginning of a new era of public spending and borrowing. With the coming of war we had three years of enormous deficits as follows:

$$
\begin{aligned}
1917 &\ldots\ldots\ \$\ \ \ \ 853,357,000 \\
1918 &\ldots\ldots\ \ \ \ \ 9,033,254,000 \\
1919 &\ldots\ldots\ \ \ 13,370,638,000^2
\end{aligned}
$$

The history of the war measured in national debt may be stated as follows:

$$
\begin{aligned}
1914 &\ldots\ldots\ \$\ \ 1,188,235,000 \\
1919 &\ldots\ldots\ \ \ 25,482,000,000
\end{aligned}
$$

State and local debts had risen from \$3,821,896,000 in 1912 to \$8,689,740,000 in 1922.[3]

This was due almost wholly to war. After that, however, in the period from 1922 to the depression of 1929, the federal government, instead of borrowing, annually reduced its debt. But the state and local authorities became heavy borrowers. However, no small part of the local debts was contracted for revenue-producing improvement and practically all of this debt was created with provisions for amortization. None of it was arranged as part of any scheme to produce national income, though it had that effect. It arose chiefly out of the demand of local communities for public utilities such as schools, education, health facilities, streets, and from the great demand for roads to make way for the stream of motorcars that poured from our factories. Whatever the purpose, however, the policy did accustom the public mind to public borrowing as a fixed policy of government.

The theory of public spending as an instrument of government to regulate the economic system first appeared in the early part of 1922. The theory was advanced by the Unemployment Conference of that year. Briefly stated, it held that during periods of prosperity, when private industry is supplying all the requirements of national income, the federal and local governments should go slowly on

[2] *Statistical Abstract of the U.S.*, 1941, p. 178.
[3] *Ibid.*, pps. 230, 251.

public-works expenditures. They should accumulate a reserve of necessary public-works plans to be put into execution when business activity shows signs of tapering off. However, it was not contemplated that the governments should go into debt for these purposes but should carry them out in accordance with the principles of traditional sound finance. This theory amounted merely to a plan to carry on public building and spending operations in periods of diminished private business activity rather than in time of prosperity.

When the depression appeared in 1929, therefore, Mr. Hoover, on December 4, 1929, sent a message to Congress proposing additional appropriations for public works. He asked an increase of $500,000,000 for public buildings, $75,000,000 for public roads, $150,000,000 for rivers and harbors, and $60,000,000 to dam the Colorado River.[4] He believed this could be done within the budget. Actually the Hoover administration provided $256,000,000 in 1929 and $569,970,000 in 1930 for agriculture, public works, and farm loans while at the same time reducing the public debt by $746,000,000.[5] The central theme of these proposals was to use public spending merely as a stabilizer. There was a pretty general agreement with the theory. But as the depression advanced there was a persisting failure of tax funds so that by 1931 there was a deficit of $901,959,000 which increased the next year to nearly three billion dollars.[6] A part of this deficit resulted from the public-works expenditures but most of it was caused by a failure of tax revenues. Hoover, of course, never planned an unbalanced budget. However, so imbedded in the public consciousness was the aversion to national public debt that the Democrats in 1932 roundly denounced the Hoover administration for its extravagances and its failure to balance the budget. The platform of June 1932 contained the following as its very first plank:

We advocate:

1. An immediate and drastic reduction of governmental expenditures by abolishing useless commissions and offices, consolidating departments and

[4]*The Hoover Administration*, by Myers and Newton, Chas. Scribner, New York, 1936.
[5]*Ibid*. Also *Statistical Abstract of the U.S.*, 1941, p. 230.
[6]*Statistical Abstract of the U.S.*, 1941, p. 176.

bureaus and eliminating extravagance, to accomplish a saving of not less than 25 per cent in the cost of the Federal Government; and we call upon the Democratic party in the States to make a zealous effort to achieve a proportionate result.

2. Maintenance of national credit by a *federal budget annually balanced* on the basis of accurate executive estimates within revenues, raised by a system of taxation levied on the principle of ability to pay.

Mr. Roosevelt, the Democratic candidate, stood strongly behind these declarations. He not only opposed heavy public spending but public borrowing as well. He advised that a "government, like any family, can for a year spend a little more than it earns, but you and I know that a continuation of that means the poorhouse." He warned that "high-sounding phrases cannot sugar-coat the pill" and begged the nation "to have the courage to stop borrowing and meet the continuing deficits." Public works "do not relieve the distress" and are only "a stopgap." And having asked "very simply that the task of reducing annual operating expenses" be assigned to him, he said he regarded it as a positive duty "to raise by taxes whatever sum is necessary to keep them (the unemployed) from starvation."[7]

The party itself plastered the nation with huge posters warning that the Republican party had brought it to the verge of bankruptcy and calling on the voters to "throw the spendthrifts out and put responsible government in." The candidate and the party were quite sincere in these declarations and promises. They were in accordance with the most orthodox American convictions. But practical political leaders, in search of power, besieged by resolute minorities with uncompromising demands for results and bombarded by cocksure merchants of easy salvation, find themselves forced along courses of action that do not square with their public proclamations of principle. Just as Mussolini and Hitler denounced their predecessors for borrowing and spending and then yielded to the imperious political necessity of doing the thing they denounced, so the New Deal, once in power, confronted with a disintegrating economic system and with no understanding of the phenomenon

[7] *Public Papers and Addresses of Franklin D. Roosevelt, 1928–36*, Random House, New York, 1938.

175

that was in eruption before its eyes, turned to the very thing it denounced in Hoover. But there was a difference. Hoover's deficits were the result of failure of revenue and were unplanned. Mr. Roosevelt's *first deficit was a deliberately planned deficit.* Within a few months of his inauguration he approved a proposal for a $3,300,000,000 public-works expenditure with borrowed funds in the NRA Act of May 1933. He then turned in the following deficits: $3,255,000,000 in 1933–34; $3,782,000,000 in 1934–35; $4,782,000,000 in 1935–36; and $4,952,000,000 in 1936–37.

Nevertheless, despite this record, the administration persisted in its theory that budgets should be balanced. Its platform in 1936 said:

> We are determined to reduce the expenses of the government. . . . Our retrenchment, tax, and recovery program thus reflect our firm determination to achieve a balanced budget and the reduction of the national debt at the earliest possible moment.

In January 1937 the President triumphantly presented what looked like a balanced budget. He said:

> We shall soon be reaping the full benefits of those programs and shall have at the same time a balanced budget that will also include provisions for the reduction of the public debt. . . . Although we must continue to spend substantial sums to provide work for those whom industry has not yet absorbed, *the 1938 budget is in balance.*

The whole tone of this message was pitched on the growing importance of a balanced budget. Nevertheless, notwithstanding this amazing statement, the budget of that year was not in balance. It showed a deficit of $1,449,626,000. Immediately there was a tremendous drop in the rate of business activity. We began to have what was called a recession, while the President continued to talk about "the extreme importance of achieving a balance of actual income and outgo." I recall all this now in order to make clear that up to this time no party in this country seriously approved the practice of borrowing as a definite policy. I think it illustrates also with complete finality that the men who were guiding national policy knew nothing about the workings of our economic system. The

President made it clear that he was spending and borrowing purely as an emergency device. As late as April 1937 he said:

> While I recognize many opportunities to improve social and economic conditions through federal action, I am convinced that the success of our whole program and the permanent security of our people demand that we adjust all expenditures within the limits of my budget estimate.

He then delivered himself of the following extraordinary opinion:

> It is a matter of common knowledge that the principal danger to modern civilization lies in those nations which largely because of an armament race are headed directly toward bankruptcy. In proportion to national budgets the United States is spending a far smaller proportion of government income for armaments than the nations to which I refer. It behooves us, therefore, to continue our efforts to make both ends of our economy meet.

Here was a clear recognition of the fact that in Europe for many decades governments had been doing what our government was then doing, spending great sums of money and going into debt for it, but doing it on armaments instead of on peacetime activities as Mr. Roosevelt was doing. But nations which borrow money and pile on vast national debts can go into bankruptcy whether the debts be for armaments or roads, parks and public buildings. European nations were far more deeply stricken in crisis and had been for years. The armaments had become an *economic* necessity to them. They were not to us. Our government was delivering lectures on sound fiscal policy, deploring the deficits, yet planning new and more extravagant means of spending money, soothing the Haves with promises of balanced budgets and lower taxes, and stimulating the Have-nots with promises of security and abundance. The government was doing, in fact, what Depretis was doing in Italy between 1876 and 1887. Let the reader turn back to the first part of this volume for a description of that record:

> He promised every sort of reform without regard to the contradictions among his promises. He promised to reduce taxation and increase public works. He promised greater social security and greater prosperity. When he came to power he had no program and no settled notion how he would redeem these pledges. His party was joined by recruits from every school of

political thought. He found at his side the representatives of every kind of discontent and every organ of national salvation. The oppressed tenants along with the overworked and underpaid craftsmen of the towns crowded around him beside the most reactionary landowners and employers to demand the honoring of the many contradictory promissory notes he had issued on his way to office.

Depretis then, for lack of any other weapon, proceeded to do what he had denounced his conservative predecessors for doing—to spend borrowed money on an ever-larger scale. When he did *"every district wanted something in the way of money grants for schools and post offices or roads or agricultural benefits. These districts soon learned that the way to get a share of the public funds was to elect men who voted for Depretis. Men who aspired to office had to assure their constituencies that they could get grants for these constituencies from the Premier."* I quote again what the Encylopaedia Britannica said of this episode:

In their anxiety to remain in office, Depretis and the Finance Minister, Magliani, never hesitated to mortgage the financial future of the country. No concession could be denied to deputies, whose support was indispensable to the life of the cabinet, nor under such conditions was it possible to place any effective check upon administrative abuses in which politicians or their electors were interested.

Miss Margot Hentz, writing of the same episode, said:

Pressure was brought to bear through the organs of local administration who were given to understand that "favorable" districts might expect new schools, public works, roads, canals, post and telegraph offices, etc.; while the "unfavorable" might find even existing institutions suppressed.

Depretis' policy was pursued on a larger scale by his successors, including Giolitti whose administration brought Italy to the eve of World War I and the threshold of bankruptcy. Those who have read the chapter in this volume on Germany will not fail to see the resemblance first on a small scale to the performances of the old imperial government and then on a larger scale to the policies of the republican government that preceded Hitler.

All this, however old, was a new chapter in American policy.

When, therefore, these vast expenditures were made, the noblest and most heroic explanations were offered. Having denounced timid deficits, the administration embarked upon a program of huge deficits, but it did it in characteristic American fashion, with proclamations of righteousness as if America had suddenly discovered something new. In fact, it was called a *New Deal*. Actually, it was America dropping back into the old European procession.

The recession of 1937-38 marked a turning point of the greatest importance in American public policy. Up to this point spending had been done on the pump-priming theory. That is, public funds, flowing out into business, were expected to produce a resumption of business activity. But business utterly failed to respond to this treatment. Apparently the pump itself was seriously out of order. From this point on we hear no more about balanced budgets. We find the administration committed to the same policy that marked the fiscal programs of republican Germany. It turned to the device of public spending and borrowing as a continuing and permanent means of creating national income.

There was a renewal of depression, and the President himself had to admit in his 1939 message that his expectations of recovery when he reduced expenditures were overoptimistic. It had become plain to the political elements in the government that there was something wrong, that the idea of public works during an emergency, used even on an enormous scale, had not produced recovery and was merely a stopgap. The situation of the administration was critical in the highest degree. Almost all its plans had been discarded. The AAA was declared unconstitutional; the NRA was scrapped by the Supreme Court just as it was falling into utter chaos; the devaluation of the dollar and the idea of a managed currency, as well as the gold-buying plan, had proved ineffective; social security was an aid to the unfortunate but did nothing to make the economic system work. Apparently nothing was holding back a tidal wave of deeper depression save the spending and borrowing program which everyone had either denounced or apologized for. The public debt had risen as total depression deficits amounted to 19 billions. What possible avenue of escape opened for the government in the presence of rising unemployment, rising taxes at last, farmers, workers, the aged, investors all clamoring for swift and effective aid and the land filling up again with messiahs and their easy evangels?

About this time a group of young men published a little book—*An Economic Program for American Democracy* (Vanguard, 1938). It got little enough attention at the time. Its authors styled themselves Seven Harvard and Tufts Economists. It proclaimed boldly that the capitalist system as we have known it was done and that, instead of balancing budgets, the government should adopt the unbalanced budget as a permanent institution; that the only salvation of the nation was in a greater and ever-expanding program of national expenditures met with revenues raised by borrowing.

Completely unknown at the time, these men were actually announcing in this small book the theories that had been worked over by John Maynard Keynes in England and Dr. Alvin H. Hansen in this country. But they were by no means the inventors of them. They had already had a vogue in Germany under the republic, which indeed had been influenced by them in its fiscal policies.

Their theory, very briefly stated, is as follows:

The present capitalist system is no longer capable of functioning effectively. The reasons for this are as follows:

The dynamic element in the capitalist system is investment. Since millions of people save billions of dollars annually, these billions must be brought back into the stream of spending. This can be done only through investment. When private investment is either curtailed or halted, these savings remain sterilized or inert and the capitalist system goes into a depression. Nothing can produce a normal revival of the capitalist system save a revival of investment.

Private investment cannot be any longer revived on a scale sufficient to absorb the savings of the people. Hence recovery through private investment is hopeless.

Private investment cannot be revived because there are no longer open to savers adequate opportunities for investment.

Opportunities for investment are not open any longer for three chief reasons: (1) because the frontier is gone, with its opportunities for territorial expansion and the discovery of new resources; (2) because population increase has slowed down to a snail's pace; (3) because technological development has matured. That is to say, there is no longer in sight any such great inventions as the railroads, the automobile, etc., which will change all the arrangements of our social life and call for huge money expenditures.

The present capitalist system is therefore incapable of recovering its energy. This is not a mere emergency condition but is a characteristic of the system which will continue indefinitely.

For this reason we must adopt a new type of economic organization. This new type is called the Dual System or the Dual Consumptive System. Under this system the government will become the borrower of those savings funds which private business will not take. It must then spend these funds putting them again into circulation. What we must look forward to, therefore, is a "long-range program of government projects financed by borrowed funds."

Of course such a program means borrowing perpetually by the government. It means that each year the government debt will increase. When the war ends we will owe not less than $300,000,000,000. Thoughtful men are gravely disturbed as to what course we shall pursue to mitigate the immense burden of this debt. These gentlemen say our course is clear—borrow more. Borrow endlessly. Never stop borrowing.

Of course one asks: What will be the end? How will we ever pay the debt? They reply: It is not necessary to pay public debts. As long as the bondholder gets his interest he is satisfied, and when he wants the principal he can sell his bond, which is all he asks. But how long will this ability to sell his bond last with a government that never stops borrowing and whose credit can become exhausted? This they say, despite all the lessons of history, cannot happen because the more we borrow the higher we build our national income and hence the greater is our ability to borrow. But what about the interest? we ask. Will that not rise to appalling proportions? If our debt is $300,000,000,000 when the war ends, the interest, when we refund the debt, will be at least $9,000,000,000 a year. Before the depression this government never collected more than $3,500,000,000 in taxes. The greatest amount of taxes ever collected by the federal government in peacetime, even after we began to spend on war preparations, was $7,500,000,000 in 1941. But we will have to collect that much in taxes—and an additional $1,500,000,000—just to pay the interest on the national debt. Yet the advocates of this system say that when the war ends we must go on borrowing at the rate of 5 or 10 or even 20 billions a year. Mr. Tugwell estimated it must be around $12,000,000,000 a year in peacetime.

This theory has, in greater or less degree, been adopted by those most influential in the present government. It is not an idea that has infected a few choice spirits on the perimeter of the New Deal. It has become a part of the New Deal—indeed its most essential part. The evidence of this is that the job of planning for the postwar problems of America was taken over by the President himself, was not committed to any of the departmental bureaus, but was installed in his own executive office under his own eyes. For this purpose he organized as a department of his own office the National Resources Planning Board. The man who is the leading exponent of this theory, Dr. Alvin H. Hansen of Harvard, was brought to Washington as economic adviser of the Federal Reserve Board and installed as the chief adviser of the National Resources Planning Board. Six of the seven Harvard and Tufts economists who prepared the published plan were brought to Washington and made economic counsel of various important agencies. Mr. Richard V. Gilbert, one of them, and one of the most vocal apostles of this theory, is at the moment I write guiding the economic destinies of the OPA, which is supposed to be leading the battle against inflation. Most of the others have been given posts of importance in the government. Dr. Hansen has been described by such journals as the *New Republic* and *Fortune* as the man "whose fiscal thinking permeates the New Deal." The board has put out a series of pamphlets designed to outline its guiding ideas. The most important of these was written by Dr. Hansen. Everywhere in Washington, in the most important key positions, are men who have been indoctrinated with this theory.

It is interesting to note that as early as 1936 a little book appeared called *Uncommon Sense*, by David Cushman Coyle. The book, however, was circulated by the Democratic National Committee and one wonders if the hard-headed men who paid the bills realized what they were doing. It contained this amazing passage:

There are two ways to get out of depression. One is for business to borrow ten or twenty billion dollars from investors and build a lot of new factories, loading itself with debts that the investor will be expected to pay. The other is for the Government to borrow money and build public works, loading itself with debts that the investors will have to pay out of their surplus incomes. Some kind of taxpayer has to carry the debts either way. But business debts have to be paid mostly by the poorest taxpayers, whenever they go to the store to buy a cake of soap. Federal debts have to be paid by the people with better incomes who would not spend all their income anyway. That is why it is better for business and consumers if we get out of the depression by having the Government borrow than by having business do all the borrowing.

It is this incredible yet dangerous piece of nonsense which is at the bottom of the postwar plans that are being made in Washington. Recently Congress, to its amazement, became aware of these plans. It had provided funds for the National Resources Planning Board to work out a program for the postwar period. Of course everyone is in favor of that. It had been hearing about the "projects" which that board was blueprinting. It learned, finally, that the great project upon which the board was working was a project for recasting the whole economic and social system of America along the lines outlined here and based primarily upon a settled conviction that the capitalist system is dead. And it was doing this in the office of the President of the United States. It was the discovery of this fact which led to one of the first congressional revolts in 1943 and compelled the abolition of the National Resources Planning Board by Congress. The liquidation of this Board, however, does not in any particular alter the theories upon which the present government is proceeding. It is merely forced to transfer its revolutionary planning activities to other bureaus and departments.

All this is nothing more than a conscious imitation of the German experiment. Some of the political leaders, including the President, may not realize this, since they are not students. But the men who have been publicizing and promoting the program do. Thus, for instance, we find an article in *Harper's*[8] describing with a good deal of gusto the financial operations of the Hitler regime. We are told that we must not let the brutality of German political policy "divert our attention from the German financial program. *It is revo-*

[8]"The German Financial Revolution," by Dal Hitchcock, *Harper's Magazine*, Vol. 182, February 1941.

lutionary and it is successful." The author then tells us that if we will look behind the dictatorship we may possibly find "clues to the nature of our own recent financial ills, indicating what has been wrong and *what can be done* to strengthen economic democracy now and in the future." The men who built this German system are called men of unquestioned genius. It is becoming clear that "Germany's internal financial program is removing the limitations of her financial environment on rates of productive activity. For years prior to the present war German industry operated at capacity. To do these things she is changing capitalism but she is not destroying it."

Of course there is nothing new about Hitler's financial operation, as anyone who has read the German chapter of this volume will remember. It is merely the adoption by Hitler of the spending and borrowing tactics of his predecessors, whom he so roundly denounced. Hitler was doing little more than Mussolini was doing, than the republicans and Social Democrats did before him in Germany, and what the old Italian and German Ministers did before the last war. There has been altogether too much nonsense printed about the great financial wizardry of Schacht. Schacht did no more than any banker with his knowledge of modern banking might have done, caught in the same squeeze. Being an experienced financier and having seen one devastating inflation at work, Schacht introduced some clever devices to mitigate the effect of his fiscal policies. For instance, he arranged that when financial or industrial concerns of any category had accumulated large cash reserves, they were compelled to invest them in government bonds, thus relieving the government of the necessity of making inflationary bank loans. Better still, when the government decided that a new steel or munitions plant should be built, the operation would be carried on by a private corporation. It would issue its securities. In this country the government takes those securities through the Reconstruction Finance Corporation, buying them with funds raised by government borrowing on its own bonds or notes, thus plunging the government into debt. Schacht would force large financial institutions to take the securities of the private corporation directly, keeping the government completely out of the financial transaction. This was possible in Nazi Germany under a dictator. A dictator can order such things. A democratic government cannot. The author of the article from which I have quoted tops it off with the admiring observation that "the Nazis by experimentation were learning what to do while Keynes was discussing these theories in England." This is what is being offered to America. I quote once more:

> The irony of this financial revolution that has been unfolded in Germany lies in its implications for the future of economic democracy. What the Nazis have done, in essence, is to begin to chart the unknown realms of the dynamic use of government securities. Tragically for Germany and the whole world the brilliant contribution of her financial genius has been obscured by its diversion to the uses of tyranny and destruction. But can any of these financial methods be utilized so that a wise, self-governing people, determined to preserve individual freedom and anxious to make full use of individual initiative, could make private enterprise and capitalism better serve the purposes of economic democracy? If this is so—and I believe it is—we shall do well to examine the potentialities of this new arithmetic of finance as carefully and dispassionately as we should study, let us say, those of a new German development in aircraft manufacture, and seize upon whatever we can use for our own democratic ends.

This was written in 1941. The author was painfully behind the times. For already in 1938 the administration had practically seized upon this theory of finance.

It is a little astonishing how far the parallel between our fiscal theories and those of Germany go and how, once adopted, quite without design, they led off into the same weird bypaths. For instance, Italy before World War I had already learned how to increase the charges of social security in order to provide the government with money, not for social security but for its regular expenditures, and the same thing appeared in Germany. The present administration did that here until it was stopped by Congress in 1938, and now it is energetically trying to do the same thing again. Recently the New York *Sun* reported that when auditors got into the books of Mussolini's treasury, after his fall, they discovered that a large part of his deficit was due to the paying out of huge sums in subsidies to conceal the rise in the cost of living—a plan industriously urged here by the Hansen group and adopted by the President but as yet resisted by Congress. It is a singular fact that at this moment the battle against inflation is in the hands of these Perpetual Debt economists who look upon government spending and borrowing—which are the cause of inflation—as things good and necessary, and who look upon the objections to huge government spending and deficits as "old-fashioned superstition."

How the funds will be spent or "invested" by the central government is a point upon which all the advocates of this system are by no means agreed. Generally they fall into three groups:

1. The first group insists that the government shall not engage in any activities that either compete with private industry or impinge on its province. The government should put out its funds upon projects outside the domain of the profit system—such as public roads, schools, eleemosynary institutions, playgrounds, public parks, health projects, recreational and cultural activities of all sorts. A possible exception might be the development of power across state boundaries. Another exception would be public housing or housing for the underprivileged, which would not actually compete with private industry since private investors never put any money into housing projects of this kind. They would leave the whole subject of producing and distributing goods to private enterprises.

2. Another group proposes to invest these government funds in the shares and bonds of private enterprises. An eligible list of public investments would be established. The government would thus become the chief investor in private enterprise and in some cases—the railroads, for instance—the government might own all the bonds and perhaps much of the stock. Thus we would have a private corporation operating the utility in which much if not most of the funds would belong to the government. This plan, of course, would enable the general government, as the largest stockholder or holder of the mortgage, to exercise over properties a whole range of authority and power which it could not possibly exercise as a government *per se*.

3. A third plan is outlined by Mr. Mordecai Ezekiel, economic adviser of the Agricultural Department. He proposes an Industrial Adjustment Administration patterned on the lines of the Agricultural Adjustment Administration. It would work as follows: Indus-

try, organized into local groups united by national councils, would plan each year not the amount of goods it could sell but the amount needed by the nation. This estimate, approved by the government, would be authorized as the production program of the year. Each region and each unit in the region would receive its allocation of what it might produce. Prices would be fixed and all the producing units would proceed to turn out their respective quotas. The government would guarantee the sale of everything produced, underwriting the whole program and taking off the hands of all producers their undisposable surpluses. The risks of business would be transferred almost entirely to the government.[9]

What is stewing in Washington is a potpourri of all these ideas. The National Resources Planning Board in its report to Congress did actually propose that the government should become a partner in railroads, shipping, busses, airlines, power, telephone, telegraph, radio, aluminum, and other basic industries. It proposed also government participation in the financing of industry without setting very much limitation on it. John Maynard Keynes—now Lord Keynes and a member of the Board of Governors of the Bank of England and the most distinguished English-speaking exponent of these theories—speaks of this as "a somewhat comprehensive *socialization of investment.*" By this he means to distinguish his plan from the *socialization of industry.* Industry would be operated by private groups but the *investment* in industry would be socialized. "It is not the ownership of the instruments of production which it is important for the state to assume. If the state is able to determine the aggregate amount of resources devoted to augmenting the instruments and the basic rate of reward to those who can own them it will have accomplished all that is necessary," says Lord Keynes. The government will interpose itself between the corporate enterprise and the investor. The government will sell its securities to the investor, and as these will be guaranteed securities, the government can fix the rate of interest and therefore the rate of reward to the investor. The government will then invest these funds in industry. The industry is "owned" by a private corporation. But the government owns its bonds, perhaps much of its stock. Thus Lord Keynes thinks

[9] *Jobs for All,* by Mordecai Ezekiel, Knopf, New York, 1939.

he avoids statism or government ownership of industry. What is perfectly obvious, however, is that in one form or another these men are attempting to fabricate a system that will not be communistic and will not involve state ownership but will put in the hands of the all-powerful state not only through institutions of public regulation but through financial investment complete control of the economic system, while at the same time running up vast debts against the government and utilizing the public credit to create employment.

Of course this is fascism. For this principle of the Dual Consumptive Economy, as Dr. Hansen calls it, or the principle of planned consumption, as the fascists call it, by whatever name it is called is in fact one of the ingredients of the fascist or national socialist system. And if we will add to it the other ingredients of fascism or national socialism, we will then have that baleful order in America.

Whether this is a sound system or not is a matter for discussion. But sound or not, as Mr. Dal Hitchcock points out, it is the Nazi system. Whether we shall adopt it or not is hardly any longer a question. We have adopted it. The question is, can we get rid of it, and how? And if we are to continue it, the next question is how can we do so while at the same time continuing to operate our society in accordance with the democratic processes? This point we shall consider later.

America has now stumbled through the same marshes as Italy and Germany—and most European countries. Her leaders had proclaimed their undying belief in sound finance and balanced budgets while they teetered timidly on unbalanced ones. The public clamor for benefits, the cries of insistent minorities for relief and work, the imperious demand of all for action, action in some direction against the pressure of the pitiless laws of nature—all this was far more potent in shaping the course of the administration's fiscal policy than any fixed convictions based on principle. An unbalanced budget, after all, is a more or less impersonal evil, not easily grasped by the masses; but an army of unemployed men and the painfully conspicuous spectacle of shrinking purchasing power are things that strike down sharply on their consciousness. It is not easy, perhaps, to eat one's words about balancing the budget. But it is easier than facing all these angry forces with no plan. It is easier to spend than not to spend. It is running with the tide, along the lines of least resistance. And hence Mr. Roosevelt did what the premiers of Europe had been doing for decades. Only he called it a *New* Deal.

III · The Righteous Autarchy

THE LAST SEVENTY YEARS of American history have been a struggle between the ideal of "free enterprise" and the determination to restrain and regiment it. Beginning with institutions like the Interstate Commerce Commission and the Sherman Anti-Trust Law, the public set out to "regulate" industry and followed that soon with the state regulation of public-utility monopolies. Business leaders called this interference in business. Actually it was not. It was precisely the reverse. Business itself comprises the whole immense web of producing and distributing enterprises. Some men, for various reasons, set out to interfere in the natural workings of this immense organism. They organized first trade associations, then secret combinations, then trusts, then holding companies, then cartels to control production, distribution, trade practices. Some of this proceeded from sheer greed and predatory ambition. But some of it also took its rise in the effort of producers to protect themselves from the unruly hazards of trade. Thus the first combinations in oil were formed not by Rockefeller and the refiners but by the little producers in the oil regions who wanted to protect themselves from overproduction which forced the price of oil down to fifty cents a barrel when they thought by combination they could keep it to five dollars.

Rockefeller took the same course, uniting the bigger men with more brains, more capital, and more combining power to do the same thing for the refiners, but more intelligently. That feverish, helter-skelter, and dramatic episode of American business between 1870 and 1911 was not what so many have painted it—a mere assault by rapacious men upon the nation's wealth. It was that, but it was something more and also of more importance. There was a definite conviction that the economic system needed control and direction and there was also the conviction, as there was in Europe, that that control and direction should be supplied by the producers. And by producers was meant businessmen. The laws passed by the federal government and the states—particularly the anti-trust laws—were not intended to supply control and direction. They were designed to prevent the control and direction that businessmen attempted to impose. They were laws not to interfere in business but to prevent interference in business by businessmen.

What is more significant, however, is that despite the presence on the statute books of the anti-trust laws the whole development of combinations through trusts, cartels, trade associations, had its highest activity after the passage of these laws. Which is merely one more illustration of the fact that there are always present in the society certain powerful currents of opinion and desire against which even highly organized government makes headway with difficulty.

World War I had a profound effect upon this development. Immediately preceding it President Wilson had carried through the most determined assault upon the whole trend yet made. At the same time, however, the movement took another turn. The operation of an outright monopoly by a single great corporation had become difficult under the laws. But by 1912 business gave the movement another direction. The idea of self-rule, not by one great monopoly, but by great numbers of competitors in a given trade combining to regulate the trade became the new order. This was just making some progress when Wilson leveled an attack upon it with the Clayton Act and the Federal Trade Commission. But then came the war, which suspended the attack and actually brought the very government which had denounced self-rule and combination to the necessity of bringing competitors together for the war effort. This experience shook the whole system of free enterprise to its foundations, as it did in Germany under Walter Rathenau. When the war ended, the new cry for self-rule in business became the central doctrine of organized business. A whole library of books, magazine articles, and pamphlets blossomed into print setting out the necessity of changes in our laws to encourage business groups to unite to establish better systems of ethics, more intelligent supervision of production, prices, credit, labor standards, and all the other features of competition.

Many labor leaders began to be aware of the blessings of combination if it would include the unions. Thus Mr. Matthew Woll, vice-president of the American Federation of Labor, came out around 1924 for the repeal of the anti-trust laws. Labor leaders thought they saw a condition favorable to labor in large combinations of employers on one side and large and powerful unions on the other. Getting together would be easier. There were plenty of instances of employers' associations and unions entering agreements for mutual protection, labor getting recognition and the closed shop on one side and employers getting complete control of the trade through labor's refusal to work for employers who refused to co-operate with the combination.

During the administration of President Coolidge at least two-score industries adopted what were called codes of practice. Under cover of agreements to eliminate unethical practices, prices, production, and competition were controlled. This was done under the protection and sponsorship of the Attorney General's office and the Federal Trade Commission. Herbert Hoover put an end to it when he became President.

In all this we see the development of the syndicalist idea—that the economic system must be subjected to planning and control, that this planning must be done outside the political state, that it must be committed to the hands of the producing groups. In the United States, as in Italy and Germany, employers through their trade associations and workers through their unions were approaching a common ground by different routes. They differed with increasing violence on many points—wage and working conditions—but all the time were drawing closer together on the central idea of syndicalism.

After the depression of 1929 got under way a new school of reformers made its appearance. They were known as the Planners and their theories appeared in books by George Soule, of the *New Republic,* Stuart Chase, and Dr. Charles Beard. Russia's Five-Year

Plan had excited the admiration of the world. Why could not America have a plan—five years or some other span at least? In fact, what could be said against a community of intelligent beings, which had the means of producing abundance, yet suffered from want, sitting down with forethought and fabricating a plan to possess itself of the abundance within its reach? Thorstein Veblen had infected many younger thinkers with his lucubrations on the capitalist preoccupation with the creation of scarcity through employer sabotage or the withdrawal of efficiency in production to keep down production. Why, therefore, does not America set about working out a five-year plan of its own to set all its producing instruments to work to produce not scarcity in the interests of profits but abundance in the interest of the people? Everyone saw that economic laws were working blindly against us, and there was a powerful appeal in the demand that we control and direct economic law to work for us, as we control the law of gravity, for constructive purposes. The idea of planning is filled with artful suggestion. No one can think of an argument against planning.

I have already outlined briefly the character of the problem involved in business planning and in communist planning. I shall take the risk of repetition to point up again this theory which it is so important for us to understand. For instance, the United States Steel Corporation is an immense holding company, which operates mines, steel plants, railroads, steamships, fabricating industries. It is unthinkable that its directors would not sit down at intervals and determine on their future course—what plants should be operated, what plants should be slowed down or closed or replaced, what products should be pushed most vigorously, what new merchandise should be offered, what prices should be, what markets should be exploited, how funds should be obtained, if at all, by shares or bonds or bank credit. In short, the intelligent directorate of this corporation must operate on a plan. The same is true of Russia. The Soviet is an immense political organization. But it is something more. It is a gigantic holding company which owns every railroad, utility, manufacturing plant, every farm and store in the land. It is an operating enterpriser—the only one—in Russia. Therefore, of necessity it must and can sit down at intervals and lay out a plan for the management of its multitudinous enterprises just like any other owner. Indeed it cannot escape this because, as the price and profit regulator is not there to determine the movement of goods, this has to be done by deliberate fiat of the government entrepreneur. But the United States Government is not a holding company, does not own the producing units of the country. Planning for the economic system by the United States Government would involve a very different problem. It would have to plan for factories, farms, stores, utilities which it does not own, which are owned by private individuals, which private individuals must finance, and in which they must risk their funds in the hope of profits. Such plans would ultimately take the direction of coercion of investors, producers, and distributors, which is unthinkable in a free society. A communist dictatorship can do this. A fascist dictatorship may for a limited time. But a free democratic society cannot do it. Such a society might attempt to tell the laborer where he would work. In a grave enough emergency it may take a worker by the neck and set him down in an arms plant or behind a store counter. But it could never succeed in compelling a man to go into business or to expand a business with his own funds. Only dictators can do this, and then only for a limited time.

The Planners got a good deal of support from unthinking people on the simple score of common sense in the idea of planning as a wise course for all human beings. But the promoters of the idea of planning were thinking of something quite different. They were thinking of a change in our form of society in which the government would insert itself into the structure of business, not merely as a policeman, but as a partner, collaborator, and banker. But the general idea was first to reorder the society by making it a planned and coerced economy instead of a free one, in which business would be brought together into great guilds or an immense corporative structure, combining the elements of self-rule and government supervision with a national economic policing system to enforce these decrees.

This, after all, is not so very far from what business had been talking about. Business wanted the anti-trust laws suspended to enable it to organize into effective trade groups to plan its common activities. It was willing to accept the supervision of the government. This was the general objective of the codes of practice. Critics objected that business wanted to plan for scarcity—they called it protecting themselves against overproduction. Business said that orderly self-government in business would eliminate most of the causes that infected the organism with the germs of crises.

An example of this planning would be that outlined by Mordecai Ezekiel, chief economic adviser of the Agricultural Department, and also one of Vice-President Wallace's advisers. Under this plan— which he called "Jobs for All"—industry would be organized into categories, that is into trade associations. The planning would actually be done by the employers. In the shoe industry, for instance, the producers and distributors in each locality would determine the number of shoes needed by the people in that community. All the local groups would unite in a regional council which would coordinate these estimates. The regional councils would be brought together in a national council or federation or commission or corporative where employers and employees would be represented. A program of shoe production for the whole period under survey would be outlined together with all the related problems of labor, financing, etc. Sitting over all this would be the government commissar. A program would be agreed on including the number and kinds of shoes to be produced, each region would receive its allocation or quota which in turn would assign to each community and its producers their quota. Then the whole industry would be directed to produce that many shoes, and the government would underwrite the operation, taking off the hands of the producers the surplus, if any, which they could not sell. Thus "full-blast employment," to use a favorite phrase, would be assured in the shoe and every other industry. This is one type of what is called planning for abundance rather than scarcity.

The vogue of the Planners cannot be explained without attention to one or two features of the passing show of the last twenty-five years. For a long time socialism had made a powerful appeal to the intellectuals. Though he voted consistently the Democratic or Republican ticket, the "intellectual" felt called upon to avow a spiritual acceptance of the socialist philosophy, at least in principle. But the dark history of the Russian experiment, the seeming durability of the old capitalist villainy and the rise of the New Era, contrary to all the best prophecies, shook profoundly the faith of many of the Park Avenue, Greenwich Village, and academic savants who had flirted with the Red dream. Thorstein Veblen, an erratic grumbler, who had a flair for discovering to his own great surprise commonplace truisms that practical men had always known and clothing them in the language of philosophy, exercised a powerful influence over the minds of the youth of the early twenties with his theories about the dictatorship not of the proletariat but of the engineers, along with this device of planning. Veblen added, as a sort of afterthought, the economists to the engineers, and his disciples later took in the whole tribe of professors. Most of his followers were either socialists or the material from which socialists were made. And so they expunged from the philosophy the hateful words of "dictatorship" and "Soviet" which Veblen had used so frankly. They were for "democracy" and, of course, for the dear people and, of course, they were against the businessman as the prime villain of the capitalist system. But they were for capitalism, and they set up as the saviors and planners of a nobler and better form of capitalism which would be organized in the interest of their beloved masses, but would be managed for them by a legion of trained public servants—actually an elite of the professors.

When Mr. Roosevelt came into power it is entirely probable that he never heard of Veblen and certainly knew nothing of his theories. But it fell out that the economist-member of the brain trust was one of Veblen's most devoted disciples. He proceeded to indoctrinate the candidate and the brain trust with ideas for a capitalist system cast in the mold of Veblenian fascism. This was Mr. Rexford G. Tugwell. Accordingly we find Mr. Tugwell saying, about the time he became Mr. Roosevelt's chief economic adviser, that "America might have had some such organization as the German cartel system if we had not set out so determinedly forty years ago to enforce competition."[1] He called attention to the fact that factory managers had learned how to link their machines up in series, so that the product moved from one process to another without interrup-

---

[1] Speech before American Economic Association, December 1931.

tion. In this he saw the model for the economic system in which whole industries, indeed the whole nation, would be thus linked into what Tugwell, adopting Veblen's idea, called an "operational whole." The idea of anything being left to chance and to individual initiative seemed to him appalling. All this would pass away. Society, he said, will be organized just as a great factory is organized. There will be no progress toward "unseen" industries. There will be no railroad or electric industry springing into existence out of the little laboratories of scholars and scientists. There must never again be such a thing as an automobile industry leaping out of the initiative of individual pioneers. The future ahead must be planned always, and the technicians will be set to work to realize the dream in the blueprints. A blueprinted world—this is the vision—the organized, disciplined, planned, and blueprinted society.

This, of course, differs little from the dream of Fichte in Germany over one hundred and fifty years ago which captivated the German mind and exercised so great an influence over such different beings as Wilhelm II and his Social Democratic successors. Nothing will be left to chance, nothing will be left to the individual. Everything will be foreseen, planned, organized, and directed by the state. Tugwell concluded this speech with this statement:

"From what I know of human nature I believe the world awaits a great outpouring of energy as soon as we shall have removed the dead hand of competitive enterprise that stifles public impulses and finds use only for the less effective and less beneficial influences of man. When industry is government and government is industry the dual conflict deep in our modern institutions will have abated."

The wide appeal these ideas made to intellectual groups that were presently to have great influence in the government can hardly be overestimated. Here one finds a singular intertwining of the ideals of socialism and the ideas of capitalism. There is an appalling confusion. Yet confusion was the prevailing state of the time. The capitalists, after the debacle of 1929 and still more after 1932, were in hopeless confusion. But, oddly enough, so were the socialists whose whole case had been shaken first by the prosperity of the twenties and then by the brutalities of the Soviet government. This cult of planning offered to minds that in happier days would have yielded to socialism the perfect escape from surrender to orthodox capitalism. They could be for a kind of capitalist socialism without being just socialist.

When Mr. Roosevelt was elected it was as the representative and champion of the liberal wing of the Democratic party. Strangely enough, his predecessor was an engineer with an orderly mind running toward habits of surveying and planning. As a result he had set up a number of commissions to make studies and carry out policies. This practice of Mr. Hoover seemed to excite Mr. Roosevelt's especial scorn. He denounced regimentation not only when carried on by trade associations but "when it is done by the government of the United States itself."[2] He scored Mr. Hoover for "fostering regimentation without stint or limit." In March 1930 he said:

> The doctrine of regulation and legislation by "master minds" in whose judgment and will all the people may gladly and quietly acquiesce has been too glaringly apparent at Washington these last ten years. Were it possible to find master minds so unselfish, so willing to decide unhesitatingly against their own personal interests or private prejudices, men almost Godlike in their ability to hold the scales of justice with an even hand, such a government might be in the interest of the country. But there are none such on our political horizon, and we cannot expect a complete reversal of all the teachings of history.[3]

But when Mr. Roosevelt came into power it was not the philosophy of his party as expounded in his pre-election addresses that was put into practice, but measures which corresponded more closely with the teachings of the planners. Which is to say simply this, that the Democratic platform of 1932 shared the fate of the eleven points of Mussolini and the twenty five points of Hitler. The President entered the White House in the midst of a tremendous economic crisis and the measures he adopted were suggested not by the formal declarations of policy made by politicians based on ideas they supposed to be popular but by the necessities of the times.

[2] *Public Papers and Addresses of Franklin D. Roosevelt, 1928–36,* Random House, New York, 1938.
[3] *Ibid.*

The reasons upon which Mr. Tugwell's opinions about planning were based were very different from those of the Chamber of Commerce or the American Federation of Labor. But the idea that there was something wrong in the economic system, that there was disorder, that there ought to be planning of some sort, and that there should be a conscious control and management of the economic system was deeply rooted in all these groups in one form or another. And so as the President settled down to the task of putting policy into effect he ran not with the stream of his oratory, but with the stream of opinion and desire in the minds of the important and dynamic minorities which controlled the thinking of the nation. And so the President who denounced Hoover for his slight, fragmentary efforts at control brought into existence the NRA and the AAA—two of the mightiest engines of minute and comprehensive regimentation ever invented in any organized society. And the masses of the people who had cheered what Mr. Roosevelt had said about regimentation now cheered lustily when he proceeded to impose the regimentation he had denounced, while labor unions and Chamber of Commerce officials, stockbrokers and bankers, merchants and their customers joined in great parades in all the cities of the country in rhapsodical approval of the program.

It is not necessary here to go into the details of the National Recovery Administration (NRA). It was based, not consciously but in fact, almost wholly on the principle of the guild or corporative system which Mussolini was in process of perfecting at that very time. It adopted the Chamber of Commerce's favorite theory of self-government in industry under government supervision. It suspended the anti-trust laws which the President had vowed to enforce. The codes of practice, which had been drawn up and approved under Mr. Coolidge and which Mr. Hoover had ended, were gotten out, polished up, and strengthened with all sorts of devices to control prices, production, competition in the interest of scarcity and profits. Mr. H. I. Harriman, then president of the Chamber of Commerce, had said a little before:

A freedom of action which might have been justified in the relatively simple life of the last century cannot be tolerated tóday, because the unwise action of one individual may adversely affect the lives of thousands.

We have left the period of extreme individualism and are living in a period in which the national economy must be recognized as a controlling factor.[4]

Of course the NRA proved to be a colossal failure. The reason was obvious. The innumerable regulations adopted were designed to dictate the behavior of men in the operation of their factories and stores where they had always enjoyed the fullest freedom. However the country may have approved the experiment in theory, in practice enterprisers found themselves subjected suddenly to directives endless in number and complexity, to espionage, and finally to coercions against which they rebelled. Nothing could make this work save the iron hand of a dictatorial and ruthless government that could exist without the approval at the polls of these enterprisers. A dictator in Germany and Italy, answerable to no one save his own mailed fist and with his storm troopers to enforce compliance with his decrees, may, perhaps, operate such a system. But in a democracy it is impossible. Long before the Supreme Court, by a unanimous decision, declared the NRA unconstitutional, it was falling apart for lack of effective compliance machinery.

Thus we saw this experiment in corporativism, planning, and autarchy upon the same general model and for the same reasons as in Germany and Italy. The first condition of a planned economy is that it shall be a closed economy. The perfect example of autarchy would be a nation with an impenetrable wall around it, keeping out everybody and every kind of goods and striving for a complete self-sufficiency. Of course this is not practicable anywhere. Despite our great resources there are essential materials, such as rubber, tin, tungsten, quinine, etc., we do not possess. We must buy them from other nations and in turn sell things to them. But there is a theory that nations should develop their own resources to be self-sufficient as far as humanly possible. The tariff has been used in some measure toward this end, but in a very modified form. However, when planners set out to manage the society, not for self-sufficiency primarily but in order to speed up the economy, it is inevitable that they move toward autarchy. If you seek to plan your economy you must lay

[4]*Report of the Committee on Continuity of Business and Employment,* H. I. Harriman, chairman. U.S. Chamber of Commerce, Washington, D.C., 1931.

down rules for the behavior of manufacturers and distributors and farmers with the object of getting the highest production with the highest wages and the best standards of living. Obviously you cannot let anybody inside that economy compete who does not comply with these regulations. All must pay the agreed wages, work the short hours, provide the minimum health and cultural conditions, pay compensation, old-age, employment, and health insurance, pay the same schedule of high corrective income taxes. Having required this of the producers in your own economy you cannot permit the producers of Germany or Japan or Britain or any other country to bring their products into our market and sell in competition with our producers upon whom we have imposed all these costly regulations. You cannot impose these regulations on the producers of Japan and Germany and Britain. Hence you must exclude their producers for the same reason that you would exclude an American producer who refuses to produce under the requirements of your planned society. Planning means autarchy, and it is interesting to find the adventure of the New Deal in 1933 hailed as such by one of the ardent supporters of its economic policies—indeed the man who was the author of its title, the New Deal. Mr. Stuart Chase said in September 1933:

> Autarchy . . . is distinctly thinkable and it is probably coming. It is unthinkable unless it be controlled. It must be planned and planned by the Federal government . . . To introduce it in a society of *laissez-faire* is economic suicide. It can only be undertaken when governments take power and speculative profits away from businessmen and bankers. Vast and delicate problems of adjustment are entailed, which cannot be left to the clumsy hands of high finance. New industries must be set up; old industries liquidated; industrial research for substitute commodities encouraged on a large scale; millions of potential unemployed steered to new jobs; colossal capital shrinkage adjusted in some fashion; such foreign trade as remains rigidly budgeted by central authority. National planning and economic nationalism must go together or not at all. President Roosevelt has accepted the general philosophy of planning. Under his guidance we may move toward an inevitable autarchy with less trepidation than if we were pushed into it while a Hoover or a Mills still gazed dreamily at the logical harmonies of the nineteenth-century free market.[5]

[5] "Autarchy," by Stuart Chase, *Scribner's Magazine*, September 1933, Vol. XCIV.

Since the war effort got under way all the dreams of the planners have been realized. Everything they advocated has been brought about—an economy supported by great streams of debt and an economy under complete control, with nearly all the planning agencies functioning with almost totalitarian power under a vast bureaucracy manned and in many cases guided by the favored elite of the planners. It is no longer a question whether we shall adopt this kind of economy. We have it. The question is, can we get rid of it? It may be a little surprising to ingenuous people now when it is a little late to find that this is precisely what the planners had in mind. Only a few days after the war started, September 20, 1939, Mr. George Soule, most indefatigable planner, was saying in the *New Republic:*

> Under old conditions (of peace) it would have been necessary to wait much longer for the growth of national planning before international planning could be attempted on a large scale. But the war will leave the nation with its own kind of planning agencies and with full economic controls.

Mr. Soule's statement quoted above is followed by a rather curious observation. It is that when the war is over "the first thing to do is to know how to adapt these to peace objectives and to make the transition smoothly." The transition, of course, is to an international planned economy. In Washington the Board of Economic Warfare, before its demise headed by Vice-President Wallace and his *fidus Achates*, Milo Perkins, the State Department, and several other groups have been making their blueprints for what may be called an international WPA, an international PWA, an international AAA, and an international RFC. More than this, they are toying with the idea of carrying on international trade on the national socialist model, that is between nations organized as great trading corporations rather than between the individual importers and exporters of nations.

And while the war is in progress and the minds of the people are upon that vast enterprise and while on a broad range of subjects their thinking is more or less suspended and they are giving to the present government the fullest measure of loyalty, the administration is taking advantage of their trust to advance, through elaborate plans and extensive propaganda carried on with war funds, its proposals for a new economic order in which public debt and economic regimentation will be the central principles—an incredible mixture of autarchy with internationalism, which will never work, which probably can never be started, but which will entangle the nation in a futile and destructive effort toward an impossible end.

What the administration is planning has been made abundantly clear. The National Resources Planning Board was headed by the President's aged uncle, Colonel Frederic Delano. Its guiding intelligence, however, was Dr. Alvin H. Hansen, who is the leading exponent of the theory of persistent borrowing and deficits as an instrument of public policy. This board has issued a number of pamphlets and reports and has carried on an extensive propaganda in newspapers and colleges for its theory of creating abundance through endless public borrowing. In 1943 the board made an elaborate report to Congress in which it outlined its grandiose program when the war ends. Dr. Hansen had already said in an interview in the Chicago *Journal of Commerce* that "it is folly to think we can return to normal after the war." The official report, transmitted to Congress through the President himself, proposed the most amazing and extensive government control when the war ends.

Briefly it proposed (1) that certain war plants which, though not essential, employ many people, shall be kept going to keep up employment and that manufacturing plants financed during the war in regions where no plants existed before shall be kept going; (2) that wartime controls and priorities shall be continued on all scarce materials and plants turning out producers' goods; (3) continued federal control of industries based on raw materials, or on raw materials whose reserves are diminishing, or industries supplying fuel and power and transportation and other public services; (4) a joint partnership of government and business in aluminum, magnesium, shipbuilding, aircraft, communications, including radio, telephone and telegraph, air transport, synthetic rubber, and certain chemicals; (5) joint partnership and/or government assistance in urban development, housing, transport, terminal reorganization, river-basin development, agricultural rehabilitation, all transport facilities including terminal reconstruction, highway transport, pipe lines, electric power, water power, and rural electrification.

The joint partnerships will be by means of those mixed corporations which Walter Rathenau originated in Germany during World War I and which became the most fruitful means of control under the republic and, on a great scale, under Hitler.

The appearance of this report produced an immense irritation upon the congressional mind, already alarmed at the grandiose schemes of totalitarian government in America, and the National Resources Planning Board, against the most vigorous protests of the President, was abolished. Congress did not object to making plans for postwar problems. It objected to the President utilizing this idea to make plans not to save the present system but to junk it.

IV · Democratic Militarism

AT THIS MOMENT we are at war. There is not much difference of opinion among Americans as to the propriety of a national army raised on the principle of universal service during war. But when the war ends we may be sure that a powerful movement will spring up for a continuance of the principle of universal service during peace. It may be recalled that I defined militarism as a system of conscription in time of peace. If we go in for that we will have militarism, whatever excuse we may offer for doing it.

When the original selective service bill was passed in 1940 the chief argument made for it was the imminent need of a large army because we were in danger of being attacked. Many of those who urged the measure were careful to say that they did so purely as a war measure. But a great many were equally careful to insist that universal compulsory military service was a good thing in itself and something peculiarly suited to the purposes of democracy. A favorite argument, as Representative Mary T. Norton of New Jersey said, was that it would "take our youth and improve it physically and morally and teach it obedience and discipline." The Minneapolis *Spokesman*, a colored journal, saw in it "a fine opportunity for colored youth. It will take up some of the slack of the conditions resulting from unemployment and may possibly give them some of the discipline so noticeably lacking among today's youth, black and white." Congressman Whittington of Mississippi was especially concerned over our softness. College students by the thousands watch football. Only "twenty-two play and are trained and hardened while thousands watch and remain soft." Congressman Hobbs, thumping the same drum, declared: "That is what this bill is—a voluntary surrender of our right to grow soft and flabby so that we may strengthen and train ourselves." Congressman Cox of Georgia mourned the disintegration of our moral fiber. "Since the quest of the frontier," he declared, "there has been a gradual, yet definitely perceptible attenuation of our individual physical development reflecting the demand for physical strength and well-developed bodies. . . . In my opinion we are witnessing the attenuation of the moral fiber of the nation as we are witnessing the attenuation of its physical fiber. . . . Let us train the young men of the nation to be strong in body and mind. Let us reawake the spirit of our ancestors, let us kindle the flame of loyalty to home and fireside, let us reinspire the youth of the nation with the faith of our forefathers"—those robust individualist forefathers who would have chased the conscription officer in peacetime away from their doors with a squirrel gun.

Many others, like Congressman Sabath, saw in universal military training an opportunity for young men to acquire training in skilled trades. And General George C. Marshall, Army Chief of Staff, told Americans that "it is only through discomforts and fatigue that progress can be made toward the gradual triumph of mind and muscle over the softness of the life to which we have all been accustomed." Thus we can depend on a considerable number of very respectable people who have no wish to engage in aggressiveness to support the institution of militarism because they like armies, feel the taste for them in their blood, and look upon them as a great school of discipline and order and as an expression of our national power.

Bills for universal military service when the war ends as a permanent peacetime policy of the United States have been introduced. Many of those who urged the policy for the war crisis now urge it for the peace. Mr. Arthur Sulzberger, one of the original advocates, and Congressman James Wadsworth, of New York, have both taken a formal stand for the institution. Mr. Wadsworth puts it on the interesting ground that we must show our might to the world. The New York *Herald Tribune*, which industriously belabors New Deal extravagance, nevertheless says: "The interests of security, of national health and of democratic citizenship, alike point strongly toward the wisdom of maintaining universal compulsory training thereafter as a permanent feature of our peacetime life." (November 19, 1943.) The *Daily News*, at the other end of the journalistic spectrum in New York, is equally eager for peacetime conscription. *Collier's Magazine* has recently come out for it both for national defense and for the physical good of the youth and for the additional amazing reason that "it is democracy in action." That is a reason for it which the German generals never thought of. Of course the President has been for it throughout his life.

It is a fact that the first resistance to spending programs by the government will always come from the conservative groups who are as a rule also the taxpaying groups. After all, a long-continued program of government borrowing inevitably ends in a heavy national debt which calls for ever-increasing taxes to service it. Moreover, if the spending and borrowing are continued there is always the threat of inflation. This is always a source of apprehensiveness to people who have money and who are expected to invest it. Inflation threatens the stability of the dollar and holds out to investors the fear that their investments will be returned to them, if ever, in dollars which have lost their purchasing power. And so they can be depended upon to avoid investment. And they can also be depended upon to raise a very potent voice against continued borrowing and spending by the government.

There is another barrier to continuous spending on peacetime projects by the central government. In this country our central government is a federal government. It is not charged with carrying on governmental activities within the states. Almost any public function one can name will be found outside the constitutional limits of federal power. The central government may build schools but these will belong to the states or their government units—counties or towns. Hospitals, playgrounds, roads, eleemosynary activities of all sorts fall within the purview of state and local power. In times of emergency some latitude will be tolerated for the federal government, but even this is greatly limited and is temporary. If the federal government builds schools it must be done through the state authorities, and the same thing applies to almost every other public enterprise. One important consequence of this is that these schools, roads, hospitals, playgrounds, health and recreational activities when completed are in the hands of the local governments and must be maintained by them.

The capacity of the states and cities to support these extravagant public enterprises is limited. Most states and a very large number of cities plunged gaily into debt in the lush days of the twenties and now find themselves saddled with an intolerable burden of debt charges. To this is added the maintenance of those numerous institutions and facilities built for them with federal funds. The states and cities are pretty generally at the end of their rope. The war, with its flood of federal expenditures pouring into the states, on a strictly federal project—war—has, for the moment, rescued the states and cities from the unequal struggle against debt charges and city costs on one side and the dwindling state and city tax resources on the other. But this will not last. When the war ends, states and cities will resume their battle to carry on the activities to which they are now committed. The building of any more institutions or roads or parks or playgrounds, hospitals and various educational and welfare utilities will impose upon them a burden they cannot support. This point had been reached in 1939. At that time the federal government was studying, preparing, and urging on cities and states projects of all sorts, and the states were in a growing number of cases refusing them because they were already pressed to the wall to operate existing facilities. The cities and states wanted federal money but they wanted it without having it flow into new and expanded local and state institutions the support of which would devolve upon these authorities.

As part of the whole theory of spending in a political system such as ours the federal system becomes an almost insuperable barrier. Either the spending program will bog down for lack of projects or the federal system will be itself slowly liquidated. But this has not occurred yet. However, even were it otherwise, the spending government must sooner or later encounter stubborn resistance to spending of borrowed money because of the burden which this policy imposes on taxpayers. I am not concerned with the merits of the taxpayer's lament; merely with the fact that it inevitably develops and with the further fact that in the end the taxpayer is a very powerful person. The rise in public debt creates a growing interest charge which must be met by taxes. When this war ends, that interest charge alone will be greater by nearly 200 per cent than the whole cost of government before 1929.

These two stubborn forces—the lack of federal projects for spending, with the resistance of the states to spending on local projects that will complicate their already perilous fiscal position, and the resistance of the conservative groups to rising expenditure and debt—will always force a government like ours to find a project for spending which meets these two conditions: It must be a strictly federal project and it must be one upon which the conservative and taxpaying elements will be willing to see money spent. The one great federal project which meets these requirements is the army and navy for national defense. And this, of course, is quite inadequate unless it is carried on upon a scale which gives it all the characteristics of militarism. I do not propose to examine the psychological basis for this devotion of the conservative elements to military might. The inquiry is interesting, but here we are concerned with the fact and it is a fact. It is a fact that military outlays, at least within limits, generally can be counted on to command the support of those elements which are generally most vigorous in the opposition to public spending. At the same time those elements among the workers who are generally opposed to militarism are weakened in this resistance by the beneficial effect which war preparation has upon employment. Thus militarism is the one great glamorous public-works project upon which a variety of elements in the community can be brought into agreement.

This economic phase of the institution, however, is not always stressed, being smothered under the patriotic gases pumped out in its defense. Nevertheless, this economic aspect is never absent from the consciousness of most people who champion militarism. Thus, for instance, in 1940, when the drive for conscription in peacetime was running into some obstacles, the New York *Post*, which, like all militaristic champions, was for the measure only for the noblest reasons, perceived that a large number of our dumb proletarians resisted the infection. It felt that they should be given a shot of the more sordid ingredients of the militaristic dialectic. It therefore urged that the yokels should be given a dose of the economic argument and that the debate in Congress should be "concentrated on the entire program of 500,000 youths to be trained, with pay, by the National Youth Administration, of the score of new airports to be built by the Work Projects Administration, of the rise of the number of jobs which will follow the letting of ten billions of defense contracts."

Mr. Edward Hallett Carr, of the London *Times*, puts his finger on the central idea in this subject. He sees with clarity that war has performed and still performs a social purpose, even though it be not a moral one. The wars of the last century were gilded with an oblique moral purpose even though they were raw aggressions because nations suffering from scarcity made it a high moral purpose to possess themselves of Asiatic and African territories to provide their people with the necessities of life. There is not too solid a foundation to this pretense, but it was made nevertheless. Now, however, we are told that scarcity is a thing of the past, at least among the great favored nations. But war now finds its social purpose in the struggle against unemployment and inequality. "Against these evils, which democracy and *laissez-faire* capitalism cannot cure," says Mr. Carr, "large-scale war provides an effective if short antidote."[1]

This is the central idea, but it is a mistake to suppose that it is war itself which is the chief weapon used against unemployment and unequal distribution of wealth. War does wipe out unemployment and does create and distribute widely new money income. But far more important than war is the *preparation for war*. Indeed war itself is often a by-product of this preparation and of the circumstances which lead to preparation. Preparation for war is far more

[1] *Conditions of Peace*, by Edward H. Carr, Macmillan, New York, 1942.

effective than war as an antidote against unemployment. War produces a more complete result but it is temporary, passes swiftly, and leaves behind it immense dislocations. But preparation for war can go on for a long time—for forty years in Germany and France and Italy. War or preparation for war establishes the government as the one big customer for the one big industry to which almost all industries become tributary: the armament industry. Preparation for war —national defense, it is called—can take a million or more men in this country in peacetime out of the labor market and put them in the army while at the same time three times as many can be drawn into the industries which provide them with tanks, planes, guns, barracks, food, clothes, etc., all paid for by the government with funds raised largely if not altogether by debt.

It has been the pacifist, the liberal, and the radical who have been supposed to be the bulwark against militarism—here as elsewhere. Yet even in their armor is a flaw, which originates in the profound economic necessity upon which the true-hearted militarists have floated. A good many years ago William James, an avowed pacifist, could twist out of his own mind an argument for universal service. He wrote:

> Reflective apologists for war at the present day all take it religiously. It is a sort of sacrament. Its profits are to the vanquished as well as to the victor, and, quite apart from any question of profit, it is an absolute good, we are told, for it is human nature at its highest dynamic. Its "horrors" are a cheap price to pay for rescue from the only alternative of a world of clerks and teachers, of coeducation and zoophily, of consumers' leagues and associated charities, of industrialism unlimited and feminism unabashed.

Here was an excellent half-ironic statement of the shallow nonsense that was spread around Great Britain, which was tackling the White Man's Burden and singing Kipling's *Recessional*. But, alas, James was to add:

> So far as the central idea of this feeling goes no healthy-minded person, it seems to me, can help to some degree partaking of it. Militarism is the great preserver of our ideals, of hardihood, and human life with no use for hardihood would be contemptible. Without risks or prizes for the darer, history would be insipid indeed. So long as anti-militarists propose

no substitute for war's disciplinary function, no *moral equivalent* for war, analogous one might say to the mechanical equivalent for heat, so long they fail to realize the full inwardness of the situation.[2]

And so James proposed a conscription of youth for a war upon nature. But James had not put his finger on the mark. It is not war as a discipline and a field of glory for which we must find a substitute. It is war as a source of economic energy for which apparently we must find a substitute, if we are to look upon the subject in that way. Mr. Carr examines this subject more intelligently. War as an economic instrument is possible because it is possible to work up a moral support for war—or for national defense. War produces its economic effects wholly by sending the government off upon a gigantic spree of spending borrowed funds. It would be possible to obtain the same effects by spending borrowed funds on any other sort of project. But there is, as yet, no project behind which the necessary moral energy can be generated. Mr. Carr thinks it can be found. And the eternal liberal or liberal-radical, whatever is the precise name for him, toys dangerously with this idea—dangerously to the point of falling out of whatever cloud he happens to be riding into the militarist band wagon when his support is most helpful to his warrior brothers. Thus such a journal as the *New Republic,* which, between wars, cries out with indignation and scorn every time the Navy asks another yard of rope for a warship, has to find a crack in its philosophy through which it can squeeze when militarism becomes a more or less realizable ideal. The *New Republic* allowed, when the issue was presented, that it would like to see something different from the conscription of 1917. It wanted conscription organized as a sort of glorified CCC that would teach young men arts useful in peace as well as in war. However, it had to concede—falling into step with its intellectual predecessors of Italy and Germany and France—that after all democracy was safer with a citizens' army rather than a professional one. If worst comes to worst democracy is safer "when everyone knows how to shoot than when only a professional minority knows." This last incredible morsel belongs to the age when every citizen knew how to handle a rifle and had one over the mantel or

[2]*The Moral Equivalent of War,* by William James. American Association for International Conciliation, February 1910, No. 27.

in the corner. The knowledge of the machine gun and the 75 mm. howitzer will do the citizen in a democracy very little good when no one possesses these expensive toys save the state. And thus the *New Republic* came out for guns *and* butter. Actually it was with some such bait that the first conscription proposals were launched. I quote from the New York *Times*, June 23, 1940, in an article by Luther A. Huston, describing the plan:

> The argument of proponents of the plan is that the nation must put itself under discipline within the framework of our democracy or it cannot escape an enforced discipline imposed by autocratic tyrants. They contend that there is a place in democratic society for a communal effort which will enhance the educational resources of the country, strengthen its physical facilities, and preserve its essential democratic principles. Their program, they contend, will provide industry with a reservoir of labor which will enable it to step up production to meet the requirements of the defense program and provide millions of young people with training which will bulwark their position in the national economy. It will provide the armed forces of the nation with the man-power needed to operate the expanded military machinery for the protection of the nation.

Here is a collection of words and ideas to make the angels gasp, but they were admirably adapted to oiling the consciences and reasoning apparatus of the pacifists and radicals who were rapidly sprouting muscles and fangs and raging for a great crusade of some sort. Here was a kind of economic equivalent for war—several million youths inducted by universal service into glorified, militarized CCC camps which would turn them at the same time into skilled artisans and skilled soldiers for use in whatever direction they had to be sent. This is what Mrs. Roosevelt and the *New Republic* were asking for. And this is what Mrs. Roosevelt is asking for now and what Mr. Roosevelt has always been for from his earliest years. Fundamentally it takes its root in the search for some scheme that will enable the nation to drain off each year a million or two men during peace from the unemployed by putting them into labor camps and soldier camps while putting another three or four million to work in a gigantic arms industry. All sorts of people are for it. Numerous senators and representatives—of the Right and Left— have expressed their purpose to establish universal military training when the war ends; and the companion institution—labor camps—to train youth in military and industrial activities—is a part of the same purpose. The National Resources Planning Board in one of its official pamphlets, sent out from the executive office of the President, estimated an expenditure of five billions a year on defense when the nation returns to peace. This will be plus the nine billions for interest on the war loans.

The great and glamorous industry is here—the industry of militarism. And when the war is ended the country is going to be asked if it seriously wishes to demobilize an industry that can employ so many men, create so much national income when the nation is faced with the probability of vast unemployment in industry. All the well-known arguments, used so long and so successfully in Europe, in Germany, in Italy, and in France, will be dusted off—America with her high purposes of world regeneration must have the power to back up her magnificent ideals; America cannot afford to grow soft, and the Army and the Navy must be continued on a vast scale to toughen the moral and physical sinews of our youth; America dare not live in a world of gangsters and aggressors without keeping her full power mustered; America can find a moral equivalent for war in a great peacetime army which will primarily train our youth for life and health with adequate military training thrown in, and above and below and all around these sentiments will be the sinister allurement of the perpetuation of the great industry which can never know a depression because it will have but one customer—the American government to whose pocket there is no bottom.

Let no one soothe himself, therefore, with the assurance that we in America, having gone in for spending and autarchy, will not add the third fascist or national socialist ingredient to our society—militarism.

V · American Imperialism

EMBARKED, as we seem to be, upon a career of militarism, we shall, like every other country, have to find the means when the war ends of obtaining the consent of the people to the burdens that go along with the blessings it confers upon its favored groups and regions. Powerful resistance to it will always be active, and the effective means of combating this resistance will have to be found. Inevitably, having surrendered to militarism as an economic device, we will do what other countries have done: we will keep alive the fears of our people of the aggressive ambitions of other countries and we will ourselves embark upon imperialistic enterprises of our own.

Two words have come into extensive use since the present war began. One is "isolationism"; the other is "internationalism." Curiously internationalism has come to be a synonym for interventionism. Intervention was a word used to describe the policy of those who insisted that America should intervene in the European war. There were many lifelong and sincere internationalists—men who were warm supporters of the League of Nations or similar plans for world co-operation—who were opposed to American entry into the war. The two words represent wholly different ideas.

Imperialism, too, has come to describe a kind of internationalism, so that one who opposes it is scornfully called an isolationist. Imperialism is an institution under which one nation asserts the right to seize the land or at least to control the government or resources of another people. It is an assertion of stark, bold aggression. It is, of course, international in the sense that the aggressor nation crosses its own borders and enters the boundaries of another nation and what results is an international clash—a clash between two nations. It is international in the sense that war is international. An imperialist nation, therefore, is one which acquires interests as a result of its aggression in territories outside of its own boundaries. These interests by their very nature bring the aggressor nation into clash with other nations across whose aggressive ambitions it cuts. We have clashes between Germany and England and France and Japan over their respective aggressive ambitions in Asia. We have clashes between Germany and Russia over their respective ambitions in the Balkans; between Italy and France over their hostile objectives in northern Africa, and so on. This is internationalism in a sense, in that all the activities of an aggressor are on the international stage. But it is a malignant internationalism.

There is another internationalism which finds its extremist view in the dreams of those who look for the Parliament of Man and the Federation of the World. Pacifists, for instance, who see in the possibility of a world government the hope of world peace are internationalists of this type, and they look upon imperialism as its greatest foe. A curious confusion has arisen out of all this, which should be simple enough to understand. There are several nations which have engaged in extensive imperialist aggression. As a result these nations have colonies all over the world. Having gotten possession of their prizes and acquired a kind of semi-legal claim upon them and having perfected a kind of international tolerance for them through a sort of squatter's sovereignty, they are now interested in preserving the *status quo*. This *status quo* is the result of aggression, is a continuing assertion of aggression, an assertion of malignant internationalism. Now they appeal to this other benevolent type of internationalism to establish a world order in which they, all leagued together, will preserve a world which they have divided among themselves and in which the combined forces and might of the allied aggressors will hold for each what they have. This benevolent internationalism is taken over by the aggressors as the mask behind which the malignant internationalism will be perpetuated and protected. And it is now offered to the world in all the phrases of benevolence and as a dream of world peace.

I have outlined these views chiefly for the purpose of clearing up the ideas and the meaning of words which I am using here. I wish to speak of imperialism and internationalism, but I want to be sure that the two ideas are kept separate and are understood.

I do not see how any thoughtful person watching the movement of affairs in America can doubt that we are moving in the direction of both imperialism and internationalism and that this internationalism is curiously, indeed incredibly, mixed up with the wholly contradictory idea of autarchy. Who can doubt that with the planned economy which is being fabricated for the United States, similar to the planned economies already existing in other countries, we will have an autarchy like our international neighbors and allies? As we have seen, autarchy is very nearly the last word in isolationism—a nation enclosed in a completely planned and managed economic system, whose planning must be protected as of necessity from the impact of external economies. These planned economies will all be brought together into a great international planned economy the members of which will be autarchial states. The problem will be to maintain the isolated autarchial system in each constituent state and to unite all these autarchies in an international economy. This is not the place to discuss the feasibility of this hybrid system. But I throw the idea out here for the benefit of those who think they see a world order based, at least roughly, on the league of American states in the United States of America. The union of the American states was a union of free economies from which all possibility of autarchy was banished by the terms of the Constitution. If tomorrow these states of ours, despite their long union, could be transformed into self-planned autarchies, this union would not last half-a-dozen years. Yet it is an administration in Washington which from the beginning has been struggling toward autarchy here, and which broke up the London Economic Conference in 1933 because it threatened our own autarchial arrangements, which now calls itself a great international regime and actually smears its critics as "isolationists."

And now of imperialism. This is, of course, nothing more, as I have said, than a form of bald and naked assertion of might. Its origin in the human mind is by no means clear. It does not find its roots wholly in the greed of the merchant adventurers or in the ambitions of military leaders or the dreams of dynasts for extension of their glory. It has had an abundance of support at the hands of gentlemen who hold themselves out as philosophers. Certainly it is unnecessary here to repeat the innumerable declarations made by British historians, philosophers, poets, and publicists in support of Britain's divine right to seize land anywhere. There is not a statement that has ever been made by a German imperialist that cannot be matched from the pen of a highly respected and highly honored British imperialist. You will find an acquisitive industrialist like Rhodes saying "We are the first race in the world, and the more of the world we inhabit the better it is for the human race." But you can also find a liberal statesman like Earl Grey saying "In so far as an Englishman differs from a Swede or a Belgian he believes he represents a more perfectly developed standard of general excellence

—and even those nations like ourselves in mind and sentiment—German and Scandinavian—we regard as not so excellent as ourselves." And a scholar like Ruskin, who spent so much time weeping over the poor, could say that England "must found colonies as fast and as far as she is able; seizing every rod of waste ground she can set her foot upon and then teaching these her colonies that their chief virtue is fidelity to their country and that their first aim is to advance the power of England by land and sea."

But we need not go to England. Professor Washburn Hopkins of Yale said in 1900, when America was considering her first feeble steps in imperialism, "What seems criminal aggression in a large nation against a weak one is justifiable if it conduces to the advantage of the race," and with characteristic American piety he called this the "higher morality." We need not suppose that the seeds of this dangerous and malignant philosophy do not lurk deeply in our own national nature. America broke very definitely with her great democratic tradition in 1900 when she decided to hold the Philippine Islands. This was an assertion of power, the power of conquest, the right based wholly on might. At the time some of America's most distinguished men, statesmen like Senator George Hoar, for instance, warned America that she was introducing a poisonous organism into her system, that she was throwing away principles of human justice which she had asserted with complete confidence and belief in the past, and that, furthermore, she was pushing her western frontier like a long, thin salient into the Orient where every cat-and-dog fight in the future between aggressor nations of Europe and Asia might involve her in a war.

The Philippines turned out to be a very bad bargain from the point of view of imperialist profit, which is the basis on which we remained there, though the bargain was wrapped up in moral gold paper. It was more than thirty years later that we decided to leave the Islands, fixing five years as a period of our departure. But we were too late. We are at war, and we are at war in Asia because we possessed the Philippine Islands. That was the break with our great tradition, and that break had the approval of the American people in 1900 when the presidential campaign was fought almost exclusively on that issue.

Americans of today can hardly realize the nature of the chauvinistic elation which came to us as a result of our new colonial world. I listened to almost all the debates in Congress on that subject. For the first time in our history men began to roll under their tongues the phrase "American empire." It would be an interesting example of verbal statistics if someone were to go through those debates and number the times the imperialists of that day referred with growing pride to the great American "empire." The advocates of that policy scoffed at the attempts to apply the principles of the Declaration of Independence and of the Constitution to our new situation. There was no end of statements by the leaders of the day calling attention to the fact that the new American empire had outgrown these simple-minded illusions of the fathers who uttered them. The world had changed and grown and America had expanded and was now an empire. There was a great deal of solid pride in that fact.

As an example of this let me quote what one of the leaders in this movement had to say. Senator Albert Beveridge, on January 9, 1900, made his first speech in the Senate.[1] He began it with this extraordinary sentence:

> The times call for candor. The Philippines are ours forever—country belonging to the United States—as the Constitution calls them, and just beyond the Philippines are China's illimitable markets. We will not retreat from either. We will not repudiate our duty in the archipelago. We will not abandon one opportunity in the Orient. We will not renounce our part in the mission of our race, trustee under God, of the civilization of the world. And we will move forward to our work, not howling out our regrets, like slaves whipped to their burdens, but with gratitude for a task worthy of our strength and thanksgiving to Almighty God that He has marked us as His chosen people to lead in the regeneration of the world.

Here is the whole complex gospel. Our duty under God to lead in the regeneration of the world on one side, and to stay in the archipelago "beyond which are China's illimitable markets." He told the Senate that the Pacific is "our ocean" although half a dozen other large nations had extensive territories along that ocean. And

[1] 56th Congress, 1st Session, Vol. 33, p. 704.

then the senator proceeded with a dramatic and eloquent catalogue of the magnificent resources, extent, and wealth of the Philippine Islands "beyond which lies China's trade" which he valued at $285,738,000 of which we were getting only 9 per cent and of which "under God," as we "regenerate the world," we should get 50 per cent. Lifting his arm aloft, holding a lump of gold in his hand, he exclaimed dramatically: "I have a nugget of pure gold picked up in its present form on the banks of a Philippine creek. I have gold dust washed out by the crude process of careless natives from the sands of a Philippine stream." And then he said that it must be our great objective "to establish the supremacy of the American race throughout the Pacific and throughout the East to the end of time." Self-government for Asiatics, people with savage blood, Oriental blood, Malay blood, and Spanish example—this was not to be thought of. He prophesied that "self-government and the internal development of the country have been the dominant notes of our first century; administration and development of other lands will be the dominant notes of our second century." And he ended with this rhetorical flourish:

> This question is elemental. It is racial. God has not been preparing the English-speaking and Teutonic people for a thousand years for nothing but vain and idle contemplation and self-administration. No! He has made us the master organizers of this world to establish system where chaos reigns. He has given us the spirit of progress, to overwhelm the forces of reaction throughout the earth. He has made us adepts in government that we may administer government among savage and senile peoples. . . . And of all our race He has marked the American people as the chosen nation to finally lead in the regeneration of the world. This is the divine mission of America. . . . We are the trustees of the world's progress, guardians of its righteous peace. The judgment of the Master is upon us: "Ye have been faithful over few things. I will make you ruler over many things."

When the senator had finished this strange mélange of world duty, world glory, world opportunity, regeneration of savage and senile peoples, 50 per cent of the trade of China and gold nuggets on the banks of streams, imperial destiny and treasure, the venerable Senator Hoar of Massachusetts, who had been shocked at the spectacle of the eloquent young senator summoning America to her imperial destiny and duty and holding aloft a torch of gold to light the way, rose in the Senate and said:

> I could hear much calculated to excite the imagination of the youth charmed by the dream of empire. . . . I could think as this brave young republic of ours listened to what the senator had to say of but one sentence:
> "And the Devil taketh Him up into an exceeding high mountain and showeth him all the kingdoms of the world and the glory of them.
> "And the Devil said unto Him, 'All these things will I give thee if thou wilt fall down and worship me.'
> "Then saith Jesus unto him: 'Get thee behind me, Satan.'"

But, alas, the American people did not make the reply to Senator Beveridge that Jesus made to the devil. Indeed as Beveridge ended his address he was greeted with "long and continued applause" in good earnest and senators crowded around him to shake his hand. I have chosen the Beveridge statement because it was the clearest and most eloquent of numerous speeches made in the House and Senate at the time. For instance, Representative Gibson of Tennessee said what others were saying on the stump and in the pulpit:

> Our race has a mission. No devout student of history can misread it. We are the preachers of a new evangel of government; we are the missionaries of a new and higher civilization; we are the apostles of the New World to the Old; and a part of our mission is to evangelize Asia and the islands of the sea.

But this was to be only a beginning, as the congressman made abundantly clear. He continued:

> The progress of our race can never be stayed. You can never fix its bounds. No one continent can suffice it. No one ocean can satisfy it. No one zone can contain it. No one hemisphere can circumscribe its powers and activities.
> The world is its area and the lands of the world its only boundary. Its destiny is to dominate the entire face of the earth, to include all races and all countries and all lands and all continents.[2]

The Springfield *Republican* lamented that the religious press of the country was almost a unit in support of the imperialism of which these gentlemen were the spokesmen. Dean Farrar said that "impe-

[2]*Congressional Record*, February 6, 1900, pp. 1565–66.

rialism is a natural evolution of *vital and aggressive Christianity.*"³

These were not the utterances of black reactionaries. Beveridge became a leader of the rising progressive movement. And here is a singular collection of views from one who can by no stretch of the imagination be called a reactionary. A year before Beveridge spoke America was having trouble with her new ward, Cuba. A most solemn pledge—the Platt Amendment—bound us to respect her independence at the end of the Spanish War. In the midst of these difficulties the following editorial appeared on March 20, 1899:

> Riots against the police are occurring in Havana. They will keep occurring. No Latin country governs itself. Self-government is the most difficult thing in the world for a people to accomplish. It is not a matter that a nation acquires by adopting a set of laws. Only Anglo-Saxons can govern themselves. The Cubans will need a despotic government for many years to restrain anarchy until Cuba is filled with Yankees. Uncle Sam, the First, will have to govern Cuba as Alphonso, the Thirteenth, governed it if there is any peace in the island at all. The Cubans are not and, of right, ought not to be free. To say that they are, or that they should be, is folly. Riot will follow riot. Anarchy will rise to be crushed. And unrest will prevail until the Yankee takes possession of the land. Then the Cubans will be an inferior—if not a servile—race. Then there will be peace in the land. Then will Cuba be free. It is the Anglo-Saxon's manifest destiny to go forth in the world as a world conqueror. He will take possession of all the islands of the sea. He will exterminate the peoples he cannot subjugate. That is what fate holds for the chosen people. It is so written. Those who would protest, will find their objections overruled. It is to be.

That is from the pen of William Allen White in his Emporia *Gazette*. More than ten years later he was to write in a volume published in 1910 the following paragraph:

> The best blood of the earth is here—a variated blood of strong, indomitable men and women brought here by visions of wider lives. But this blood will remain a clean, Aryan blood, because there are no hordes of inferior races about us to sweep over us and debase our stock. We are segregated by two oceans from the inferior races, and by that instinctive race revulsion to cross-breeding that marks the American wherever he is found.⁴

³*Literary Digest*, October 27, 1900.
⁴*The Old Order Changeth*, by William Allen White, Macmillan, New York, 1910.

And now, nearly forty years later, is not this what we hear? Are we not being told that it is our high destiny to regenerate the world, to administer savage and senile peoples? Senator Beveridge was liberal enough to include the Teutonic along with the Anglo-Saxon peoples as the "master organizers of the world." Now, of course, the Teutonic peoples are ousted from the great fraternity of the master race and we alone—with our junior partners, the British—claim that proud distinction. We have been chosen by God to establish system where chaos reigns, to overwhelm the forces of reaction throughout the world. We are the trustees of the world's progress and the guardians of its righteous peace—the "we" referring to the Anglo-American peoples, since our former partners, the Teutons, have been discovered to be criminals for holding these same views though, of course, some of our most generous-souled commentators are willing to acquit them on the plea of insanity. But "we" Americans, above all, are chosen as God's missionaries to bring freedom and civilization and three square meals a day to all lands everywhere. What Beveridge and his colleagues were talking about were those first feeble steps of ours in the direction of American imperial destiny. Beveridge said prophetically that our first century was taken up with self-government and that the development and administration of other lands will be the dominant note of our second century. Now Mr. Henry Luce, who probably never read this Beveridge speech, bobs up with the glorious evangel and gives to this century its proper name—the American Century.

Nothing could be further from the truth than to suppose that these ideas spring up in the minds of only wicked people. And nothing could be more dangerous than to imagine that these fatal illusions cannot be generated here among men and women who in all the relations of life appear to us as good human beings and good citizens and who can, yet, nourish a philosophy that is not one whit different from that which has driven European aggressors along their careers of cruelty and disaster.

Of course these ideas may be conveyed in the soft, scholarly terms of high religious duty by a scholar like Ruskin or they may be shouted at us in the raucous tones of Hitler in the *Sportpalast*. When we announce our racial mastery and our intention to use this high privilege for any purpose we do so with a careful choice of words in order to exhibit our intentions in the best light. When we ascribe the same sentiments to some hostile alien aggressor we do it in words designed with equal care to express precisely the same ideas in the worst possible light. The enemy aggressor is always pursuing a course of larceny, murder, rapine, and barbarism. We are always moving forward with high mission, a destiny imposed by the Deity to regenerate our victims while incidentally capturing their markets, to civilize savage and senile and paranoidal peoples while blundering accidentally into their oil wells or metal mines. The truth is that the hateful and destructive doctrine takes its root in different minds in different ways—for religious or racial or commercial or political or economic reasons or for the sake of glory. The urge that in the end drives us forward may be compounded of all these reasons. Generally the condition which is essential to such adventures is economic. But the economic factors are usually subordinated in the public discussions to the ethical and adventurous. The practical men let the preachers and the poets do the talking.

I have called attention, in the chapters on Italy and Germany, to the rise, in times of distress and frustration, of these dangerous ideas. In one form or another the d'Annunzios appear under widely differing manifestations to inflame the imagination of youth and to play upon the strings of national and racial greatness. In Italy it was the philosopher Gentile saying "faith in the necessity of the advent of an ideal reality, a conception of life which must not enclose itself within the limits of fact," or socialists like Papini taking up the cult of the "dangerous life" talking to Italy of the great anvil of fire and blood on which strong people are hammered and who could see in war "the great reawakening of the enfeebled—as a rapid and heroic means to power and wealth." Here is the same mixture of glory, spirit, power, and wealth as in the Beveridge evangel. Here is that same spirit Josiah Royce identifies: "Trust your genius, free your noble heart." Here come the "excellent men" for whom life has no savor unless it has something in it—something transcendental in which they sweep themselves to the achievement of some great purpose, when the normal pursuits of men are sneered at and the nation is summoned off in pursuit of "greatness." All that is here.

In a period of depression—and we have had this now for fourteen years—facts become after a while exceedingly irksome and bleak companions. Poverty, unemployment, bitter controversy, hatreds, the frustration of the middle classes, the seemingly hopeless struggle between labor and capital, all floating upon a precarious tide of government debt which might run out on us any minute leaving us stranded on the beach—the whole thing seems so difficult, so impossible, so insoluble that men run away from these facts after a while. Young people who in 1929 were twenty years old are now thirty-five. These fairest years of their lives have slipped away from them—the opportunity to build, to make homes, to have children, to get definitely started in some hopeful direction is gone. Little businessmen who for fifteen years have struggled to hold onto their shops and their stores, who were twenty-eight or thirty when the depression started and were moving toward that state of security which is their great objective, are now past forty, moving into middle age. Hundreds of thousands of them have gone under. Hundreds of thousands more have gotten nowhere and middle age approaches with the dream of security almost completely broken and the future for them darker than ever. These are the conditions which make the going easy for the romanticist. Men who run away from facts, from these dark and foreboding facts, do not like to run away frankly. They prefer to give their retreat the character of a great advance in another direction. It is the advance to "greatness." When the romantics leap up with their bugle calls and banners inscribed with florid slogans summoning to greatness, to high adventure, it is possible to perceive the incredible spectacle of men who have failed to operate their own society and are now in defeat and retreat sounding the drums and raising the banners for a great crusade to do for the whole world what they could not do for themselves.

Thus we find these very poorly disguised admirations of Adolf Hitler:

A few years ago the "practical men" and the economic scholars were saying that Hitler was the greatest money crank of all. They announced that he had bankrupted Germany. In fact, he had bankrupted the experts and the practical men. Today in the dark continent of his contriving, the experts are demoted to the job of finding ways and means of serving Hitler's will (in the democratic world they are allowed to spend their time explaining why it is impossible to do what man desires) and the practical men in Hitler's continent can now be divided into three classes—those who have been interned, those who have been in jail, and those who have been blackmailed into becoming Quislings. It would seem that in our forcing-house of history the practical view of life is not a success.[5]

Here is Mr. Herbert Agar, one of our leading apostles of the cult of greatness, who cannot help observing that Hitler has succeeded and that the practical men who said he could not succeed have been liquidated. I know Mr. Agar does not like to see practical men or others murdered, but he reveals clearly at least implied acceptance of Dr. Gentile's theory that the world cannot be enclosed in fact and that some kind of leader must arise who does not believe in facts, who does not believe in money, who does not believe in budgets, who does not believe in arithmetic, and who does not believe in history, and who will set the experts and the practical men not to advising him but to contriving means to achieve his ends. There is also the singular illusion in this quotation that the experts who predicted that Hitler would bankrupt Germany were wrong. It all depends upon what one means by the word "bankrupt." If ever there was a bankrupt nation in this world it is Germany, whether we take the orthodox or the moral meaning of the word.

Yet it is this spirit, brewed in the minds of a frustrated strong people, that will provide the dynamic element which will enable the more pragmatic imperialists to unfurl the banners and weave the philosophies and produce the slogans behind which the nation may be drawn away from its own unsolved problems to the regeneration of the world.

To sum it up, what I am trying to say with as much emphasis as I can is that the germs of a vigorous imperialism are here among us—I mean the moral germs. And if the economic problem of the nation should seem, when the war ends, to lead us off into some imperialist adventures, the moral support of such adventures will not be lacking. Our peculiarly happy geographical situation has in the past kept us free from the powerful temptations to aggression that

[5] *A Time for Greatness*, by Herbert Agar, Little, Brown, New York, 1942.

have overwhelmed other nations. Nevertheless, we have managed to run up a little history of imperial adventure upon a small scale of which we may well be ashamed. It is a long story, but the whole unpleasant business may be summed up in a single short paragraph uttered by the military commander who led most of our little imperialistic expeditions. The late Major General Smedley Butler, who was commander of the Marines, said some years before his death:

> I spent thirty-three years and four months in active service in the country's most agile military force, the Marines. I served in all ranks from second lieutenant to major general. And during that period I spent most of my time being a high-class muscle man for Big Business, for Wall Street and the bankers. Thus I helped make Mexico, and especially Tampico, safe for American oil interests in 1914. I helped make Haiti and Cuba a decent place for the National City Bank boys to collect revenue in. I helped in the raping of half-a-dozen Central American republics for the benefit of Wall Street. The record of racketeering is long. I helped purify Nicaragua for the international banking house of Brown Brothers and Co. in 1909–12. I brought light to the Dominican Republic for the sugar interests in 1916. I helped make Honduras "right" for American fruit companies in 1903. In China in 1927 I helped see to it that Standard Oil went its way unmolested.

These were strong words from a man who felt a deep devotion to and pride in the Marines but resented the uses to which they had been put.

We have managed to accumulate a pretty sizable empire of our own already—far-spreading territories detached from our continental borders—Alaska, Hawaii, the Philippines, Puerto Rico, Guam, American Samoa, Panama Canal Zone, Virgin Islands, with a territorial area of 711,000 square miles or as much as Germany, France, Italy, Belgium, and Holland all combined, and a population of 19,000,000.

We have now managed to acquire bases all over the world—islands as distant as the Australian Archipelago which President Roosevelt seized in 1938 without so much as a by-your-leave from Congress. There is no part of the world where trouble can break out where we do not have bases of some sort in which, if we wish to use the pretension, we cannot claim our interests are menaced. Thus menaced there must remain when the war is over a continuing argument in the hands of the imperialists for a vast naval establishment and a huge army ready to attack anywhere or to resist an attack from all the enemies we shall be obliged to have. Because always the most powerful argument for a huge army maintained for economic reasons is that we have enemies. We must have enemies. They will become an economic necessity for us.

VI · The Last Mile

THERE REMAINS the final ingredient—the totalitarian state. Surely that cannot come here! Let us see.

We have seen that already we have introduced:

1. The institution of planned consumption or the spending-borrowing government.
2. The planned economy.
3. Militarism as an economic institution, and
4. Imperialism as the handmaiden of our militarism.

But what of the totalitarian state? Can it be that America will ever complete that job? It may be, I hear the critic say, that we have embraced four of the elements of the fascist state but we will not have fascism or national socialism until we add the fifth—the totalitarian political idea. Between a democratic state seeking to plan and manage its economic life and supporting it by means of national debt, even though it becomes militaristic and imperialist, and the fascist state managing these things through a dictatorship there is a world of difference.

Let us say at once that there is at least a difference—even though it be not a world of difference—between an autarchial public-debt-supported militaristic state managed by a democratic parliament and one managed by a dictator. But let us also admit frankly that the two are perfectly alike in all but that. Let us say to ourselves frankly that we have now adopted four of the factors of the five which make fascism. This may be called the prologue to fascism. Having adopted these four I now lay down the proposition that we must adopt the fifth or abandon the other four. And this I assert because it is impossible to operate a public-debt-supported autarchy save by means of a totalitarian government. The system of planning calls for interferences and intrusions into the private affairs of business organizations and of private citizens. It implies of necessity the multiplication of rules and regulations upon an oppressive scale. It involves endless improvisation of these regulations and the administration of them by vast bureaucratic organizations. All this must be on a scale that will inflict so many irritations and annoyances and oppressions that men will not submit to them save in the presence of overwhelming and ruthless force. No democratic society will submit to them. Only the dictator with the last ounce of coercion in his hands and the willingness to use it can extort compliance.

At this moment we have a planned and managed society. We have but to recognize that fact and survey the scene. Its harrying oppressions are endured because this country is at war. In such a time men surrender upon a large scale their individual interests and personal autonomy in the face of a great national effort. Does anyone really believe that these intrusions, limitations, interferences, regimentations would be submitted to in peacetime in this country under our present form of government, where businessmen, workmen, and citizens can put pressure on their congressmen and senators to resist the regulations of the public managers? They will use their political power to wreck the whole thing, as they did during the NRA episode of evil memory, which was ready for the scrap heap before the Court administered the *coup de grâce*. It fell down upon the issue of compliance. Let the planners and the autarchists wring their hands in lamentation over that fact. Maybe it is a sad fact that men will not submit more tamely to being thus ruled. But it is a fact which settles definitively the proposition that planning must be carried on by a totalitarian government with unlimited powers of coercion and in which the citizen is powerless to express or enforce his resistance, or the idea must be abandoned.

The same holds true in the matter of public spending to support such a regime. Public spending necessitates heavy taxes to begin with. But under this fascist system a large part of the public spending is made possible by public borrowing. The spending of borrowed money as a permanent policy with a continuous rise in the public debt can have only one effect. As the debt rises, the yearly interest charge increases. In time the interest charge gets to be more than all the other costs of government. Funds for interest can be obtained only by taxes. A rising public debt means a continuously rising interest charge and persistently rising taxes to service the debt. When this war ends, this government will have to collect more money just to pay interest on the debt than it has ever collected for every other purpose in any year up to and including 1941. And this is only the beginning. For as the war ends, the government is planning new and more adventurous and, as it likes to say, "dynamic" uses of public debt than ever. Of course businessmen and individuals will resist such taxes. The free society knows such a device as the "tax strike." We have seen that happen in our cities within the last dozen years when in some places—Chicago noticeably—schoolteachers had to go unpaid for several years because the payment of taxes ceased. Only in a totalitarian state can these oppressive levies be imposed and enforced. And even in such a state there is a limit. But the limit in the free society is swiftly reached. Mussolini could operate a system like this for twenty-one years in Italy. But he would have come to an end long before if Italy had had a free parliament answerable to the people to make its laws. It is for this reason—and there are other reasons as well—that I make the statement that this managed public-debt-supported autarchy must turn to the totalitarian government or abandon its plans.

1. The Totalitarian State

Does anyone seriously believe that a totalitarian government will appear here? Where is this dictator to come from? Is not our Constitution an impassable barrier to dictatorship? Are we likely to amend it—which requires the consent of thirty-two states—to invite a dictator to govern us? If not, then where is he to come from? Is he to spring out of the ground? No. He will not spring out of the ground. And probably we will not amend our Constitution to oblige him. I say *probably,* because one cannot be sure. Before the last war, when prohibition by constitutional amendment was proposed, it seemed the most fantastic thing in this world. But a little touch of crisis—a war crisis—and the thing was done with bewildering swiftness. Then men said repeal was impossible. It would never be possible to get the assent of thirty-two states. Clarence Darrow, doughtiest anti-dry, said the hope was utterly illusory. Prohibition, he said, would die by the dead-letter route. Then came another crisis—the depression—and the Eighteenth Amendment vanished almost as swiftly as it came. Crises have a way of dissolving many things—often very old things and sometimes very precious things. Before us now lies another crisis—a momentous one—as great, at least, and perhaps greater than the Civil War crisis, though in a different way. What will vanish amid its dislocations we cannot say.

However, a great deal may be done without constitutional amendment. Here is another point at which we will do well to choose our words with caution. The words dictatorship and totalitarianism are used very loosely as perfectly synonymous. This is not so. The totalitarian government is one which possesses in itself the total sovereignty of the nation. In our government that total sovereignty resides in the people. Only parts of it are delegated through the Constitution to the federal government. A very great part of it—indeed the greatest part—is reserved to the states. And very vital portions of the sovereignty are delegated neither to federal government nor to states but are held wholly by the people.

Our government, then, is the antithesis of the totalitarian government. However, it is possible to imagine a parliamentary government in which the central government would have practically unlimited or total sovereignty. That is true of the English government. The Parliament in England is pretty nearly supreme. It could change the form of government from a monarchy to a republic. It is subject to being elected by the people. But even this limitation is not absolute. Members of Parliament are elected for five years. But that term of office is fixed not by a constitution but by an act of Parliament. Parliament can change it from five to seven or to ten. Indeed in the past Parliament has called off elections and lengthened its life to twelve years once. In this war crisis Parliament by its own vote has deferred general elections until the crisis is over. Parliament could call off elections indefinitely if there were enough votes to support a cabinet in such a course. Our House of Representatives must be elected every two years. That is fixed by the Constitution. There is a long series of popular rights established by tradition and law in England, but Parliament can change the law on every one of them.

A totalitarian government, therefore, is one—whatever its form—which possesses the power to enact any law or take any measure that seems proper to it. That government may consist of a dictator, or a king and cabinet, or a king, cabinet, and parliament, or just a parliament and a president. Provided that government is clothed with the power to do anything without any limitation on its powers, it is totalitarian. It has total power. Now with us the federal government consists of a president and congress. Even if the President and Congress agreed on a measure it could not be adopted unless under the Constitution they have the express or implied power to adopt it. The powers conferred on our federal government are very limited. The governments of our states possess powers which in England reside in the central Parliament. And there are great powers which are not granted either to federal government or state, but are reserved to the people. Not only are the powers of the central government divided among Congress and the President and the Court, but there is an immense range of sovereign powers which the federal government does not possess at all. If our system could be changed so that all the powers of the state legislature could be vested in the central government and all the limitations set out in the Constitution could be repealed, we would have a totalitarian government here even though we preserve the presidency and the Congress and the Court to determine the division of powers among themselves. In theory such a change could not take place here without a constitutional amendment. But it is possible for the powers of states and of Congress itself to be lost by non-use, by slow abdication under powerful economic pressures. It is possible for the central government, under one pretext or another, to draw slowly to itself these powers. We have seen this happen on a limited scale under limited pressures. What may happen under more irresistible pressure we can guess.

We have a dictator when the unlimited powers of a totalitarian government are deposited with the executive or an executive council. No one will admit that he wants a dictator in Washington. But there are many who say with complete frankness that they want the central government to have whatever power is necessary to carry out its will—to have absolute power, some are willing to admit. Of course they do not advocate the abolition of the bill of rights protecting the citizens against abuses by the central government. But no less a person than Vice-President Wallace has expressed the fear that we have put too much emphasis on "bill-of-rights" democracy.

There is a powerful school in Washington that wants to make great fundamental changes in the structure and powers of our federal government which will remove if not all, at least all of the important, restrictions upon its powers. They will not call the product of these changes a totalitarian government. But that is what it will be. They wish to endow the central government with vast powers over every phase of our social and economic life. A dictatorship is a totalitarian government in which all the powers of sovereignty are centered not in a balanced government but in a single man. Our fascist-minded "democrats" want a totalitarian government. No one will admit he wants those powers lodged with a single man—a dictator. Nevertheless, they play even with that fire.

2. The New Order

When our government was formed, the great tyrant was the tyrant state. Its founders had seen the tyrant state operated by an absolute monarch like Louis XIV and XV or a parliamentary monarchy like England. They were determined to make an end of the tyrant state in America.

But a state must have power. How endow it with power and yet prevent it from becoming despotic through the abuse of that power? The problem was solved by splitting up the powers of the state and lodging those fractional parts in different agencies. Each agency, the founders rightly believed, could be depended on to guard with jealous vigilance their several possessions of power. The federal government would have a fraction. That fraction would be divided among the

Congress, the executive, the Court. Another fraction should be deposited with the states—each in its own territory. Still another should remain, undelegated to anyone, in the source of all power, the people.

This made state despotism impossible. In a world where free societies began to blossom and representative government flourished until the last war, this country almost alone held fast to its freedom. Almost everywhere else those hard-won freedoms have been withering. Now men—men of good will, as they like to think themselves, lovers of freedom as they proclaim themselves, the monopolists of freedom—are busy with plans to junk the structure of government which alone in the world has resisted the erosion of tyranny. The anointed lovers of free government propose to scrap the government which has remained free and to replace it with some pale imitations of the governments which were the first to lose freedom. Incredible? It is no more incredible than the spectacle of social democrats in Germany supporting Von Hindenburg, the Junker, and Junkers supporting Hitler, the iconoclast.

Nevertheless, those men who are in positions of the highest power have now grown utterly weary of the present structure of government in America. The functions of government, they say, are now different. Government must take upon itself the redemption of the economic life and the organization of the whole social structure of the people. It is not just a police force, an army and a navy, a postal system, a diplomatic service along with some minor dabblings in farm and river and harbor aid. Now it is responsible for creating the purchasing power of the nation. Now it must preside over the organization of industry and supervise through great bureaus the prices and distribution of the products of farms, mines, factories. It must engage in vast enterprises of its own, the production of power, the management of transportation by air, sea, and land. Above all, it is to become the great banker and investment trust and finance holding company. It is to be the great insurance company bringing security to old and young, employer and employee, the widow, the maimed, and the halt. It will have billions—incomprehensible billions —to invest. It will build dams and roads and schools and highways and seaways. It will manage our exports and imports. It will do a hundred other things, including educational and recreational and cultural and scientific things.

Obviously such a government, dominating and guiding such vast enterprises, cannot be run by a Congress such as ours. The thing is unthinkable. We must now see the imperious necessity of efficiency. It was only the other day when the same kind of men were pointing with scorn and hatred to our great holding companies and denouncing them as instruments of the devil. They were telling us these evil things must be dissolved, that the stockholders who were the owners must be emancipated and given power over their properties which had been taken out of their hands by bankers and managers. We had won political democracy in which the common man conquered control of his political life. But it was a futile conquest because he did not possess the control of his economic life. We must, they said, set up economic democracy in which the owner of industry, as well as labor, will have something to say about these great corporations. But all that is changed. Now the magnificent efficiency of the great corporation and holding company has fascinated them. Instead of modeling the corporation on the pattern of the democratic state, they wish to alter the state to form it on the model of the totalitarian corporation.

"How many subscriptions," asked Professor Henry J. Ford, one of the pioneer exponents of this theory, "would a promoter of a new joint stock company get if he used the argument that the interests of the stockholders would be perfectly secured because it had been arranged that they themselves would elect all the employees?" Can citizens, they conclude, suppose themselves to be any more secure because they are called on to elect all their public officials? The point seems to be that the management of a joint stock company and a community of citizens is quite the same thing. The primary end is efficiency of operation. And this view has been expressly approved by our current New Dealers. But, after all, efficiency in the corporate management and efficiency in the state are two very different things. And this for the reason that the product in each case is different. The corporation executives are asked to produce goods and profits. But one of the products of government is social freedom. The corporate management is not called on to secure to all its employees the perfect atmosphere in which to follow their own aspirations and methods of working. All this is laid down for them and the severest compliance is exacted in the most efficient corporations. The government's objective is to create a climate and an environment in which free men may follow their own dreams and ambitions and forms of living and striving. It will be efficient in proportion as it makes that fully possible. It must, of course, in a modern state, do other things too. But it must never interfere with this greatest and primary aim.

While talking endlessly of freedom, these planners forget it when they make their blueprints for our new state. For they have political blueprints quite as definite as for the economic system. Generally their program is based on the following principle:

The government of divided powers is no longer suited to the modern economic state.

It is necessary that we erect a strong central government whose powers are unlimited.

These powers of the central government should be concentrated in the executive with the Congress acting as a mere supervisory body.

We have made the mistake up to now, so the argument goes, of scattering power in order to weaken the government that it may not oppress us. We have weakened it so that it cannot serve us. The correct principle is to concentrate power, supply the government with unlimited power and adequate force, and then make that government responsible. The way to achieve such government, says Mr. Herbert Agar, one of the more vocal New Dealers, is to "make the responsibilities of the executive *absolute and public*." He argues the point thus: "The problem of constitutional government, however, is not merely the problem of how to restrain the use of power. It is not force which is to be feared, but force in the hands of rulers who cannot be held responsible by their fellow men. *A government must have unlimited power to act*, and at times act fast, or it cannot survive the emergencies of our unquiet world."[1]

[1] *A Time for Greatness*, by Herbert Agar, Little, Brown, New York, 1942.

Something like this has already happened in the British Parliament. Mr. Harold J. Laski, economic adviser to the British Labor party, who enjoys peculiarly intimate relationships with our White House, tells us that the British Parliament is hardly to be classed as a formal legislative body any more. "Its real business is to act as the Cabinet's organ of registration."[2] And Mr. Carr, of the London *Times*, confirms this view by assuring us that "the best Parliament can do is to confine itself to vague pronouncements of its intention and then give wide powers to the executive to carry this intention into effect."[3]

If this is true, it is easy to understand Mr. Laski's characterization and Mr. Carr's assurance that the Parliament is "rapidly losing power to the Cabinet and the Prime Minister." There is, of course, no doubt that the objective of our New Dealers is a government nearer this type—where almost unlimited power is in the hands of the central government but with that power centered mostly in the hands of the executive.

It must not be supposed that these are the views of men who are outside of the New Deal high command. On the contrary. As I have pointed out, the New Deal has had, up to recently, a great planning agency—the National Resources Planning Board. It was a bureau of the President's own executive office. It was headed by his uncle, a very aged but highly respected gentleman who was mere window dressing. It was supposed to be making blueprints for projects in the postwar world. Actually it was making a blueprint for the new social order. It was this board which was propagandizing the program of Dr. Alvin H. Hansen for unlimited postwar spending of borrowed funds. But it had views also respecting our political mechanisms. Dr. Hansen himself outlined them. In an interview printed in the Chicago *Journal of Commerce* he said:

> Congress will surrender to the administration the power to tax, keeping to itself the right only to establish broad limits within which the administration may move.
> Congress will appropriate huge sums; will surrender the power of directing how and when they will be spent.

[2]*The American Presidency*, by Harold J. Laski, Harper's, New York, 1940.
[3]*Conditions of Peace*, by Edmund H. Carr, Macmillan, New York, 1942.

235

Other extraordinary powers such as, for instance, to effect wholesale social reforms, will be delegated to the administration *which will retain most, if not all, of its present extraordinary wartime controls.*[4]

The same view is supported by Dr. Charles Merriam, of Chicago University. Dr. Merriam was vice-chairman of the President's personal planning body—this same National Resources Planning Board. He insists that our government must be streamlined. By this he means that Congress must withdraw as a formal legislative body. It must adopt a few very general directives at each session instead of passing laws. It must do what Carr says is the very most the British Parliament can do—express a "vague pronouncement of its intention and then give wide powers to the executive to carry it into effect." It must limit itself to granting to the President large lump sums leaving it to him to allocate them as he pleases. Drs. Lewis Meriam and Laurence F. Schmeckebier indicate that the manner of attaining this new form of government will be "to have Congress delegate some of its powers to the President and by having it forego the exercise of some of the powers it possesses. The argument advanced in support of this change is briefly that the President alone represents all the people; the people hold the President responsible for the success of the government; and consequently the President should have power commensurate with that responsibility."[5]

These views represent the opinions upon which the President's planning boards operated. They represent the views of most of that group of economists, political scientists, and lawyers who for the last six years have moved around from one bureau to another as their guides and philosophers and who generally are looked upon in Washington as the thinking element of the New Deal. It was, indeed, the rather slow and even reluctant discovery by Congress of the persistence and virility of the drive for these ideas which had much to do with the revolt of Congress, the indignant sweep with which it destroyed the National Resources Planning Board and later turned its wrath upon the Board of Economic Warfare in such a way as to end in its liquidation.

[4]*Chicago Journal of Commerce,* June 27, 1942.
[5]*Reorganization of the National Government,* by Lewis Meriam and Laurence F. Schmeckebier, Brookings Institution, Washington, 1939.

There is something in all this alarmingly like those ideas which flourished in Hitler's Germany. "The principle of unconditional connection," said Hitler, *"between absolute responsibility and absolute authority* will gradually breed up a choice of leaders inconceivable today in the era of irresponsible parliamentarianism." The state, he conceded, will not be able to do without these things called parliaments. They, however, "will give counsel, but responsibility can and must be borne by one man."[6]

In the light of this movement it is easy to understand the persistent, concerted attacks upon Congress which have featured the last two years of our history. Men like Herbert Agar ask: "In a world that must be first class or nothing can we afford a congress?" He looks upon congressmen as buffoons. Mr. Raymond Clapper, who has leveled a good many rather dull-edged shots at Congress, has informed us that "99 per cent of what you hear in Congress is tripe, ignorance, and demagoguery." The crime Congress commits is twofold. It disagrees with the columnist and indulges in what is sneeringly called "talk." Congress would have great difficulty agreeing with columnists since they disagree among themselves as vigorously as congressmen do. And how a democratic chamber is to arrive at any kind of conclusion without discussion, which is carried on by means of talk, it is difficult to say. As a matter of fact, more sapient students and critics of our House of Representatives have complained that debate has been dangerously curtailed. However, no man familiar with the Washington scene and the often weird phenomena of capital propaganda can have the slightest doubt that many columnists, radio announcers, and newspaper editorial columns lent themselves, some unwittingly, to an inspired and directed attack upon the institution of Congress for the purpose of discrediting it in the interest of this new theory of the centralized executive government.

3. THE POWER OF THE PURSE

The greatest weapon in the hands of the people against the irresponsible state is the power of the purse. That power was the instrument by which the commoners of England first drew from

[6] *Mein Kampf.* Reynal & Hitchcock, American translation, 1940.

the King a recognition of their rights and then erected those rights into a House of Commons and from there went on to possess themselves of complete domination of the government, including the power of life and death over the King. In our Constitution that power is deposited in the Congress and even the Senate is denied the right of originating money bills. Now it is proposed to put the origination of such bills in the hands of the executive, to limit the Congress to a mere approval of large lump-sum or blank-check appropriations, giving to the President the power to allocate those funds. Mr. Harold Laski has suggested that the Congress should "by a self-denying ordinance, which has worked admirably in the House of Commons, deny any member the right to ask for appropriations that is not sought under the direct authority of the President." Imagine what would be the final result of such a plan. We have seen what can happen when this blank-check method is used, that is, when the Congress grants to the President four or five billions, leaving to him the power to say how it shall be spent.

For many years every session of Congress was featured by what was called a pork-barrel bill. "Pork" was a colloquialism for those appropriations which congressmen asked for their own districts. Every congressman had a pet project for his district which might cost from a few thousand to a few hundred thousand. The district wanted a new post office or federal building, an agricultural experiment station or a fish hatchery, a drydock or army post, a naval station, or some appropriation for roads or other projects within the limited functions of the federal government. All together these appropriations amounted to little more than sixty or seventy millions and probably two thirds of the money appropriated was for useful purposes. Yet each year these pork-barrel bills, exposed to pitiless publicity, evoked a storm of criticism. To get such an appropriation the congressman or senator merely introduced a bill or made application to the Appropriation Committee and the subject was passed on by the whole House.

But in 1933 Congress passed its first "blank-check" bill, handing over to the President $3,300,000,000 to be spent as he chose. When it did that something very fundamental, which nobody bargained for, happened in this country. After that, instead of appealing to

Congress for an appropriation, the congressman and senator had to go with his hat in his hand to get his share of the public funds from the President. Overnight that measure put the Congress into the hands of the President. The Congress, indeed, still possessed the power of the purse. But it had handed the purse over to the President filled with money. Now congressmen had to sue at the feet of the President for handouts. Governors and mayors of cities, instead of petitioning Congress, were forced to go as mendicants to the President, who became the dispenser of all good things. The great question in every congressional district was—can our congressman get us our share from the President? How does our congressman stand at the White House? Why, asked constituents, is it that we get nothing while in the next district the people are enjoying all sorts of rich benefits? The answer was simple. The congressman over in that neighboring district votes with the President; our congressman fights him. How can we expect to get anything? What we need in this district is a man who can get along with the President, who will get us playgrounds, high schools, parkways, a magnificent post office, a great dam, and other millions besides.

Congressmen—even Republicans—had to convince their constituents that even though they were in the opposition they were "playing along" reasonably with the administration. Of course the billions voted to the President would one day be exhausted and, presumably, Congress would get a chance to emancipate itself. But the President always had countless hundreds of millions of unexpended balances in his hands from the old bill for which congressmen and senators were scrambling.

Amid the many tons of abuse heaped upon Congress, it must be said in good truth that none was so richly deserved as that which was directed at the Congress from 1933 to 1939. Never in the history of congressional government in this country had Congress sunk to so low a level. It threw away its dignity, its self-respect; it discarded its functions to such an extent that it had to be rebuked by the Supreme Court—unanimously in the NRA case. Congress literally abdicated. Its leaders became the pliant office boys and messengers and stooges of the White House. The President publicly sent "must" bills to it. He lectured it. And his bureaucrats openly sneered at its members. The congresses of those years must remain as monuments of weakness and docility. Worse, they supply to us the complete proof that when the power of the purse is surrendered to the President, the Congress becomes a mere rubber stamp. This is the plan which the remodelers of our government propose to fasten on the nation as its permanent form.

4. The Bureaucratic State

Congress is being incessantly badgered because of its failure to deal to the satisfaction of everyone with all the innumerable problems that demand its attention. The explanation of this takes us to the very center of the great problem of national government, which cannot longer be ignored. For a good many years the people in local communities and in states have been calling upon government to assume first one and then another function hitherto belonging to private arrangement. The problems of farmers, of little and big businessmen, of human welfare, of education, of all sorts of things have been saddled on the government. Along with these has gone another movement to push all those problems toward Washington. Under the interstate-commerce clause of the Constitution almost everything under the sun, including taking a girl on a party across a state line, has been held to be interstate commerce. The most fantastic manipulations of that phrase—interstate commerce—have been invoked to bring the matter under the jurisdiction of the federal government.

The effect of this has been to pile upon the desk of Congress a mountainous heap of problems with which no human beings ever created can possibly deal. The only escape from this impossible assumption of tasks has been to pass them on to some subordinate agency. Congress, therefore, began to create bureaus. And as fast as new functions were thrust upon Congress it expanded the bureaus already created and then created new ones. This practice began before the last war. The war gave the movement a great impetus. The problems of the postwar world added to the tendency. The Great Depression of 1929 gave an immense push to the whole movement. This war has finally completed the job until today, under the pretense of interstate commerce or of emergency or the "general welfare," the central government has taken jurisdiction over almost every phase of our national life.

Against these bureaus a storm of public damnation has broken. And the very word "bureaucrat" has come to express an extreme brand of public odium. As a matter of fact, there is plenty of justification for this criticism. At first the growth of this bureaucracy was one of those unplanned stratagems which an overworked and bewildered Congress turned to in a spirit of frustration. But now the bureaus are defended by a new school which looks upon this institution as the model form of government. This word "bureaucrat" must not be confused with the same word as used in former days. Once upon a time anybody working in a public office was called a bureaucrat and, in its most odious sense, it described nothing more than the official who lived on red tape. The present-day meaning, however, comprises a significance of far more serious character. The old bureaucrat was a public employee who carried out the laws and orders of Congress. But today he is something very much more than this. Congress, in its impotence to deal with the multitude of its assignments, delegates to these bureaus great gobs of its own legislative power, clothes them with the authority to make laws which they call "regulations" and more recently "directives." But these regulations and directives are actually laws and have the force of law. The grand result of this is that the bureau officials who are appointed by the President are answerable to him and pliant in his hands. And as they have this power through "directives" to enact laws, a vast sector of the power of Congress to legislate has passed to the hand of the executive. Judge Hatton W. Sumners, distinguished chairman of the Judiciary Committee of the House, says that today more law is being enacted by these bureaus than by Congress itself.

More recently the President has taken to creating bureaus without any authority of Congress and without so much as notifying it. With vast sums of money voted to him in lump sums by Congress, he can allocate any amount he chooses to these bureaus, which exercise over the lives and fortunes and affairs of the people the most extensive supervision. This practice has led to a curious experiment in extraconstitutional activity by the executive. The President creates these bureaus, endows them with the most arbitrary powers and the most generous supplies of money. If Congress does not like the bureau or wishes to destroy it, then Congress must pass a law forbidding its continuance or stripping it of its powers. When Congress does that, the President can veto the law and Congress, to pass it over the veto, must have a *two-thirds vote*. This executive technique of usurping powers he does not possess, until stopped by Congress, is putting into the hands of the President the power to govern without congressional collaboration.

Little by little these bureaus are exercising power over a multitude of subjects that were once the province of the states. They may be exercising unconstitutional powers, but states and individuals and cities are often powerless to resist their ordinances because the executive has in his hands the distribution of such immense sums that the local authorities cannot afford to challenge the power.

This vice takes its origin, however, in the great drift of states, towns, trade and labor and welfare bodies, and every kind of pressure group toward taking their problems to Washington and demanding solution at its hands. As long as this continues, Congress must abandon most of its work to bureaus. And bureaus will always be under the domination of the executive. The whole tendency plays into the hands of the champions of highly centralized executive power. From this there is no escape but to begin to reverse the tendency—to begin to send all those non-federal powers back to the states and the cities where they belong.

5. Liquidating State Powers

Perhaps nothing in this whole movement seems so unlikely to come to pass as the liquidation of the powers of the state. But it will not do to overlook the power and sweep of the forces against which true free government is tending in this world—even in America. The corrosive power of the Great Depression has wrought greatly upon the whole structure of our society—far more than is generally supposed. We have yet to feel the full shock of the war crisis and the far more terrible blow from the postwar crisis which is yet to come.

We must take note here of the plans that are being made for our new order. Under our Constitution the authority of the federal government is very severely restricted. However, the federal government, beginning around 1881, has been slowly extending its power under the general-welfare clause, the interstate-commerce clause, and the so-called "inherent-rights-of-sovereignty" theory during times of emergency. If you will consult the various acts under which the national government has usurped so many powers you will see it is always done under one of these guises. If the general-welfare or the interstate-commerce clauses are not adequate excuse for the invasion, the assumption of emergency will do the work. But generally the proposal to pay federal money to the tune of hundreds of millions into the states or to relieve the states of their own fiscal burdens is sufficient to paralyze all resistance to the invasion. Thus the government, under a color of constitutional observance, has enormously stretched its power over a vast terrain. However, there is a limit even to this sort of thing. Hence some new means of control must be invented. And these means have been found.

A great Wall Street banker who does not own a share of stock in a railroad or utility company and who has no constitutional grant of power to regulate it may, nevertheless, acquire over it an almost autocratic power. He can dictate its policies, name its officials, and elect its directorate. One of the great problems of the last fifty years has been the ascendency of a few powerful banking houses over our railroad and utility systems. This they acquired first by capturing control of the pools of national savings—the banks and the insurance companies and finance companies. They could withhold or grant financial aid to these industrial corporations. They could make available on short notice funds for stock and bond issues by the companies in sums they could get in no other way.

Now the President's planning groups have been outlining the program of the administration to become the partner or financier or both of transportation, communication, shipping, shipbuilding, radio, basic metals, and other enterprises. By these means it will unite to the vast powers it exercises by political agencies those almost equally great powers it may exercise as investor and banker.

The government, if it carries out its plans for universal insurance with security from the cradle to the grave, will soon be in possession of the great bulk of the savings of the United States. As for private insurance companies—in what will they invest? Private investment will gradually disappear from the scene and they, along with almost every other kind of investment agency, including the savings and commercial banks, will be forced to buy United States bonds.

If you want some mortgage money on your house or wish to buy a home, it will be federal funds which will provide the money or at least the federal government will control its flow through its guarantee and mortgage-insurance agencies. If you have a farm and want to borrow money, it will be from a financial institution either owned or controlled by the federal government.

Most of the states are at the end of the road financially. The same thing is true of the cities. Yet when the war is over the demands upon these local government agencies will be beyond their power. How will the states and cities meet the enormous costs of education? The answer is simple. The government is already laying plans to become their banker and financial fortress—the banker of the states and cities and school districts and counties. Governors, county commissioners, mayors, and school-board members will stand in line at the federal treasury for their handouts. They will stand in line not before Congress but before a federal bureaucrat with almost absolute powers in his hands. Will it be necessary to amend the Constitution to give that bureaucratic spendthrift power over the object of his philanthropy? He will have no constitutional power to require either a state or a city or a school district or an industrial corporation or a building company or a local utility to do anything. But he will have the power to give or not to give, to open the treasury door or not to open it to the suppliant governor, mayor, or corporation executive. The pass admitting them to the vaults of the treasury will be a certificate of compliance with the conditions which the bureaucrat makes for the federal gift.

The Supreme Court held, in the AAA case in which that famous creation of Mr. Henry Wallace was held unconstitutional, that it was based on this very theory, that it undertook to do by indirection what the federal government could not do under a direct grant of congressional power—to govern the farms of America through the power of appropriation, enforcing compliance with otherwise illegal orders by withholding funds. But the Court that made that decision is no more—a new batch of judges owing their appointment to the present executive is in power.

If the present movement should succeed and the powers of the federal government should be pushed to the last limit under the new interpretations of the interstate-commerce and the general-welfare clauses and emergency theories, and these powers should be supplemented with a great bureaucratic structure empowered to engage in almost every kind of enterprise, including chiefly the great enterprise of banking and investment, the power of the federal government over every phase of our national and local functions will be complete. If, along with that, the Congress should consent to forego the exercise of many of its powers while delegating others to the President, contenting itself with the role of a mere supervising and critical agency, making great lump-sum appropriations and adopting yearly a few vague directives instead of laws, then indeed we will have in this country a centralized government with practically unlimited powers, and with those powers for all practical purposes lodged in the hands of the executive. This is as near totalitarian government as the present advocates of our American brand of national socialism believe is necessary. Though, if we arrive at this point, there will be no barrier save an explosion of public resistance to prevent the central government from going to any limit it desires.

6. Can It Happen Here?

I have already observed that no idea is more deeply rooted in the American consciousness than the belief that nothing can deprive us of our long-established freedoms. For this reason it is difficult for us to give very much credence to the possibility that the objectives outlined here will ever be realized. Let us see.

Generally these objectives are:

1. To make appropriations to the executive in lump sums for major purposes and to leave him free to work out all the detailed allocations to specific organization units.

2. To have the Congress, instead of adopting specific legislation, delegate to the President the authority to make the laws within the framework of a general congressional directive.

3. To give the President a complete free hand over the structure of the government.

4. To repeal all the laws that govern procedures in administration and have all this determined by regulations proclaimed by the President.

5. To put the Comptroller General under the authority of the President instead of Congress.

6. To put all the quasi-legislative and quasi-judicial establishments, like the Federal Trade Commission, under the direct authority of the President.

This is the program. Now in respect to this I think the following is a fair statement: That some of these objectives have been already completely achieved, others partly achieved, and that there is not one of them we have not already either done wholly or in part at some time in the last ten years. It is not a question whether or not these things can happen in this country. They have happened.

1. Take the first proposal to have the Congress make appropriations in lump sums leaving it to the President to allocate this money, that is, to spend it as he sees fit—leaving it to him to determine who shall get it. In the last ten years from 40 to 50 per cent of all federal appropriations have been made in that way. The budget of 1933-34 amounted to $7,105,000,000. Of this amount $3,300,000,000 was voted in one big lump sum to the President, leaving it to his judgment (save for a very minor exception) to pay out to whom and in such sums as he chose. This was the beginning of the most dangerous tendency this country has ever known. This practice has been continued to the present time. The blank-check appropriation is not, then, a vague fear of something that may come to pass. It is here and has been here for ten years.

In the last days of the session before the summer recess of Congress in 1943, Secretary of Commerce Jesse Jones was testifying before the Banking and Currency Committee of the Senate. The senators were somewhat surprised to learn that the Board of Economic Warfare had spent about $1,500,000,000. Not one cent of this money had been appropriated by Congress, which had given the board a mere $12,000,000 for administrative expenses. Where did the money come from? asked the astonished legislators. Mr. Jones informed them the money had been appropriated by the Reconstruction Finance Corporation of which he is chairman. Where had it gotten the money? From the Treasury, from which it borrowed it at 1 per cent interest. This vast sum it had handed over to Vice-President Wallace to be spent at his sweet will, without even so much as an accounting. The Reconstruction Finance Corporation had appropriated $34,000,000,000 in the same way to various bureaus. What, asked Democratic Senator McKellar, acting chairman of the Appropriations Committee, is the need around here for such a functionary as myself—an appropriation committee chairman—if Mr. Jones can appropriate $34,000,000,000? What function do I perform? The fact fell upon the minds of the senators with a sense of shock.

Senator Joseph C. O'Mahoney, also a Democrat and for long a supporter of the New Deal, wrote recently:

> Lend-Lease, which was created by Congress as a war measure, has become a gigantic financial instrument of the Executive by which, without the advice or consent of Congress, the global shape of things to come is being prepared. Congress has appropriated 18 billion dollars for Lend-Lease. But from funds appropriated by Congress for other purposes some 50 additional billions have been transferred to this agency by Executive order.

It is, of course, sheer nonsense to speculate on whether this feature of the plan to erect the President into a powerful appropriating agent has been made effective. It has been made effective. The job is done. It is the secret of the immense power which the present executive has exercised over the affairs of this country for ten years.

2. The second item in this subversive program is to have Congress adopt a few general directives leaving the President to fill in the details. In other words, to have Congress delegate to the President its constitutional powers of legislation. Surely we have not forgotten the National Recovery Administration—the incredible NRA. In our modern society it is at least a fair assumption to say that two thirds of the domain in which important legislation is enacted is economic.

Laws affecting industry and labor and agriculture constitute the most important phase of congressional activity. In 1933, suddenly, with little or no consideration in the great disorder and fever of the collapse, Congress passed the National Recovery Act. That act authorized the President to bring about a complete and comprehensive organization of industry and to make rules and regulations governing every phase of its activities. Under practically every category of industry and finance the entire nation was organized into what the Italians would call "corporatives"; what we called code authorities. These code authorities, under the authority of the President, were empowered to make rules, to regulate production, prices, distribution, competition in all its phases. These regulations had the force of law and under them men could be haled into court on civil and criminal liabilities. Some men were actually jailed for violating them. It is, I think, a fair statement that the President, under the NRA, exercised the right to make laws over at least half, if not more, of the domain within which Congress ordinarily legislates. The Supreme Court, in a unanimous decision, declared this law unconstitutional and based its opinion entirely on the proposition that Congress had *delegated its legislative power to the President,* who in turn had delegated it to the code authorities. It was an abdication by Congress, said the Court. If there was any part of the legislative power over economic life that remained undelegated, Congress effectively turned that over to the AAA, which was also declared unconstitutional, and to several other bureaus that escape judicial annulment because Congress had divested itself of its powers in somewhat more artful language.

Of course the NRA decision has not put an end to this practice. On the contrary, it has grown. The delegations have been cloaked in seemingly constitutional language. Senator O'Mahoney said recently that in the last ten years the executive branch has adopted and proclaimed from 110 order-issuing agencies over 4,000 executive orders with the force of law, and that this was as many as Congress itself had passed in that time.

The Constitution declares that the President "shall have power by and with the advice and consent of the Senate to make treaties, provided two-thirds of the Senators present concur; and he shall nominate and by and with the advice and consent of the Senate shall appoint ambassadors, other public ministers and consuls. . . ." Yet this constitutional provision, plain enough beyond misinterpretation, is ignored by the present executive. Agreements of all sorts covering almost every field of international arrangement are made by the present executive and the Senate is not always even apprised of the agreements. Mr. Wallace McClure, a member of the staff of the State Department, has just published a volume, *International Executive Agreements* in which he writes: "The President can do anything by executive agreement that he can do by treaty, provided Congress by law co-operates, and there is a very wide field of action in which the co-operation of Congress is not necessary; indeed where Congress possesses no Constitutional authority to dissent." And Senator O'Mahoney says that we have today a far greater number of executive agreements than we have treaties.

In the same way the President has begun to ignore the constitutional requirement that diplomatic agents shall be appointed by him with the advice and consent of the Senate. The President names what he calls "his envoys" or "his personal representatives" to various countries without ever submitting their names to the Senate and escapes the necessity of even getting an appropriation to pay them by taking the funds out of the blank-check grants with which Congress has endowed him. He has, upon an extensive scale, done the same thing in the field of domestic appointments, naming men like Mr. Harry Hopkins to the very highest functions in the state, even outranking in importance cabinet officers, without any provision for the office or any appropriation for it or any confirmation of the appointment by the Senate. To these usurpations Congress has bent a compliant neck, shamefully suppressing its own dignity, muttering under its breath until recently when, to the great disgust of the President's drove of radio and columnar storm troopers, Congress has shown signs of recovering its constitutional self-respect.

3. The third item in the program is to take the hand of Congress completely off the whole subject of the structure of the government. Always Congress has determined, with the approval of the President, how the government shall be organized. Now it is pro-

posed that the President shall have full and free hand, unrestrained by Congress, to determine what departments, bureaus, boards, and commissions shall exist, with power to change or shift powers around from one bureau to another, change the number and character of bureaucrats in those bureaus, and decide what funds shall be allocated to each. The reorganization bill which excited such a violent attack just after the court fight and brought the President a second defeat, involved this feature. The attempt to do this has already been made by the President. And, though beaten in his first attempt, he did succeed in getting some portion of it in the second attempt. Nevertheless, the determination to effect this change has never departed from the program of the New Dealers, and, under cover of the war crisis, the President has accomplished a good deal of this plan. The same observation applies to Number 4, the proposal to have Congress abdicate also the right to make laws affecting administrative procedures.

5. The Comptroller General is an official created by Congress as an agent of Congress to follow and audit and scrutinize all expenditures of money to determine whether or not money is being spent in accordance with the legislative authority granted by Congress. One of the first moves of the present administration was against this office. The Comptroller General's office stood as a barrier to the free-and-easy expenditure of funds by the executive. The battle against this last shred of congressional power over appropriations once they had been made was finally abjectly surrendered by Congress in one of those very low moments of servile abnegation of which it gave so many exhibitions until its recent redemption. This item in the program has been accomplished and now the Comptroller General is a mere stooge of the executive.

6. The final item is to enable the executive to get rid of those independent quasi-judicial and quasi-legislative bodies such as the Federal Trade Commission or to bring them completely under his control. At present he can appoint their members, which gives him an adequate measure of control. But he cannot direct their activities once they are appointed. One of the earliest acts of the President was to dismiss a Federal Trade Commissioner who refused to obey him. For that act he was rebuked by the Supreme Court. But,

once again, let us repeat that the Court has changed. We shall soon see another attempt at control on this same front.

In view of this, what point can there be in asking whether or not the abdication by Congress of its power to the President can happen here? It has happened. It was defeated by a Court which stood on the Constitution. But that Court has changed its face and its character radically. And let it not be forgotten that, because the Court had dared to balk the President in his illegal usurpation of power and his subservient Congress in its illegal abdication, the President attempted in the famous attack upon the Court to acquire complete control over its powers by a packing process. Congress had not been sufficiently subdued to surrender on this point. The surrender was never complete. There was always a considerable body of resistance. But the dark precedents have been established—reactionary precedents of the worst type—and by a so-called liberal regime.

VII Final Note

IF WE WILL LOOK over the scene in America we will see clearly enough that, despite many differences in the character, customs, laws, traditions, resources of the peoples of Italy, Germany, and America, we have been drifting along identical courses and under the influence of the same essential forces. We have been moving away from free enterprise and from the essential features of constitutional government. This movement has been going on for a long time, more slowly here for many years than abroad, because our basic conditions were better, but more rapidly in the last ten years. We have, without knowing it, been turning first to one and then another of those devices for escaping our economic difficulties to which Italy and Germany turned before us. We have been doing this because each of these devices offered the political administration the easiest escape. The alternative has been to make difficult and sacrificial corrections in our system and to make unpopular alterations in our course. These sacrificial measures and these hard corrections are possible and might be made under a courageous and heroic leadership. Instead we have had a confused, selfish, and utterly political leadership which has sought out, not the remedies, but the special demands of great and powerful minorities and set about satisfying those demands—running with the streams even though the streams are running over the abyss. The end of it all is that we are experimenting here with precisely the same economic and political measures which fascist Italy and national socialist Germany have been using. Of course we refuse to admit that. Always we adorn those measures here with decorative and patriotic names, while giving to the same measures in Italy and Germany odious names.

If you would know, therefore, who are the fascists in America, you must ask yourselves not who are the men and women most vocal in their denunciations of Hitler and Mussolini. The most ardent enemies of those two leaders were some of their rival fascist dictators in Europe. The test of fascism is not one's rage against the Italian and German war lords. The test is—how many of the essential principles of fascism do you accept and to what extent are you prepared to apply those fascist ideas to American social and economic life? When you can put your finger on the men or the groups that urge for America the debt-supported state, the autarchial corporative state, the state bent on the socialization of investment and the bureaucratic government of industry and society, the establishment of the institution of militarism as the great glamorous public-works project of the nation and the institution of imperialism under which it proposes to regulate and rule the world and, along with this, proposes to alter the forms of our government to approach as closely as possible the unrestrained, absolute government —then you will know you have located the authentic fascist. By all means let us liquidate the few hundred or thousand bundists who are Hitler's ridiculous fifth column in America. Let us locate and point out and, where overt acts are committed, disarm any other fifth columnists playing the game of Italy or Germany or any other foreign country here.

But let us not deceive ourselves into thinking that we are dealing by this means with the problem of fascism. Fascism will come at the hands of perfectly authentic Americans, as violently against Hitler and Mussolini as the next one, but who are convinced that the present economic system is washed up and that the present political system in America has outlived its usefulness and who wish to commit this country to the rule of the bureaucratic state; interfering in the affairs of the states and cities; taking part in the management of industry and finance and agriculture; assuming the role of great national banker and investor, borrowing billions every year and spending them on all sorts of projects through which such a government can paralyze opposition and command public support; marshaling great armies and navies at crushing costs to support the industry of war and preparation for war which will become our greatest industry; and adding to all this the most romantic adventures in global planning, regeneration, and domination all to be done under the authority of a powerfully centralized government in which the executive will hold in effect all the powers with Congress reduced to the role of a debating society. There is your fascist. And the sooner America realizes this dreadful fact the sooner it will arm itself to make an end of American fascism masquerading under the guise of the champion of democracy.

It should be equally clear that all this is in no sense communism. It must stand as a strange commentary on our times that almost all of the criticism leveled at the current course of government in America has been on the theory that it was surrendering to communism and was moving in the direction of Moscow. Nothing could be further from the truth. But it is easy to understand why this is so. In the first place, great numbers of communists have found their way into government service—some of them into key positions. Communist groups have been vocal and, at times, violent in support of what was being done. The explanation of this is perfectly simple once one understands the communist strategy in this as in all countries. Lenin laid down the principle. In a country like America, where communists are only a handful of the population and where there is literally no support for their theories—but a deep hatred of them—it would be folly to suppose they could actually put any portion of communism into effect. The Communist party is utterly different from the old Socialist party. That party was democratic and reformist. It fought honestly and valiantly for various kinds of social and political reforms because it was moved by an interest in the welfare of the masses as well as a devotion to this country. Since it could not force socialism out of hand it battled for such mitigations of the lot of the common man as seemed possible, and it collaborated with the liberal groups to that end. The Communist party fights for no reforms. It takes up various sore spots and irritants in American society. But it has no thought of trying to remedy these evils. On the contrary, it seeks to expand them and use them to further activate them as great irritants. It would be easy to give examples of communist agitators leading movements for perfectly reasonable reforms, yet all the time doing everything possible to make those reforms impossible. The evils aimed at serve the communist purpose as long as they exist as sores into which they can rub sand. In addition to this, the general objective of the party is to produce confusion—confusion everywhere and about everything. The presence of communists in various spots of the New Deal naturally led people to identify New Deal policy as communist.

Another reason for the confusion is the character of the men who are authentic and honest New Dealers but who were not communists. Many of these men are ex-socialists or academic or parlor pinks who had never become outright socialists. This gentry, numerous in New York City, used almost all of the socialist diagnosis of the evils of capitalism and, when on that subject, seemed to be talking the doctrine of socialism. But they always held themselves a little above socialism. They were a kind of radical elite. They flourished on the circumference of the radical movements, never quite forming part of them. The black history of Moscow settled their hash as potential communist philosophers. But it did not end their careers as radical aristocrats. They began to flirt with the alluring pastime of reconstructing the capitalist system. They became the architects of a new capitalist system. And in the process of this new career they began to fashion doctrines that turned out to be the principles of fascism. Of course they do not call them fascism, although some of them frankly see the resemblance. But they are not disturbed, because they know that *they* will never burn books, *they* will never hound the Jews or the Negroes, *they* will never resort to assassination and suppression. What will turn up in their hands will be a very genteel and dainty and pleasant form of fascism which cannot be called fascism at all because it will be so virtuous and polite.

These are the persons from among whom the present government has recruited whole regiments of its bureaucrats—young lawyers steeped in black ignorance of economics and even of history, young economists fascinated by the schemes of Lord Keynes and Dr. Hansen, other young pundits equally fascinated by the guild theories of Dr. Hobson and G. D. H. Cole and a whole train of well-meaning but confused persons whose central doctrine is that the world can be made perfect by the sheer will to make it perfect—men of the Henry Wallace school, a kind of fevered evangelistic school, having almost no doctrines at all, but hating evil and loving goodness, yet withal willing to plunge the world into flames to bring to reality their vague utopias. There has been a tendency to group all such persons together and brand them as communists. That would not matter if it were not that it distracts us from their real character and the direction in which they are actually going, which is not toward communism but toward national socialism or fascism.

At this moment, in the midst of the war, we have a very close approach to national socialism. Congress has passed simple and vague directives delegating vast powers to the executive, and what powers it failed to give he has taken under the shadow of the needs of war. The lives of the people, the affairs of industry, the local concerns of the states are prescribed, ordered, and supervised by the central government, while the greater part of the industrial system is supported by the raging floods of purchasing power created by the government through the medium of national debt, all of it expended on huge military enterprises, while the government dreams of great programs of world management to lengthen out the crisis of war. The nation endures this because it is at war and looks upon it as a temporary dislocation of its normal life which patriotism demands but which will very soon pass away. But is it not apparent that if the war were to end, people would very soon refuse to submit to such an order and that nothing could induce them to submit but superior force?

Nevertheless, it is part of the government's plan to continue this new and abrasive order. "Normal" is precisely the condition to which we will not be permitted to return. Its spokesmen have said so a score of times. "We cannot think of discontinuing the wartime controls," they add more specifically. But in view of the inevitable resistance of the people, how can such a system be continued? The answer is ready. We began this experiment in 1933 under the pressure of an internal economic crisis. We continue and extend it under the stern necessities of a war crisis. When the war ends, with its inevitable chaos, unemployment, and world commitments, we must continue it under the inexorable compulsion of the postwar crisis. And there, indeed, is the secret of this whole black chapter. It is born in crisis, lives on crises, and cannot survive the era of crisis. By the very law of its nature it must create for itself, if it is to continue, fresh crises from year to year. Mussolini came to power in the postwar crisis and became himself a crisis in Italian life. Then he conjured up new crises—the imperious need for Italy's domination of the Mediterranean, the need for further colonial expansion that produced the Ethiopian crisis, after which crises were produced for him in the aggressions of Hitler to whom he instantly attached himself. Hitler's story is the same. And our future is all charted out upon the same turbulent road of permanent crisis.

We would do well to cease our storming at bureaucrats and at the small fry of briefless lawyers, youthful instructors, and social-welfare practitioners who flourish in Washington and are supposed to be at the bottom of all this. They are in Washington because they sing the song that is wanted there, because they prattle the theories which conform to the policies our rulers in Washington want and which they adopt not because these little national and planetary remodelers preach the doctrine but because these policies represent the estimate of the administration as to the easiest line to take with the American people.

It was the easiest line ten years ago. However, it is no longer. When the policy of government spending is first launched it produces nothing but benefits—benefits to the man on relief and the man on the PWA job and to the merchant and manufacturer with whom he spends his government pay. But after a time the burdens pile up. The loan of 1933 that pumped three billion dollars into the cash registers of America is now a debt, calling for interest payments, and on top of it are piled all the other debts of the depression and the war. Continuing this policy will no longer run with the great current of desire in America. Regulating business, cutting in as the partner of industry, repressing the labor unions that were encouraged to action, satisfying the aged who were lured on to dream of abundance—all this will present a problem that will call for such drastic impositions upon every section of the population that nothing short of a totalitarian government supported by the weapons of ruthless coercion and the will to use them will bring compliance from the people. We shall presently be presented with the final crisis—the necessity of taking the last few steps of the last mile to fascism in some generated crisis, of ending the prologue and running up the curtain on the swelling theme—or of calling off the whole wretched business in some costly, yet inescapable, convulsion.

If national socialism is not the answer to the troubles of the capitalist system—then what is? The question is a fair one. My own answer is that as between the troubles of the capitalist system and national socialism I will take the present system no matter how great and difficult its troubles. Anything rather than the degenerate, the degrading forms of existence which fascism requires. However, I know that the difficulties of the capitalist society are such—weighing as they do upon the least favored elements of the population—that some intelligent and rational solution must be found or the fraudulent messiahs will have their way. I am convinced that it is possible to formulate a program for the regeneration and salvation of the present system of society and for the preservation of our essential political liberties. But it must be in a wholly different direction from national socialism toward which we now move. This system of society cannot possibly be saved by men who do not believe in it, who are convinced that it is washed up, and who are contriving plans that have been tried over and over again in Europe and always with the same result—despotism and disaster. I did not undertake this book in order to outline a program of action, so that this is not the place to indicate such a program. My only purpose is to sound a warning against the dark road upon which we have set our feet as we go marching to the salvation of the world and along which every step we now take leads us farther and farther from the things we want and the things that we cherish.

Bibliography

ITALY

Amoruso, Vincenzo, *Il sindicalismo di Enrico Corradini*, Palermo, 1929.
Ascoli, Max, and Feiler, Arthur, *Fascism for Whom?* W. W. Norton, New York, 1938.
Ashton, E. B., *The Fascist: His State and His Mind*, Wm. Morrow, New York, 1937.
Bonomi, Ivanoe, *From Socialism to Fascism*, London, 1934.
Borgese, G. A., *Goliath*, Viking Press, New York, 1937.
Brady, Robert A., *Business as a System of Power*, Columbia University Press, New York, 1943.
Cambridge Modern History, Vol. XII, Modern Age Books, New York.
Crispi, Francesco, *Memoirs*, London, 1912.
Croce, Benedetto, *History of Italy* (translated by Cecilia M. Ady), Clarendon Press, New York, 1929.
Ebenstein, William, *Fascist Italy*, American Book Co., New York, 1939.
Encyclopaedia Britannica, Title "Italy," 14th Edition, Vol. 12.
Ferrero, G., *Four Years of Fascism*, London, 1924.
Finer, Herman, *Mussolini's Italy*, London, 1935.
Hentze, Margot, *Pre-Fascist Italy*, London, 1939.
Hullinger, Edwin Ware, *The New Fascist State*, Henkle, New York, 1928.
King, Bolton and Okey, Thomas, *Italy Today*, London, 1909.
Matthews, Herbert L., *The Fruits of Fascism*, Harcourt, Brace, New York, 1943.
McGuire, Constantine, *Italy's International Financial Position*, Macmillan, New York, 1926.
McLeah, H. C., *Italian Government Finances*, Trade Information Bulletins Nos. 116 and 130, U.S. Dept. of Commerce Reports 1923 and 1925.
Munro, Ion S., *Through Fascism to World Power*, London, 1933.
Mussolini, Benito, *My Autobiography*, Scribner, New York, 1928.
Packard, Eleanor and Reynolds, *Balcony Empire*, Oxford University Press, 1942.
Pitigliani, Fausto, *The Italian Corporative State*, Macmillan, New York, 1934.
Prezzolini, G., *Fascism*, London, 1926.
Pribram, Karl, *Cartel Problems, an Analysis of Collective Monopolies in Europe*, Brookings Institution, Washington, D.C.
Provveditorato Generale Della Stato, pamphlet issued by, *The Italian Budget before and after the War*, 1925.
Riccio, Peter M., *On the Threshold of Fascism*, Casa Italiana, Columbia University, 1929.
Salvemini, Gaetano, *The Fascist Dictatorship in Italy*, Holt, New York, 1927.
———— ————, *Italian Fascism*, London, 1938.
———— ————, "Twelve Years of Fascist Finance," *Foreign Affairs*, April 1935.

Salvemini, Gaetano, *Under the Axe of Fascism*, Viking, New York, 1936.
────── ────── and La Piana, George, *What to Do with Italy*, Duell, Sloan & Pearce, New York, 1943.
Sarfatti, Margherita G., *Life of Benito Mussolini*, Stokes, New York, 1925.
Schmidt, Carl T., *The Corporate State in Action*, Oxford University Press, 1939.
Schneider, Herbert W., *The Fascist Government of Italy*, Van Nostrand, New York, 1936.
────── ──────, *Making the Fascist State*, Oxford University Press, 1928.
Seldes, George, *Sawdust Caesar*, Harper, New York, 1935.
Sorel, George, *Reflections on Violence*, London, 1915.
Spencer, Henry Russell, *Government and Politics in Italy*, World Book Co., New York, 1932.
Vandervelde, Émile, *Socialism Versus the State*, Kerr & Co., Chicago, 1919.
Villari, Luigi, *Development of Political Ideas in Italy in the 19th Century*, Proceedings of the British Academy, February 17, 1926, Vol. XII.
────── ──────, *The Fascist Experiment*, London, 1926.
Volpi, Count and Stringher, Bonaldo, *The Financial Reconstruction of Italy*, Italian Historical Society, New York, 1927.

GERMANY

Abel, Theodore, *Why Hitler Came into Power*, Prentice-Hall, New York, 1938.
Angell, James W., *The Recovery of Germany*, Oxford University Press, 1929, 1932.
Ashley, W. J., *Progress of German Working Classes in Last Quarter of a Century*, London, 1904.
Atkins, H. G., "Thomas Mann and the Nazis," *Contemporary Review*, January 1941.
Bashford, J. L., Editor, *Life and Labor in Germany*, Report of the Gainsborough Commission, London, 1906.
Behrend, Hans, *The Real Rulers of Germany*, London, 1939.
Benns, F. Lee, *Europe Since 1914*, Crofts Co., New York, 1935.
Borkin, Joseph and Welsh, Chas. A., *Germany's Master Plan*, Duell, Sloan & Pearce, New York, 1943.
Bourke, Vernon J., "Philosophical Antecedents of German National Socialism," *Thought*, 1939, Vol. 14.
Bresciani-Turroni, Constantino, *The Economics of Inflation—a Study of Currency Depreciation in Post-War Germany*, London, 1937.
Bricker, Richard M., *Is Germany Incurable?* Lippincott, New York, 1943.
Brooks, S., "European Revolt Against Militarism," *Harper's Weekly*, November 16, 1907.
Bruck, Werner Friedrich, *Social and Economic History of Germany*, London, 1938.
────── ──────, *The Road to Planned Economy*, London, 1934.
Butler, Rohan D'O., *Roots of National Socialism*, Dutton, New York, 1942.
Cleugh, James, *Thomas Mann*, London, 1933.
Closs, August, "Thomas Mann, His Principles and Politics," *Contemporary Review*, October 1933.
Cohn, Gustav, "Financial Reform in Germany," *Yale Review*, November 1908.
Dane, E. Surrey, *A Report on the Economic Conditions Prevailing in Germany*, London, 1922.
Daniels, H. G., *The Rise of the German Republic*, London, 1927.
Dawson, Sir Philip, *Germany's Industrial Revival*, London, 1926.
Derrick, Michael, *The Portugal of Salazar*, London, 1938.
Einzig, Paul, *Germany's Default*, London, 1934.
────── ──────, *Hitler's New Order in Europe*, London, 1941.
Elkind, L., "German Imperial Finances," *Fortnightly Review*, December 1908.
Enock, Arthur Guy, *The Problem of Armaments*, Macmillan, New York, 1923.
Ericsen, Paul, *German Financial Methods 1914–26*, G. Nitze, New York, 1926.
Fay, S. B., "Causes of the German Financial Crisis," *Current History*, September 1931.
Ferro, Antonio, *Salazar: Portugal and Her Leader*, London, 1939.

Flink, Salomon, *The German Reichsbank and Economic Germany*, Harper, New York, 1930.
Haffner, Sebastian, *Germany, Jekyll and Hyde*, Dutton, New York, 1941.
Harris, Forbes & Co., *Economic Conditions in Germany at the End of 1926*, New York, 1927.
Heiden, Konrad, *A History of National Socialism*, London, 1934.
Hitchcock, Dal, "The German Financial Revolution," *Harper's Magazine*, February 1941.
Hitler, Adolf, *Mein Kampf*, edited by Dr. George N. Shuster and others, Reynal & Hitchcock, 1940.
Howard, E. D., "Condition of the German Workman," *Journal of Political Economy*, February 1906.
Kaufman, Theodore N., *Germany Must Perish*, Argyle Press, 1941.
Kircher, R., "Chancellor Brüning," *Living Age*, September 1931.
Klein, F., "Brüning of Germany," *Current History*, October 1931.
Kuczynski, R. R., "German Railways and German Public Finance," *Journal of Political Economy*, April 1924.
Le Figaro's Reports, "The Secret of Germany's Budget," *Harper's Weekly*, January 2, 1909.
Liebknecht, Karl, *Militarism*, B. W. Huebsch, 1917.
——— ———, *Speeches*, International Publishers, 1927.
Lochner, Louis P., *What About Germany?* Dodd, Mead, New York, 1942.
Lotz, W., *Present Economic State of Germany: Public Finance*, International Conciliation, April 1932.
Lowe, Charles, *Prince Bismarck*, New York, 1886.
Lowenstein, Prince Hubertus, *The Tragedy of a Nation*, London, 1934.
Lowenstein, Karl, *Hitler's Germany*, Macmillan, New York, 1940.
Ludwig, Emil, *Hindenburg*, John C. Winston Co., New York, 1935.
Mann, Erika and Klaus, *The Other Germany*, Modern Age Books, New York, 1940.
Marcosson, Isaac, "New German Leadership," *Saturday Evening Post*, May 16, 1931.
National Industrial Conference Board, *The Situation in Germany at the Beginning of 1933*, New York, 1933.
Neumann, Sigmund, *Permanent Revolution*, Harper's, New York, 1942.
Oechsner, Frederick, *This Is the Enemy*, Little, Brown, New York, 1942.
Palzi, M., "Economic Foundations of the German Totalitarian State," *American Journal of Sociology*, January 1941.
Pendle, G., "Greece, a Mature Dictatorship," *Fortnightly Review*, December 1937.
Perris, Herbert, *Germany and the German Emperor*, Henry Holt, New York, 1912.
Plutynski, A., *The German Paradox*, London, 1933.
Pope, Ernest R., *Munich Playground*, G. P. Putnam, New York, 1941.
Preissig, Edward, *Political Institutions of the Old World*, Putnam, New York, 1906.
Rauschning, Hermann, *The Conservative Revolution*, Putnam, New York, 1941.
——— ———, *Men of Chaos*, Putnam, New York, 1942.
——— ———, *The Revolution of Nihilism*, Alliance Book Corp., New York, 1939.
Reimann, Guenter, *The Vampire Economy*, Vanguard Press, New York, 1939.
Reinhold, Peter P., *Economic, Financial and Political State of Germany Since the War*, Yale University Press, 1928.
Renatus, Kuno, *Twelfth Hour of Capitalism*, Alfred A. Knopf, New York, 1932.
Reynolds, Bernard F., *Prelude to Hitler*, London, 1933.
Robertson, C. Grant, *Bismarck*, London, 1918.
Rosenberg, Arthur, *History of the German Republic*, London, 1936.
Salazar, Antonio de Oliveira, *Doctrine and Action*, London, 1939.
Schmidt, Carl T., *German Business Cycles, 1924–33*, National Bureau Economic Research Pubs. No. 25.
Schuman, Frederick L., *Germany Since 1918*, Henry Holt, New York, 1937.
Scott-James, R. A., "Greece Under the Dictatorship," *Christian Science Monitor Monthly*, October 6, 1937.

Shuster, George N., "Talk with Chancellor Brüning," *Commonweal*, April 15, 1931.
Snyder, Louis L., *From Bismarck to Hitler*, Bayard Press, Williamsport, Pa., 1935.
Sollohut, N., "Forerunners of the Third Reich," *Contemporary Review*, July 1939.
Stolper, Gustav, *German Economy*, Reynal & Hitchcock, New York, 1940.
Sydow, Reinhold, "Germany's Serious Financial Dilemma," American *Review of Reviews*, December 1908.
Thompson, Dorothy, "Will Gangs Rule the World?" (Interview with Chancellor Brüning) *Saturday Evening Post*, July 16, 1932.
Thyssen, Fritz, *I Paid Hitler*, Farrar & Rinehart, New York, 1941.
Tolischus, Otto D., *They Wanted War*, Reynal & Hitchcock, New York, 1942.
U.S. Bureau of Labor Bulletin—"Cost of Living of Working Classes in Principal Industrial Towns of the German Empire," Washington, September 1908.
Vagts, Alfred, *The History of Militarism*, W. W. Norton, New York, 1937.
Valentin, V., "Leading Factors of Modern German History," *Contemporary Review*, January 1936.
Veblen, Thorstein, *Imperial Germany and the Industrial Revolution*, Viking Press, New York, 1939.
Wagner, Adolph, "National Debt of the German Empire," *North American Review*, June 1902.
Winkler, Paul, *The Thousand Year Conspiracy*, Chas. Scribner, New York, 1943.
Woodside, Willson, "Germany's Hidden Crisis," *Harper's Magazine*, February 1937.
Young Plan Advisory Committee, "Basle Report on German Finances," *Current History*, February 1932.

United States

Angly, Edmund, *Oh, Yeah!* Viking Press, New York, 1931.
Chase, Stuart, "Autarchy," *Scribner's Magazine*, September 1933.
Coyle, David Cushman, *Uncommon Sense*, National Home Library, 1936.
Ezekiel, Mordecai, *Jobs for All*, Alfred A. Knopf, New York, 1939.
Hansen, Alvin H., *Fiscal Policy and the Business Cycle*, W. W. Norton, New York, 1941.
James, William, *The Moral Equivalent of War*, Am. Association for International Conciliation, February, 1910, No. 27.
Keynes, John Maynard, *The General Theory of Employment, Interest and Money*, Harcourt, Brace, New York, 1936.
Laski, Harold J., *The American Presidency*, Harper & Bros., New York, 1940.
Luce, Henry R., *The American Century*, Farrar & Rinehart, New York, 1941.
McClure, Wallace, *International Executive Agreements*, Columbia University Press, 1941.
Meriam, Lewis, and Schmeckebier, Laurence F., *Reorganization of the National Government*, Brookings Institution, 1939.
Myers, William S., and Newton, Walter H., *The Hoover Administration*, Chas. Scribner, New York, 1936.
National Resources Planning Board—Pamphlets and Reports, U. S. Government Printing Office, 1942 and 1943.
Roosevelt, Franklin D., *Public Papers and Addresses*, 1928–36, Random House, New York, 1938.
Seven Harvard and Tufts Economists, *An Economic Program for American Democracy*, Vanguard Press, New York, 1938.
Soule, George, "The Basis of a Lasting Peace," *New Republic*, September 20, 1939.
Tugwell, Rexford G., speech before American Economic Assn., December 1931, reported in Proceedings.
U.S. Chamber of Commerce, *Report of the Committee on Continuity of Business and Employment*, Washington, 1931.
U.S. Dept. of Commerce, *Statistical Abstract of the U.S.*, Washington, U.S. Government Printing Office (yearly).

Veblen, Thorstein, *The Engineers and the Price System*, Viking, New York, 1933.
White, William Allen, *The Old Order Changeth*, Macmillan, New York, 1910.

No examination of this subject would be complete without consulting the files of the New York *Times* and the *Congressional Record* for the period covered.

General

Agar, Herbert, *A Time for Greatness*, Little, Brown, New York, 1942.
Burnham, James, *The Machiavellians*, John Day, New York, 1943.
——— ———, *The Managerial Revolution*, John Day, New York, 1941.
Carr, Edward H., *Conditions of Peace*, Macmillan, New York, 1942.
Cole, G. D. H., *Self-Government in Industry*, London, 1917.
Ferrero, Guglielmo, *The Principles of Power*, G. P. Putnam, New York, 1942.
Hirst, Francis W., *Monopolies, Trusts, Cartels*, London, 1905.
Hunter, Robert, *Revolution—Why, How and When*, Harper Bros., New York, 1940.
Kneller, George Frederick, *The Educational Philosophy of National Socialism*, Yale University Press, 1941.
Liefmann, Robert, *Cartels, Concerns and Trusts*, London, 1932.
Ortega y Gasset, José, *The Revolt of the Masses*, W. W. Norton, New York, 1932.
Peotrowski, Roman, *Cartels and Trusts, Origin and Historical Development*, London, 1933.
Raider, Carmen, *Do We Want Fascism?* John Day, New York, 1934.
Royce, Josiah, *The Spirit of Modern Philosophy*, Houghton, Mifflin, New York, 1892.
Strachey, John, *The Menace of Fascism*, Covici, Friede, New York, 1933.

Index

AAA, declared unconstitutional, 179, 198, 248
Adenauer, Konrad, chief burgomaster of Cologne, 96
Adowa, Italian Army wiped out by Menelik, 27
Agar, Herbert, in praise of Hitler, 224; on constitutional government, 234; 22, 75
Allgemeine-Elektrizitäts-Gesellschaft of Germany, 112
Alphonso, the Thirteenth, cited in editorial in Emporia *Gazette,* 220
American Federation of Labor, 191, 198
Anarchism in Italy, 10
Angell, Dr. James Waterhouse, on German recovery, 93, 96, 116
d'Annunzio, Gabriele, mentioned, 22; evangelist of Life, 37; glorifying ancient Rome, 122
Anti-Semitism, an article of faith with Hitler, 76; 3, 129
Anti-trust laws in the United States, their effect, 190–93
A.P.A., 162
Armament production as an economic system, 102 *et seq.*
Article 48 of the Weimar Constitution, 143–44
Association for the Promotion of Peace, formed in Munich, 128
Augustus Caesar cited, 133
Austria, influence on Italy, 7, 22

Autarchy, 108, 139, 142, 147, 199–200, 212, 214
Avanti, Italian socialist paper, 39–40
Ayres, Leonard, American economist, 167

Balcony Empire, by Eleanor and Reynolds Packard, quoted, 24
Balkan wars, 126
Bank of England, 187
Barrès, Maurice, 36
Bauer, Gustav, Chancellor of the German republic, 127
Beard, Dr. Charles, 191
Benns, Frank Lee, quoted on workmen's councils, 114
Berlin Opera House, 95
Beveridge, Albert Jeremiah, on possession of the Philippines, 217–19; 220–21
Big business in Germany, moves to Hitler's side, 133
Bismarck, Otto Edward Leopold, as creator of the Imperial German state, 80–81; 86, 89, 101, 116, 133
Black Age of Italy, 22, 34
Blank-check bills, in Congress, 23?, 246
Bloom, Sol, his commendation of Mussolini quoted, 71–72
Blücher, Gebhard Leberecht von, demand for militarism, 99
Board of Economic Warfare, its demise, 201, 236; its expenditures, 246–47
Bolshevist revolution, 43

Bonomi, Ivanoe, Italian Premier, 59
Borgese, Giuseppe Antonio, on tolerance in Italy, 5–6; on the roots of fascism, 22; 27, 34, 37, 39, 69
Brookings Institution, 29
Brown Bros. & Co., bankers, mentioned, 225
Brown House, Nazi headquarters, 133
Bruck, Werner Friedrich, his *Social and Economic History of Germany* cited, 112
Bruening, Dr. Heinrich, Chancellor of Germany, 98, 143–44; dismissed by Hindenburg, 145; 148–49
Budgets, in Italy, 13, 15, 17–18, 50–51; in Germany, 87, 90; in United States, 176, 182
Butler, Nicholas Murray, praise of Mussolini, 72
Butler, Rohan D'O., on Fichte's *The Closed Commercial State*, 109
Butler, Maj. Gen. Smedley Darlington, on the service of the Marines, 225

Cambon, Jules Martin, French Ambassador to Berlin, 85
Capitalist state, in Italy, 7, 10; opposed by syndicalism in Europe, 31; general definition, 140
Capitalist system declared dead by *An Economic Program for American Democracy*, 180; 183
Carr, Edward Hallett, on armament production, 106–07; on the social good of war, 208, 210
Cartel system, its origin, 28; in the Weimar republic, 117; 29
Castor oil in fascism, 2
Catherine II of Russia cited, 85
Catholic Church, and Hitler's war, 160
Catholics in Italy, reaction to Pope's encyclical *Rerum novarum*, 10
Cavour, Camillo Bensodi, Italian statesman, 4
Chamberlain, Houston Stewart, 36, 155
Chamber of Commerce of the United States, 198
Chase, Stuart, quoted on autarchy, 200; 191
Child, Richard Washburn, American Ambassador to Italy, admiration for Mussolini, 71
Christian Fronters, 162
Churchill, Winston Spencer, his approval of Mussolini, 70, 72; calls his attack on England criminal, 73
Civil War (United States) cited, 7
Clapper, Raymond, attack on Congress, 237

Clayton Act, used in attack on monopolies, 190
Cleveland Trust Co., 167
Closed Commercial State, The, by Fichte, cited, 109
Codes of practice in industry, done away with by President Hoover, 191
Colaganni, Napoleone, Italian socialist, 38
Cole, George Douglas Howard, English socialist, 164, 255
Collapse of 1933 begins, 166
Collier's Magazine, prints Churchill's praise of Mussolini, 70; on military service, 205
Colonialism, its seeds planted in Italy, 27
Colt, Samuel, on armaments as industrial stimulant, 105
Commune of Paris, 85
Communism, manifesto on the proletariat, 31
Compensation insurance in Germany, 86
Comptroller General (United States), his functions, 250
Confederation of Workers of Italy, 41
Conscription, as a permanent institution, 99–100, 203 *et seq.*
Coolidge, Calvin, President of the United States, New Era cited, 7, 92, 96; 191, 198
Corporative state, its rise and affiliations, 54–55; in Germany, 138 *et seq.*; in United States, 192 *et seq.*
Correnti, Cesare, quoted on Italy, 7
Cox, Edward Eugene, congressman from Georgia, on military service, 204
Coyle, David Cushman, his *Uncommon Sense* circulated by the Democratic National Committee, 182
Crispi, Francesco, Italian statesman, attacks Abyssinia, is defeated at Adowa, 26–27; his death, 27; 20, 22, 25, 51, 171
Croce, Benedetto, Italian philosopher, 33, 35–36, 69
Croker, Richard, American politician, cited, 60
Cromwell, Oliver, cited, 70, 72, 85
Crowd: a Study of the Popular Mind, The, by Le Bon, 45
Cuba, and the Platt Amendment, 220
Cyrenaica, conquered by Italy, 39

Daily News (N.Y.), on peacetime conscription, 205
Dante mentioned, 22
Darré, Richard Walther Oskar, 151

Darrow, Clarence, on repeal of prohibition, 229
Dawes Plan in Germany, 92
Declaration of Independence (American), 217
Decline of the West, by Spengler, mentioned, 123
Decomposition of Marxism, The, by Georges Sorel, 30
Deficits, in Italian budgets, 15, 18, 39, 42, 50–51; in Germany, 87 *et seq.*; in the United States, 172–73
Delano, Col. Frederic, head of National Resources Planning Board, 202
Democracy, a loose term, 5
Democratic National Committee, circulates Coyle's *Uncommon Sense*, 182
Democratic party, its platforms, 170–71, 174–75
Depression of 1929, 166, 174, 191, 242
Depretis, Agostino, Italian statesman, 12; his budget policies, 13–15; 20, 22, 26, 51, 171, 177–78
Deutschland, Deutschland, über alles, German national anthem for Hitler, 132
Dictatorship, in fascism, 2, 61 *et seq.*; precedents for in Germany, 142 *et seq.*; confused with totalitarianism, 229
Dies, Martin, congressman from Texas, 3
Dingfelder, Dr. Johannes, in the German Worker's party, 128–29; 150
Dodecanese islands conquered by Italy, 39
Dollfuss, Engelbert, Austrian Premier, assassinated, 2; his fascist regime, 163
Douglas, Maj. Clifford Hugh, English economist, 169
Drexler, Anton, German locksmith, 128–29, 131, 150
Dual Consumptive Economy, of Dr. Hansen, 188
"Dynamism," as expounded by Mussolini, 56

Ebenstein, William, his figures of fascist spending on army and navy, 55
Ebert, Friedrich, President of the Weimar republic, 127
Economic difficulties in Italy, 8–9, 17
Economic Program for American Democracy, An, book proclaiming the end of the capitalist system, quoted, 180–81
Economic system, its control at base of fascism, 28
Eighteenth Amendment, and its disappearance, 229

Eisner, Kurt, Bavarian Premier, assassinated, 127
Eleven Points of San Sepolcro, 45, 49
Elite, principle of the, 66, 111–12, 154
Encyclopaedia Britannica, quoted on Italy, 14; on public spending, 178
Engels, Friedrich, German socialist, 101
Enock, Arthur Guy, on defense expenditures of Germany, 105
Esser, Hermann, German reporter, 128; his harangues on socialism and anti-Semitism, 129
Ethiopia, defeats Italy at Adowa, 27, 38
Ezekiel, Mordecai, economist, his plan for production and distribution, 186–87, 194

Farm Holiday, 169
Farrar, Frederic William, dean of Canterbury, on evolution of imperialism, 219–20
Fasci di azione Revolutionaria, organized by Mussolini, 40; disappears, 44
Fasci di Combattimento, organized by Mussolini, 44; its program, 45
Fascism, its vague understanding, 1, 74; definitions, 2, 48 *et seq.*, 67, 161 *et seq.*; growth in Italy, 3–4; as carried out by Mussolini, 1 *et seq.*; praises of, 70; 74 *passim.*
Feder, Gottfried, German engineer, 128; originator of *Federgeld*, 129; 130–32, 150, 156
Federal Reserve Board, 182
Federal Trade Commission, in attack on monopolies, 190; 191, 246, 250
Federgeld (feather money), invention of Gottfried Feder, 129
Ferrero, Guglielmo, Italian historian, 8; his *Militarism* quoted, 16
Fichte, Johann Gottlieb, his social philosophy, 108; his *The Closed Commercial State* cited, 109; 156, 196
Figaro, Le, quoted on German debt, 89
Five-Year Plan of Russia, 191–92
Ford, Prof. Henry Jones, on corporations, 233
Fortune magazine, 182
Franco, Francesco, as a dictator, 76
Franco-Prussian War, 79
Free Corps in Germany, 127–28
"Free enterprise," 189
Frick, Wilhelm, German socialist, 151
Fruits of Fascism, The, by Herbert L. Matthews, 73

Garibaldi, Giuseppe, Italian patriot, 4, 22
Gazette (Emporia, Kan.), editorial quoted, 220

General Confederation of Labor, in Italy, 29, 37, 41, 48
Gentile, Giovanni, Italian philosopher, 35–36; Mussolini apologist, 69–70; 222, 224
"German disease," 22, 75
German Workers' party, 128–29; changes name and draws up program of Twenty-Five Points, 130
Germany, as a federation, 10, 79–81; its capitalist system, 82–83; effects of loss of the war, 92–98; militarism as an industry, 102; its collapse after defeat, 113; policies of successive governments, 125–26; public debt, 134; as a bankrupt nation, 224
Gibson, Henry Richard, Congressman from Tennessee, on mission of the United States, 219
Gilbert, Richard Vincent, economist, 182
Gilbert, Seymour Parker, Agent General of Reparations, 97
Giolitti, Giovanni, Italian politician, 16, 33, 37–38, 41, 43, 51, 60, 62, 132–33, 171, 178
Gobineau, Joseph Arthur de, 155
Goebbels, Joseph, joins National Socialist party, 131; 138, 150
Goering, Hermann, joins National Socialist party, 131; 138, 150, 156
Grand Council of the Fascist party, 64
Grey of Fallodon, Earl, quoted, 215–16

Hague, Frank, Mayor of Jersey City, 151
Ham and Eggs crusade in California, 163
Hamlet, cited, 46
Hansen, Dr. Alvin Harvey, economist, 180; economic adviser of Federal Reserve Board, 182; his Dual Consumptive Economy, 188; on spending borrowed money, 235–36; 202
Harper's, on German budget, 134, 136; on the Hitler financial operations, 183, 185
Harrer, Karl, German journalist, 128–29, 150
Harriman, Henry Ingraham, president of the Chamber of Commerce of United States, quoted on the national economy, 198–99
Hentze, Margot, on Italian public spending, 14, 178
Herald Tribune (N.Y.), on Germany's public debt, 134; on military service, 205
Hess, Rudolf, joins National Socialist party, 131
Himmler, Heinrich, 150
Hindenburg, Paul von, appoints Hitler as Chancellor of Germany, 133, 146; governs by decree, 143–44; dismisses Chancellor Bruening, 145; dies, 146; 232

Hines, James, American politician, 151
History of the German Republic, by Arthur Rosenberg, quoted, 95–96
Hitchcock, Dal, on German finances, in *Harper's*, 136, 188
Hitler, Adolf, persecution of the Jews, 68; anti-Semitism an article of faith, 76; his *Mein Kampf* cited, 79; becomes a member of the German Workers' party, 128; his contribution of doctrine, 129; interest in German Army, 130; arrested in beer-hall *Putsch*, 132; appointed Chancellor, 133; creates full-blast employment, 136–37; consolidates office of Chancellor with Presidency and rules by decree, 146; his dictatorship, 147 et seq.; his financial program, 183–84; disguised admiration for him, 223–24; 1–2, 66, 74, 77, 88, 94, 98, 114, 123, 127, 131, 138–45, 221, 237, 252–53, 256
Hoar, George Frisbie, senator from Massachusetts, shocked at United States imperialism, 216, 218–19
Hobbs, Samuel Francis, congressman from Alabama, on military service, 204
Hobson, John Atkinson, English socialist, 164, 255
Hoover, Herbert Clark, President of the United States, appropriations of his administration, 174; abolishes codes of practice in industry, 191; sets up commissions, 197; 176, 198
Hopkins, Harry, 249
Hopkins, Prof. Washburn, on imperialism, 216
Hugenberg, Alfred, 138–39, 148–49, 151, 156
Huston, Luther A., N.Y. *Times* correspondent, quoted on conscription, 211

Illiteracy in Italy, 5
Imperialism, infecting Italy, 20, 22; European background, 23; in full flower in Italy, 39; 56–57; in America, 213–14
Inflation in Germany, 91–92
Inquisition cited, 35
International Executive Agreements, by Wallace McClure, quoted, 249
"Internationalism," 213–14
Interstate Commerce Commission, 189
"Isolationism," 213, 215
Italy, as the laboratory of fascism, 4 et seq.; defeats Turkey in war for Libya, 38–39; in World War I, 40; her "Beveridge Plan," 41; a land of small states, 79

Jacobins of France mentioned, 25
James, William, American philosopher, on universal military service, 209–10
Jarres, Dr. Karl, chief burgomaster of Duisberg, 95
Jaurès, Jean, French socialist, 101
Jews, persecution of, 2, 151; by Hitler, 68, 132, 152; their property in Germany confiscated, 136; 129–30, 133, 165, 254
"Jobs for All" plan of Vice-President Wallace, 194
Johnson, Gen. Hugh, and NRA, 169
Jones, Jesse, Secretary of Commerce, on expenditures of the Board of Economic Warfare, 246–47
Journal of Commerce (Chicago), interview with Dr. Hansen, 202, 235
Junkers, their dominance of Germany, 88; support of Hitler, 232; 99–101, 149

Kahn, Otto Hermann, his commendation of Mussolini quoted, 72
Kemal Pasha, Mustapha, as a dictator, 76, 165
Keynes, John Maynard (Lord Keynes), 180, 185, 187, 255
Keyserling, Hermann, 154
King, Bolton, on Italian taxation, 16
Kipling, Rudyard, cited, 36; his *Recessional* mentioned, 209
Kleinwächter, Prof. Friedrich, 109
Know Nothings, 162
Kock, Eric, German socialist, 133, 151
Krupp's, munitions manufacturer, 102, 106, 132
Kuliscioff, Anna, 38
Ku Klux Klan, 162
Kultur, its veneration, 155
Kun, Bela, headed Red government in Hungary, 127

Labor market and the army, 102–04
Labrioli, Arturo, Italian socialist, 38
Lamont, Thomas William, his praise of Mussolini, 71
Laski, Harold Joseph, political economist, on the British Parliament, 235
Leadership principle, in Italy, 66–67; 159
League of Nations, 213
Le Bon, Gustave, his book *The Crowd: a Study of the Popular Mind*, 45
Lenin, Nikolai, cited, 58
Leo XIII, Pope, his encyclical *Rerum novarum*, 10

Ley, Robert, 150, 153
Life of Bismarck, by Ludwig, cited, 101
Life of Christ, by Papini, mentioned, 36
Lion of Judah in Abyssinia, *see* Menelek
Lochner, Louis Paul, Associated Press representative in Berlin, quoted, 150
London Economic Conference, 215
Long, Huey, cited, 60; his Share-the-Wealth movement, 169
Louis XIV of France cited, 2, 133, 231
Louis XV cited, 231
Louis XVI, beheaded by the Jacobins, 25; cited, 85
Luce, Henry, and the American Century, 221
Ludwig, Emil, his *Life of Bismarck* cited, 101; 68
Luther, Hans, Chancellor of Germany, 144

Machiavelli, Niccolo, cited, 44; doctrines adopted by Mussolini, 45; 123–24
Magliani, Agostino, Italian politician, 14, 178
Malatesta, Enrico, Italian anarchist, 39
Mann, Erika and Klaus, critics of Hitler, 79, 132–33
Mann, Thomas, German novelist, father of the preceding, 155–56
March on Rome, 48
Marshall, Gen. George Catlett, army Chief of Staff, on military service, 204
Marx, Karl, doctrines cited, 30; quoted on Germany's capitalist system, 82
Matteotti, Giacomo, Italian socialist, assassinated, 48, 63–64, 70
Matthews, Herbert Lionel, N.Y. *Times* correspondent in Italy, 24; his early admiration for Mussolini admitted in his book *The Fruits of Fascism*, 73
Maurras, Charles, 36
Mazzini, Giuseppe, Italian revolutionist, 4, 22, 25
McClure, Wallace, his *International Executive Agreements* quoted, 249
McKellar, Kenneth, senator from Tennessee, on the uselessness of the Appropriations Committee, 247
Mein Kampf, Hitler's autobiography, 79, 129, 132, 138
Menelek, Lion of Judah in Abyssinia, 23; attacked by Italians, 26; defeats them at Adowa, 27
Meriam, Dr. Lewis, on presidential spending, 236

Merriam, Dr. Charles, on streamlining government, 236
Metaxas, John, as a fascist dictator, 2, 76, 164
Militarism, in Europe, its economic effects, 18–19; gains foothold in Italy; 23; in full flower there, 39; as a modern institution, 98 *et seq.*; banned by Treaty of Versailles, 127; reintroduced by Hitler, 142; advantages of compulsory military service, 203–05; bills for universal service in Congress, 205–06; 56–57, 143. See also footnote on Plutarch, p. 19
Militarism, book by Ferrero, quoted, 16
Moneta, Ernesto T., Italian pacifist, 38
Monopolies in United States under attack, 189–91
Movies as an instrument of corporative control, 65
Müller, Hermann, Chancellor of Germany, 97
Murphy, Charles Francis, American politician, cited, 60
Mussolini, Benito, editor of the *Avanti*, socialist paper, 39; establishes *Popolo d'Italia*, 40; organizes the *Fasci di Combattimento*, 44; proclaims program, 45; becomes Premier, 48; budget problems, 50–51; his Corporative State, 54–55; glorifying war, 56; beginning his dictatorship, 62; charged with assassination of Matteotti, 64; his attack on England criminal, says Churchill, 73; likened himself to Mustapha Kemal, 76; 1, 3–4, 38, 114, 123–24, 131–32, 141–43, 152, 154, 156, 159, 163–65, 171, 184, 197, 252–53, 256

Napoleon, his fall, 99–100
Napoleon III, revives conscription, 100
National City Bank mentioned, 225
National Recovery Act, 248
National Resources Planning Board, 182; abolished by Congress, 183; on expenditures for defense, 212; 187, 202–03, 235–36
National Socialism, 3; definition of, 161 *et seq.*; original program, 130; 133, 146, 156
National Socialist party, 111; becomes ruler of Germany, 131
National Socialist German Workers' party, its program of Twenty-Five Points, 130
National Youth Administration, 208
Nationalist Association of Italy, 37
Naumann, Friedrich, German socialist, 41
Neumann, Sigmund, on permanent revolution, 170

New Deal, 7, 171, 175, 179, 182, 189, 200, 235, 254
New Era, 7, 168, 195
New Republic, on militarism, 210–11; 182, 191, 201
Nicholas, Czar of Russia, cited, 2, 85
Nietzsche, Friedrich Wilhelm, his doctrines approved by Mussolini, 45; cited, 121, 123; his myth of the superman, 124; 36, 154–55
Nitti, Francesco Saverio, Italian Premier, 62
Norton, Mary Teresa, congresswoman from New Jersey, 203
NRA (National Recovery Administration) of Gen. Hugh Johnson, 169; declared unconstitutional, 179, 199, 239; a colossal failure, 199; 198, 247–48

Oh, Yeah! book on the depression, 166
Okey, Thomas, on Italian taxation, 16
Old-age pension system in Germany, 86
O'Mahoney, Joseph Christopher, senator from Wyoming, on Lend-Lease, 247; 248–49
Ortega y Gasset, José, his *Revolt of the Masses* quoted, 83–84; 85, 118, 120

Packard, Eleanor and Reynolds, U.P. correspondents, their *Balcony Empire* quoted, 24; 73
Papen, Franz von, made Chancellor of Germany, 145–46; 148–49
Papini, Giovanni, his *Life of Christ* mentioned, 36; 222
Pareto, Vilfredo, 45, 66, 111, 156
Parliament in European states, 5
Peace Conference (1898), 104
Pendergast, Thomas Joseph, Missouri politician, 151
Penrose, Boies, cited, 60
Pericles cited, 133
Perkins, Milo, 201
Perris, Herbert, on cost of the German Army, 102
Philippines, as bad bargain, 216; its resources and wealth, 217–18
Planning in society, 28, 112, 140, 142–43, 191–94, 200
Platt Amendment on Cuba, 220
Pontine Marshes, in Italy, their draining compared to America's TVA, 55
Popolari, Italian political party, 41, 48, 59
Popolo d'Italia, Mussolini's paper, 40, 44
Pork-barrel bills in Congress, 238
Post (N.Y.), on military service, 208

Power of the purse in the people, 237–38
Preissig, Dr. Edward, 78
Press in Italy, 5
Pribram, Karl, study of monopolies in Europe, 29
Progress party in Germany, 100–01
Prohibition, and its repeal, 229
Proportional representation in Italy, 61–62
Public spending, by Giolitti, 41–42; by Mussolini, 50–52; by Weimar republic, 94; by Hitler, 134; in the United States, 172–79, 205–07
PWA, 256

Quay, Matthew Stanley, American politician, cited, 60

Radio, as an instrument of corporative control, 65
Ranshoven-Wertheimer, Dr. Egon, quoted on Hitler, 152
Rathenau, Walter, German industrialist, 111–12; quoted on planned economy, 113; founded corporations, 114; 155, 190, 203
Rauschning, Hermann, break with Nazis, 150; quoted, 153; 138, 142
Recessional, by Kipling, mentioned, 209
Reconstruction Finance Corporation, 184, 247
Red terror, 127
Red Week in Italy, 39
Reflections on Violence, by Georges Sorel, 30
Reichskreditgesellschaft, organized by the Weimar republic, 115
Reichstag, of the Weimar republic, 117
Renaissance, of Italy, 22
Renatus, Kuno, his *Twelfth Hour of Capitalism* cited, 94
Reno, Milo, his Farm Holiday, 169
Rentenmark, new currency unit in Germany, invented by Schacht, 92
Republican (Springfield, Ill.), laments support of United States imperialism, 219
Rerum novarum, encyclical of Pope Leo XIII, 10
Revolt in Germany, 118–20
Revolt of the Masses, by José Ortega, quoted, 83–84
Revolution, European radicals' specialty, 63
Reynal & Hitchcock, their edition of *Mein Kampf* cited, 79
Rhodes, Cecil John, quoted, 215
Rhodes, conquered by Italy, 39
Rights of Man mentioned, 29

Risorgimento in Italy, 4, 7–8, 22
Rockefeller, John Davidson, and the oil combines, 189
Roehm, Ernst, joins National Socialist party, 131; 138, 149
Roman Empire, its re-creation a Mussolini project, 56
Romanticists, in Italy, 33; in Germany, 120 *et seq.*; in United States, 222 *et seq.*
Romondo, Italian publicist, quoted on Giolitti, 60
Roosevelt, Mrs. Eleanor, 211
Roosevelt, Franklin Delano, President of the United States, New Deal cited, 7; his planned deficit, 176; financial policy, 189; his scorn of "master minds," 197; seizure of Australian Archipelago, 225; 175, 177, 198, 211
Rosenberg, Alfred, joins National Socialist party, 131; preaches paganism, 156
Rosenberg, Arthur, his *History of the German Republic* quoted, 95–96
Royce, Josiah, on German philosophers, 121; 222
Ruskin, John, concern for the poor, 123; cited, 221

Sabath, Adolph Joseph, congressman from Illinois, on military service, 204
Salazar, Antonio de Oliveira, Portuguese dictator, 76, 77, 164
Salvemini, Dr. Gaetano, on Italian bureaucracy, 11; on Mussolini's budgets, 50–51; his book *What to Do with Italy* quoted, 72; 139
Sarajevo, Austrian Archduke shot, 40
Sarfatti, Margherita Grassini, Mussolini's biographer, 38, 44–45, 47, 49
Schacht, Hjalmar, invents the *Rentenmark* as a new currency unit, 92; his financial juggling, 135–36; 151, 156, 184
Schiller, Johann Christoph Friedrich von, quoted, 121
Schleicher, Gen. Kurt von, made Chancellor of Germany, then ousted, 146; 145, 148–49
Schlieffen, Alfred, Count von, on military economies, 104
Schmeckebier, Dr. Laurence Frederick, on presidential spending, 236
Schuschnigg, Kurt, Austrian Chancellor, imprisoned by Hitler, 2; his fascist regime, 163–64
Schwarzhoff, Col. Gross von, 104

Scott, Howard, and technocracy, 169
Selective service bill, 203
Serbian patriot, and the shot that started World War I, 39–40, 126
Shakespeare's *Hamlet* cited, 46
Share-the-Wealth movement of Huey Long, 169
Sherman Anti-Trust Law, 189
Sickness-insurance system in Germany, 86
Sinclair, Upton, and his Epic plan, 169
Smith, Alfred Emanuel, American politician, 43
Snyder, Prof. Louis Leo, on naval power, 104–05
Social and Economic History of Germany, by Bruck, cited, 112
Social-insurance law in Germany, 86
Socialism, in Italy, 10, 29–30; turns to syndicalism in Europe, 31
Socialist party, in Italy, 41; in Germany, 85
Sombart, Werner, 156
Sorel, Georges, father of syndicalism, his *Reflections on Violence* and *The Decomposition of Marxism*, 30; 35, 45, 53, 69
Soule, George, 191, 201
Spann, Othmar, 156
Spengler, Oswald, German philosopher, 121, 123, 154, 157
Spokesman (Minneapolis), on the effect of compulsory military service on colored youth, 203–04
Sportpalast mentioned, 221
Stalin, Joseph, 1–2, 58, 142
Standard of living in Italy, 8
Standard Oil mentioned, 225
Sterilization of Germans proposed, 75
Stöcker, Dr. Adolf, German court preacher, 111
Stolper, Dr. Gustav, on the German revolution, 116; on her public debt, 134; 96, 109
Strasser, Gregor, joins National Socialist party, 131, 133; murdered by Hitler, 150; 149, 151
Strasser, Otto, brother of the preceding, his description of Germany after the war, 91; 132, 138, 150
Streicher, Julius, joins National Socialist party, 131, 133; 150
Stresemann, Gustav, Premier of Germany, 92, 95, 144
Strikes in Italy, 37, 39, 43
Subsidies, 185–86

Sulzberger, Arthur Hays, advocates universal military service, 205
Sumners, Hatton William, congressman from Texas, on enactment of laws by bureaus, 241
Sun (N.Y.), on the Italian treasury's books, 185
Supreme Court (United States), declares AAA and NRA unconstitutional, 179, 199, 239, 244; 250
Syndicalism, in Italy, 10; in European affairs, 30; opposing socialism and the capitalist state, 31; its principles, 32, 52–53; 110–11, 114, 191

Taxation, in Italy, 13, 15, 17; in Germany, 79–80
Taylor, Myron Charles, admiration for Mussolini, 70–71
Thyssen, Fritz, financial backer of Hitler, 114, 133; quoted, 115, 151; 138, 148, 156
Times (London), lament over peace, 123, 208
Times (N.Y.), on Germany's public debt, 134; 24, 51, 73, 150, 211
Tolischus, Otto David, N.Y. *Times* correspondent in Germany, quoted, 150
Totalitarian government in Italy, 66–67; definitions, 229–31
Totalitarian state, its workings, 226 *et seq.*
Townsend, Dr. Francis Everett, and pensions, 169
Townsend movement, 163
Trade-unions, as a base of fascism, 28; in the Weimar republic, 116
Treaty of Versailles, 3, 129; ban on militarism, 127, 143
Treves, Claudio, Italian socialist, 38
Tripolitania, conquered by Italy, 39
Tugwell, Rexford Guy, his estimate of government borrowing, 182; views on cartel system, 195; quoted, 196; 198
Turati, Filippo, Italian socialist, 38
Turkey, defeated in war with Italy over Libya, 38–39
TVA (United States), cited, 55
Twelfth Hour of Capitalism, by Renatus, cited, 94
Twenty-Five Points, program of the National Socialist German Workers' party, 130–31, 197

Uncommon Sense, by David C. Coyle, quoted, 182–83

Unions, in the Weimar republic, 116
United States Steel Corporation, 140, 192

Vagts, Alfred, on militarism, 99, 101, 106
Vandervelde, Émile, Belgian socialist, 31–32
Vanguard Press, 180
Vatican, assured national socialism is rooted in Christianity, 156
Veblen, Thorstein, German philosopher, 192, 195–96
Verboten sign in Germany, 119
Versailles, Treaty of, *see* Treaty of Versailles
Viag (*Vereinigte Industrie Aktiengesellschaft*), holding company of the Weimar republic, 115
Victor Emmanuel II, King of Italy, 8
Villari, Luigi, fascist apologist, 50, 53, 58, 62
Volkswagen, Hitler's promise, 154
Volpe, Prof. Gioacchino, fascist apologist, 58
Volpi, Giuseppe, Italian Finance Minister, 71
von Papen, *see* Papen

Wadsworth, James Wolcott, congressman from New York, advocates universal military service, 205
Wagner, Dr. Adolph, on German government loans, 105–06
Wallace, Henry, Vice-President of the United States, his "Jobs for All" plan, 194; expenditure of money without accounting, 247; 169, 201, 244
War plants, disposition after war, 202

Warren, Dr. Robert B., and his gold purchase plan, 169
Washington, George, cited, 70
Waterloo cited, 99
Weimar republic, established, 113; enters banking field, 115; collective bargaining and unions, 116; Ebert elected President, 127; its liquidation, 143, 146
What to Do with Italy, by Dr. Salvemini, quoted, 72
White, William Allen, quoted on Aryan blood, 220
White Man's Burden, 209
Whittington, William Madison, congressman from Mississippi, on military service, 204
Wilhelm II of Germany, attempt on his life, 81, 86; on disarmament, 106; mentioned, 196
Wilson, (Thomas) Woodrow, President of the United States, his attacks on monopolies, 190
Wolff, Theodore, 68
Woll, Matthew, advocates repeal of anti-trust laws, 191
Work Projects Administration, 208
World War I, begins, 40; 58, 81, 83, 89, 90, 106, 117, 123, 151, 167, 172, 178, 185, 190. *See also* footnote on causes, 89–90

Young Plan, 133

Zarathustra, by Nietzsche, read by Mussolini, 45; 123

JOHN T. FLYNN was an author and journalist, a social critic with wide-ranging interests. Born in 1882, Flynn was a graduate of Georgetown University Law School. He made his career in journalism, working for such publications as the *New York Globe* and the *New Haven Register*. During the 1930's he wrote for the *New Republic*, and he also served as an adviser to the Senate Committee on Banking and Currency, economic affairs being one of his journalistic specialties. He was also a lecturer on contemporary economics at the New School for Social Research at this time.

As a strong critic of militarism and domestic statism, Flynn opposed America's drift towards war prior to World War II and was chairman of the America First Committee in New York. In 1940, he published one of many books, *Country Squire in the White House*, a critical study of President Roosevelt. *As We Go Marching*, his indictment of American fascism was published in 1944.

During the 1950's his views were emphatically right-wing, but still concerned with limiting the power of government. In addition to writing books on American foreign policy in Asia and other subjects, he was a network radio commentator. Flynn died in 1964 at the age of 81.

RONALD RADOSH is Associate Professor of History at Queensborough Community College, C.U.N.Y., and is a member of the Graduate Faculty of the City University of New York. He is author of *American Labor and United States Foreign Policy* (Random House, 1970). He is now completing a study of the critique of American foreign policy made by leading "conservatives," including John T. Flynn, Charles A. Beard, Oswald Garrison Villard, and Robert A. Taft. This work will be published in September 1974 by Simon and Schuster.